D1093370

Decoding the Social World

Information Policy Series

Edited by Sandra Braman

The Information Policy Series publishes research on and analysis of significant problems in the field of information policy, including decisions and practices that enable or constrain information, communication, and culture irrespective of the legal siloes in which they have traditionally been located as well as state-law-society interactions. Defining information policy as all laws, regulations, and decision-making principles that affect any form of information creation, processing, flows, and use, the series includes attention to the formal decisions, decision-making processes, and entities of government; the formal and informal decisions, decision-making processes, and entities of private- and public-sector agents capable of constitutive effects on the nature of society; and the cultural habits and predispositions of governmentality that support and sustain government and governance. The parametric functions of information policy at the boundaries of social, informational, and technological systems are of global importance because they provide the context for all communications, interactions, and social processes.

Virtual Economies: Design and Analysis, Vili Lehdonvirta and Edward Castronova

Traversing Digital Babel: Information, e-Government, and Exchange, Alon Peled

Chasing the Tape: Information Law and Policy in Capital Markets, Onnig H. Dombalagian

Regulating the Cloud: Policy for Computing Infrastructure, edited by Christopher S. Yoo and Jean-François Blanchette

Privacy on the Ground: Driving Corporate Behavior in the United States and Europe, Kenneth A. Bamberger and Deirdre K. Mulligan

How Not to Network a Nation: The Uneasy History of the Soviet Internet, Benjamin Peters

Hate Spin: The Manufacture of Religious Offense and Its Threat to Democracy, Cherian George

Big Data Is Not a Monolith, edited by Cassidy R. Sugimoto, Hamid R. Ekbia, and Michael Mattioli

Decoding the Social World: Data Science and the Unintended Consequences of Communication, Sandra González-Bailón

Decoding the Social World

Data Science and the Unintended Consequences of Communication

Sandra González-Bailón

The MIT Press
Cambridge, Massachusetts
London, England

This book was set in Stone Serif and Stone Sans by Toppan Best-set Premedia Limited. Printed and bound in the United States of America.

Library of Congress Cataloging-in-Publication Data

Names: González-Bailón, Sandra, 1977- author.
Title: Decoding the social world : data science and the unintended consequences of communication / Sandra González-Bailón.
Description: Cambridge, MA : MIT Press, 2017. | Series: Information policy series | Includes bibliographical references and index.
Identifiers: LCCN 2017011041 | ISBN 9780262037075 (hardcover : alk. paper)
Subjects: LCSH: Digital communications. | Digital media. | Social problems. | Problem solving.
Classification: LCC TK5103.7 .G747 2017 | DDC 303.48/33--dc23 LC record available at https://lccn.loc.gov/2017011041

10   9   8   7   6   5   4   3   2   1

To my parents
Mari and Julián

Contents

List of Figures   ix

Series Editor's Introduction   xi

Preface   xv

Acknowledgments   xxi

1   Introduction: Decoding the Social World   1
    1.1   Communication and Its Metaphors   2
    1.2   The Social Cryptogram   5
    1.3   Vast National Barometers   8
    1.4   The Unpredictability of Social Life   12
    1.5   Reasons and Passions   15
    1.6   Book Outlook   18
2   Old Puzzles, New Evidence   23
    2.1   The Law of Unintended Consequences   25
    2.2   Self-Fulfilling and Self-Defeating Prophecies   31
    2.3   Cumulative Effects   35
    2.4   The Power of Communication   41
    2.5   Why Focus on the Unintended?   43
3   The Effervescence of Collective Behavior   45
    3.1   The Nature of Social Facts   48
    3.2   The Rhythms of Communication   53
    3.3   The Dynamics of Collective Attention   56
    3.4   Unpacking Collective Effervescence   59
    3.5   Collective Behavior Rehashed   65
4   The Social Logic of Influence   71
    4.1   The Contagion Metaphor   74
    4.2   Milling, Herding, and Wildfires   81

4.3 Exposure and Reference Groups   86
4.4 The Double Edge of Contagion   95
4.5 The Unpredictable Paths of Influence   97
5 Networks and Social Distance   99
    5.1 Network Chains   102
    5.2 Structure and Navigation   106
    5.3 Components, Communities, and Cores   109
    5.4 Dynamics and Layered Connectivity   115
    5.5 Network Interventions   118
    5.6 Hidden Architectures   123
6 Communication in Space   125
    6.1 Collective Maps   127
    6.2 Redefining Boundaries   131
    6.3 Selection Bias and Digital Gaps   138
    6.4 Cities as Laboratories   141
    6.5 Measurement and Representation   144
7 Designing Policy and Action   147
    7.1 Crowdsourced Problem Solving   151
    7.2 Algorithms and Decision Making   157
    7.3 The Two Sides of Privacy   162
    7.4 New Forms of Activism   166
    7.5 Networked Governance   169
8 Conclusions: Questions for Now and the Future   171
    8.1 Which Form of Critical?   172
    8.2 Unintended Effects or Collateral Damage?   174
    8.3 What to Archive and Retrieve?   176
    8.4 How to Control Networks?   177
    8.5 When Is the Code Cracked?   179

References   183
Index   209

List of Figures

2.1   Illustration of cumulative effects in networks   36

3.1   Temporal profiles of communication   54

3.2   The evolving signature of collective behavior   61

4.1   Epidemic models of contagion   76

4.2   Modeling approaches to local influence   89

4.3   The unintended effects of interpersonal influence   93

5.1   Core-periphery structures   112

5.2   Network reduction with community detection   114

5.3   Temporal and multilayer networks   117

6.1   Networks of influence in space   133

Series Editor's Introduction

The good news, according to Sandra González-Bailón in *Decoding the Social World*, is that existing social theory *can* be used to analyze "big data" in valuable ways—despite claims to the contrary by those who prefer the easy and/or most immediately utilitarian, even if not reliable, route. The even better news is that we not only can continue to use the social theories that have been so important to us over recent decades, but can also use theoretically powerful theories from the past that were previously untestable. González-Bailón argues that the seminal and still-influential nineteenth-century ideas of Émile Durkheim have been much more heavily used to analyze empirical data than those of another thinker of the same period, Gabriel Tarde, for example, not because Durkheim's ideas were better but because we had the methodological tools needed to test them. Now that we have the tools of computational social science, Tarde's ideas, too, can be used, as can others whose work was previously methodologically inaccessible. The result is a significantly enriched analytical toolkit for the social sciences.

And then there is the news about the limits of empiricism: how much we can actually know. Social scientists have a history of asserting that their work results in prediction, but as González-Bailón makes clear, even the best such research can yield vision into the future only so far, because of the complexities, contingencies, and stochastic interactions of social life. This doesn't mean we should refrain from doing social science, but it does mean that the work will be stronger and more useful if unsupportable claims about the results that are produced are replaced with humility, constraints, and clarity regarding what we actually know and what we don't, where the findings are applicable and where they are not.

Decoding the Social World opens with these fundamentally important insights into the nature of social science in the twenty-first century, and goes on to explore what we know, and can learn, about social networks and the dynamics of the social processes they generate or in which they are involved. All of this has implications for information policy. The concluding chapter takes some first steps in exploring just what those may be. González-Bailón looks at the roles that technologies can play in garnering citizen input into decision making via crowdsourcing and activism, at synergies between human and machinic decision making, and at thinking through networked forms of governance.

We can build on *Decoding the Social World* to think about how social networks affect evidence that informs policymaking. The analyses of social networks and the processes they enable, or in which they engage, will be useful for understanding policy networks involving collaborations between public- and private-sector decision makers, and the globalization of legal and policy approaches via the efforts of mid-level subject-expert practitioners. Computational social science can be invaluable in the effort to develop adaptive policymaking and implementation processes so important to the effort to make law and policy fully responsive to and adequate for governance in societies as they continue to be transformed by technological innovations and other factors. Reliance upon computational social science for governance purposes may be most successful when undertaken through the lenses of complex adaptive systems theory, a growing trend in policy analysis itself.

Two other areas in which computational social science has implications for information policy need in-depth investigation. The question of how reliance on big data that includes information that is heterogeneous in nature, varies in reliability, validity, and integrity, and is of unknown provenance can serve governance purposes requiring accurate representation of those being served goes to the heart of the survivability of genuine democracies altogether. And while we have a long history of treating fictional persons (corporations) as well as biological persons (people) as legal subjects for governance purposes, networks—whether or not autonomous—do not have that status. As was unpacked in my *International Journal of Communication* article "We are Bradley Manning: The Legal Subject and the WikiLeaks Complex," the Bradley/Chelsea Manning court martial over information shared with WikiLeaks provided insight into a number of arguments the US government has experimented with for this purpose; but this is an information policy problem that is very far from being solved.

For decades, private law has been used to develop precedent for what became public law in areas in which digital technologies had made types of interactions possible for which, at the time, there was neither national nor international law in place. The developments reported on in *Decoding the Social World* are tremendously exciting from the perspective of the enormous gains in our ability to understand social processes. But they also highlight how far we have yet to go in terms of understanding what those social processes mean for, and require from, governance.

Sandra Braman
Editor, Information Policy Series

Preface

This book tells two stories: a story of change and a story of recurrence. If we look at how communication technologies have been received over the last two hundred years, a pattern clearly emerges: like a pendulum, responses oscillate from wonder to fear, from apprehension to awe. These emotions get expressed, over and over, with the visual aid of metaphors that, in their persistence, seem to have grown deep roots in our collective imagination. It is common to think of networks as planetary nervous systems, constantly responding to ever-changing circumstances; or to think of communication systems as eighteenth-century Panopticons, structures designed to watch without being watched, symbols of surveillance and control.

Metaphors like these have been used (and abused) over the years to paint evolving communication technologies with the same black and white palette. This is how the story of recurrence is written: by fitting the new into the mental schemes that were devised to make sense of the old. But there is also a story of change running in parallel. What changed significantly over the same time period was the actual potential of emerging technologies to illuminate the hidden logic of social life—and the unintended consequences that so often result from daily routines and interactions. This story of change stumbles and winds through, but it does not move in circles.

Communication has always been the force that makes a collection of people more than the sum of individuals. Now we have the tools to understand why and apply that knowledge to rethink how we live and act in society. This book offers an account of the progress made during the last few decades. This progress results partly from the digital revolution, which is, in the end, the continuation of previous revolutions—technological breakthroughs that were also received with pompous admiration (and wary regard). But progress results as well from ideas that were germinating for a long time, restrained in their growth because there was no data that could cast light on them. Our knowledge of the social world and of the unintended effects that result from human action has progressed far in recent years. New data sources have helped accelerate that progress, but there is also a past trajectory of cumulative research and blind alleys that helped us get to where we now are.

In a similar way, this book results from a particular intellectual trajectory, a path that—like most things in life—results from a combination of random chance and purpose. The purpose took the form of a DPhil in sociology, which transplanted me from the erudite and combative scholarship of Barcelona to the Oxford analytical ways. Chance materialized in the form of the many people, books, and articles that crossed my way and made me look beyond the academic boundaries that surround (and constrain) a discipline. For the last ten years, I have been trying to connect the dots of all the ideas that I saw speaking intelligently to the problem of unintended effects: why they happen, how they manifest and with what impact. Identifying that common thread took me to where I currently stand—and to the book you hold in your hands.

The pages that follow are not designed to offer a comprehensive review of all the good research that digital technologies make possible today; nor do they aim to offer a practical guide to how to conduct digital research. A single person simply does not know enough to offer a fair account of everything that is possible and worthwhile to investigate, or how to make that research happen. This is a goal that requires a collective effort. For that reason, as I was writing this book I also decided to put together an edited volume with the collaboration of more than 30 contributors. These colleagues are emerging and consolidated scholars who agreed to write a state-of-the-art review of their respective areas of work, spanning several disciplines but all concerned with the analysis of social dynamics as mediated by communication technologies (the volume, coedited with Brooke Foucault-Welles, is forthcoming in the Handbook series of Oxford University Press). That compilation offers a more complete representation of current frontiers in digital research—and also of its collaborative nature, which can only be partially acknowledged in a monograph like this.

The goal of this book is therefore not to offer a survey of research but rather to build a coherent and convincing story of why communication is core to important research problems; why these problems remained unresolved for a long time; why digital technologies allow us to confront them with more powerful data and tools; and why their resolution cannot rely on a single disciplinary approach. In selecting some problems over others I am (unavoidably) disclosing the legacy of my own research path. This trajectory has evolved mostly in the field of collective behavior and, more specifically, around the question of political mobilization through decentralized networks—communication structures, that is, that are not fully controlled by any one actor and are, therefore, a breeding ground for unintended effects. Even though the book relies heavily on my research experience in this domain, my goal here is to widen my usual focus of attention (obligatorily narrow when research is communicated through journal articles) and make theoretical connections between ideas and research approaches that do not always engage in productive discussion—to the loss of all involved.

This book vindicates the importance of sociological thinking but also of the innovative tools and methods that are being developed under the label of data science. The title of the book is a wink to those working at the intersection of an old and an emerging discipline. This is a space that is growing fast, reminding us that disciplinary boundaries are historical contingencies that, by necessity, change. And yes, the title also makes use of a metaphor long employed by scientists that look at nature as a gigantic cryptogram. As the following pages will discuss, society, unlike nature, often changes the encoding rules, sometimes with the sole purpose of misleading the observer. This makes social life all the more difficult to decode—but also all the more exciting.

The two stories told—that of change, that of recurrence—go from nineteenth-century essays on physics and politics to our twentieth-first-century discussions on social physics; from cybernetics, the science of self-regulation and control that grew in the 1950s, to the "big data" approaches to governance; from studies on the mental representation of urban landscapes, back when maps were analog and hand-drawn, to the vision of "smart cities" that has gained so much policy traction recently; from the first academic discussions about the nature of social facts during the French Third Republic, to our current research approach to collective behavior as measured through digital traces. The two stories converge around the many paradoxes that define social life, and give an account of why communication technologies allowed us to go from metaphors to explanations, and from explanations to policy and action.

This book takes a clear epistemological stance that sides with the logic of scientific discovery—which I imagine as a candid conversation between Karl Popper and Thomas Kuhn. The following pages are openly sympathetic to those who try to simplify the complexity of the world through data analysis, abstractions, and models (other than metaphors). This is where data science comes in, in its quest to find patterns where none is discernible to the human eye. But the book also tries to echo the importance of the social context to understand how we think about technologies and the things we can do with them—also to appreciate that knowledge and research often reflect the priorities of the age, not necessarily the most relevant questions.

If I had to summarize the book in one sentence, it would be that communication networks are the backbone of social life—and that they are difficult to govern when they operate from the bottom up because of their unpredictable nature. This statement, of course, is useless without the details of its many ramifications. The following chapters discuss different areas into which that root statement branches out. The territory mapped was surveyed partly because I know it well, and partly to give a response to claims about the lack of theory in data science. I hope to convey that, when the right connections are made, much of the data-driven research that is being conducted today speaks directly to long-standing (and unresolved) theoretical discussions that have kept social scientists busy since, at least, nineteenth-century debates.

In writing this book I was also motivated by the need to contextualize current discussions on the impact that technologies have on social life in the longer historical conversation to which they belong. Academic work is sometimes stranded in a shallow obsession with the here and now. This results in wheels being reinvented and in scholarship that ages fast—as fast as the technology to which it pays attention. There is a theoretical lineage to which much research seems oblivious today, and the pages that follow aim to acknowledge that history.

Likewise, the book aims to convey that while technologies change, important theoretical challenges transcend specific technologies. The unintended consequences of human action; the effects of social influence; the role of communication networks in reducing social distance—these are examples of theoretical problems that materialize in different technological eras. What matters is not the technology that dominates a given time, but how that technology can be used to crack those problems—and, by extension, the hidden code of social life. Breaking that code is important because our interventions in the world (in the form of policy or action) will have better chances of succeeding if we actually understand what we are trying to change.

The book, in the end, is a story of progress that is both humbling and encouraging. It is humbling because it demystifies the illusion that our times are more revolutionary than times past. Hyperboles, after all, are like old friends with a short memory. But the story is also encouraging because it shows that we can actually get better at decoding the complex reality of the social world. The following chapters consider why, how, and with what consequence, pointing to questions that still pulsate unresolved—and to possible directions in our search for the answers that are still missing.

Acknowledgments

This book became a reality with the support and the encouragement of many people. Many of its ideas brewed while I was still based in Oxford. I am grateful to Bill Dutton and Helen Margetts for creating and promoting a space for multidisciplinary research back when it was still not a fashionable thing to do. The years I spent at the Oxford Internet Institute gave me the confidence and the trust to work on topics that did not fall comfortably in any one research tradition. It all made sense in the end, but Bill and Helen took a chance on me for which I will always be grateful. I also want to thank Helen for her mentorship and friendship, for being a role model in many different ways, and for sharing her mirth so generously and so often. I am also thankful to Michael Biggs, my thesis supervisor, for reading the first draft version of the book (all these years after!), and for giving me, as usual, perceptive and reassuring comments. He taught me how to think and write like a sociologist, and I hope this book bears the fruits of that learning.

I thank my colleagues at the Annenberg School for Communication, my current intellectual home, for the many ways in which they support my work and offer insights: it is a great privilege to be surrounded by colleagues whose work inspires so many ideas every single day. I am particularly grateful to Michael Delli Carpini, our dean, for creating the best possible environment to allow our projects to grow, and for always having time in his busy schedule to meet and talk and give constructive feedback. I have learned a great deal from our conversations. I am also grateful to Joe Cappella, Emily Falk, Marwan Kraidy, Jessa Lingel, Carolyn Marvin, Joe Turow, Bob Hornik, and Barbie Zelizer for the advice and ideas with which they have enriched so many exchanges, in and out of the School, often in worldly places. I hope they can perceive their influence in these pages. At the end of my first year at Annenberg I was privileged to share two wonderful weeks with Elihu and Ruth Katz in Barcelona as part of the Summer Culture Program that Barbie directs. Many of the conversations we had during those two weeks keep on flashing back, always to shed light on some missing connection in my attempts to associate ideas. To this day, I treasure the little portion of their wisdom I managed to tap into.

I am also grateful to the Annenberg graduate students for their unfailing stream of interesting thoughts and for constantly keeping me on my toes: I can only hope they learn as much from me as I learn from our class discussions. In particular, I want to thank the students that took part in the Decoding the Social World seminar for their comments on a draft version of this book: Kecheng Fang, Sean Fischer, Douglas Guilbeault, Helene Langlamet, Subhayan Mukerjee, Rui Pei, and Kristin Shumaker. Thanks also to Ashley Gorham for reading portions of the manuscript and for sharing so many brilliant ideas.

The Annenberg support staff also deserve my heartfelt acknowledgment for working so diligently and with good cheer to help us make our research come alive. I want to explicitly thank Kelly Fernandez for always keeping it together, as only she can do, but also, and mostly, for her friendship—and for all those conversations full of life and comedy. Thanks also to Julie Sloane for crafting so many inspiring suggestions that help make the language of research more broadly accessible—and also, of course, for the laughs.

To my good collaborator and friend, Javier Borge-Holthoefer, I want to say thanks for all the good moments spent discussing ideas, developing projects, and writing papers, many of which helped this book have more substance and empirical roots. I look forward to the new projects that are to come, and to the jokes slipped in between mathematical explanations— I am sure some will actually be good. I am also grateful to Yamir Moreno for allowing our first collaboration to thrive and for teaching me so many things about networks. Thanks also to Alex Arenas, professor and *enfant terrible*, for allowing me to see how a physicist sees the world and for acknowledging (sometimes) that he is not always right. Our discussions are always a highlight—a treat for the mind.

Duncan Watts has been a source of inspiration for so long that I owe him a big thank-you as well. His book *Small Worlds* was one of the first non-Spanish books I bought when I was still a student in Barcelona, and his *Six Degrees* was the first book I bought when I moved to Oxford to start my graduate degree. We did not actually meet until I was finishing my dissertation but, luckily for me, we have been in touch ever since, and I never fail to learn something new from those encounters. His work simply blazed a trail that made it easier for many of us to follow.

Cristian Vaccari was kind enough to read a draft version of the manuscript during a busy time. I am thankful for his comments, which were insightful and helpful, and I look forward to future exchanges—including reading his own book manuscript, soon to come.

I also want to thank the team at the MIT Press for being supportive at all times and stages. I am very grateful to Sandra Braman for first inviting me to submit a proposal to the Press and then patiently working with me in the long process of making the book come together. She has been the most supportive editor I could hope to have. Our discussions (online or offline) were always the seed of something good: a new way of looking at ideas or a strategy to improve an argument. Working with her has made it so much easier to finish the book that I wanted to write. I am also thankful to Gita Manaktala for her professionalism, patience, and encouragement, and to Matthew Abbate for being a great adjudicator in my battles with the written word. Thanks also to the three anonymous reviewers for making suggestions that helped me improve the final version of the book.

To my friends: I thank them for keeping me sane in the whirl of academic life, for anchoring me, and for directing my attention to the things that really matter. In particular, I want to thank Tommy and Fer. They have the ability to magically show up when I need them most, and of course they did again as I was struggling to finish this book. Their company and conversation have healing powers, and I feel fortunate to have them in my life. I want to thank Berta and Silvia for the laughs and Spanish optimism with which they have filled so many nights, and for making me feel less isolated in the often daunting process of writing in a language that is still not fully mine. To Rhonda, I want to give thanks for her always timely suggestions to go to the movies—and for never forgetting to bring the bottle of wine. I am also grateful to Eline for so many good moments of deep conversation: it is energizing to discover that our friendship not only endures distance but becomes more genuine over time. And to Doug: thank you for the road trips, the soundtracks, and for sharing so many insights on work and life.

Last but not least—that is, first and foremost—I want to thank my family. They are like the North Star: often forgotten while you are busy looking down on earthly matters, but always there when you need to find direction. My parents have given me so much of that intangible force that no amount of books written could ever reciprocate fairly. But still: this book, my first, is dedicated to them, to their perseverance, example, and lifelong generosity. I also want to thank my sister, Verónica, for her unwavering support, for filling in the gaps created by my distance, and for sending me all those beautiful photos of the Mediterranean at dawn.

Philadelphia
January 2017

1 Introduction: Decoding the Social World

Communication networks have made the world smaller. They have also, paradoxically, turned it into the largest measurement instrument ever known. Journalists and commentators have filled pages discussing how technologies extend a "nervous system" around the planet that allows us to constantly monitor its pulse, regardless of location and distance. Time and space, they claim, are "annihilated" in the wired world, with rippling effects that cascade across all layers of social life, which is now more tangible, easier to measure. The local goes global, and the average person swims in a sea of information that was previously out of reach even for those wielding political or economic power. There are also critical voices accompanying this account, warning us—like a baritone in a duet—that communication networks are in fact chaining us in a perverse submission to technocrats. Technologies, they claim, blur long-standing boundaries separating the private and the public, leaving an important dimension of social life at the mercy of private interests. In the whirlwind of voices that praise and condemn, technological innovation stands like the proverbial half-glass of water: an object onto which observers project their disposition, not necessarily an accurate depiction of what they see.

As contemporary as these pronouncements might seem, they were in fact not written as a response to the digital revolution—or at least not for the first time. They were first articulated as the modern world was taking shape, and were expressed most vocally as the structures of human communication were being shaken by two tectonic shifts: the expansion of the telegraph and the invention of the telephone in the second half of the nineteenth century (Fischer 1994; Gleick 2011; Marvin 1988; Standage 2009 [1998]). Public response to those technological developments does not seem greatly different from the reception of Internet technologies today.

Given these precedents, should we consider current debates as yet another example of what philosophers call the "eternal return" of history? Or is there something new in how we think about the world that distinguishes our own communication revolution from previous ones? Much of the current discourse seems oblivious to the historical relevance of past technological breakthroughs—even though it uses the very same metaphors to describe the impact of technologies on our social life. Are we just singing a different version of the old songs: an ode to progress, an elegy for times gone? Or are we moving forward in our understanding of communication, what it reveals about the social world, and what it tells us about the societies we want to build?

This book is an attempt to answer these questions. The core of the argument, for those impatient to know, is that yes, we are moving forward—with all the caveats that any sense of direction and progress requires in the post-Enlightenment world. New ideas are shaping the way in which we think about social life and the societies we inhabit, invigorated by the availability of new data resources, the byproducts of our communication activities. Many other ideas, however, have a long shadow in the history of social research: they are loaded with analogies and metaphorical connections that we keep on using as if they offered a fresh view, thought they might in fact be trapping our imagination under the low ceilings of ingrained clichés. This is one of the main messages that connect the chapters that follow: that the metaphors we use to refer to social life, as manifested through communication, shape how we think about society and how we envision its governance and regulation. Determining what is really new in our digital revolution requires filtering out the ideas (and the analogies) that were transported from the previous revolutions like sediment in a river.

1.1   Communication and Its Metaphors

One common cliché assumes that societies are like living organisms—and so of course they have a nervous system. In his description of the Electric Telegraph Company central office in London, a journalist claimed in 1854: "Who would think that behind this narrow forehead lay the great brain—if we may so term it—of the nervous system of Britain?" A few years later, in 1880, *Scientific American* wrote about the telephone: "The time is close at hand when the scattered members of civilized communities will be as closely united, so far as instant telephonic communication is concerned, as the various members of the body now are by the nervous system" (Gleick 2011, 126). The level of telegraphic traffic in 1870 was already so high that the president of Western Union, the largest telegraph company in the United States, told a congressional committee: "The fact is, the telegraph lives upon commerce. It is the nervous system of the commercial system. If you will sit down with me at my office for twenty minutes, I will show you what the condition of business is at any given time in any locality in the United States" (Standage 2009 [1998], 170). In 1895, an English engineer compared commerce to the lifeblood of nations, claiming that roads, railways, and waterways are "the arteries through which this blood is conducted, while telegraphs and telephones may be compared to the nerves which feel out and determine the course of that circulation, which is a condition of national prosperity" (Marvin 1988, 141).

These analogies follow the spirit of the times, best represented by the intellectual of the era, Herbert Spencer, the philosopher who joined Auguste Comte in laying down the first stones of the intellectual edifice we now call sociology; a founding father who has since been largely discredited for giving to the political order a savage "survival of the fittest" philosophy. However, even he was careful to point out the limits of analogies: "Of course, I do not say that the parallel between an individual organism and a social organism is so close that the distinction to be clearly drawn in the one case may be drawn with like clearness in the other. The structures and functions of the social organism are obviously far less specific, far more modifiable, far more dependent on conditions that are variable and never twice alike" (Spencer 1873, 58). Analogies help make creative connections; but they can also draw pictures of the world that are too coarse-grained for any useful purpose.

What is surprising, then, is that 150 years later we still talk about communication technologies in very similar terms. A 2009 *Forbes* article titled "The Rise of the Social Nervous System" claims: "No technology is more transformative than the Internet. ... As ever more people get connected, we see an acceleration in the way the Internet is used to coordinate action and render services from human input. We are witnessing the rise of the social nervous system" (Ross 2009). Of course, that rise was also witnessed, and praised, more than six generations before. In 2012, a book titled *The Human Face of Big Data* relates that digital technologies are "helping the planet grow a nervous system, one in which we are just another, human type of sensor" (Smolan and Erwitt 2012, 3). What the book does not mention is that those sensors once communicated with electrical pulses and Morse code. Talking about the Internet of Things, IBM buoyantly proclaims:

Over the past century, we have seen the emergence of a kind of global data field. The planet itself—natural systems, human systems, physical objects—have always generated an enormous amount of data, but until recent decades, we weren't able to hear it, to see it, to capture it. Now we can because all of these things have been instrumented with microchips, UPC codes and other technologies. And they're all interconnected, so now we can actually have access to the data. In effect, the planet has grown a central nervous system and is developing intelligence. (IBM 2015)

This is how a giant corporation, born to rule the mainframe business only to languish under the shadow of personal computing, reinvented itself in the twenty-first century: by reigniting with awe the same old metaphors that were being used two centuries before.

These metaphors are not just marketing buzz, flashes in the current zeitgeist. They are powerful ideas that shape how we think about decision making and governance, both in the private realm of corporations and in the public domain of governments (Mayer-Schoenberger and Cukier 2013). As Susan Sontag noted in her now-classic essays on metaphors and illness, there is a "perennial description of society as a kind of body, a well-disciplined body ruled by a 'head.' This has been the dominant metaphor for the polity since Plato and Aristotle, perhaps because of its usefulness in justifying repression. Even more than comparing society to a family, comparing it to a body makes an authoritarian ordering of society seem inevitable, immutable" (Sontag 1991). Surely we have moved on since Plato and Aristotle; but metaphors still grip our imagination with the same effect, which is to make suggestive (but also misleading) connections. If actual nerves and sensory fibers stop working and channeling external stimuli into the central nervous system, the system will have serious trouble ensuring the survival of the body. But if someone decides to turn off tracking devices and shut digital signals down, this is certainly not a malfunction of the planetary body—it might create holes in the sensory experience of IBM-type brains, but the planet's survival is not at stake; it has survived so far (although bruised) without the aid of an artificial nervous system.

1.2 The Social Cryptogram

Analogies deflate when they are confronted with the limits of the associations they make—as Spencer said, the parallels between real organisms and metaphorical ones have a horizon beyond which there is not much insight left. So is there a metaphor that might trigger more imaginative associations in how we think about the social world? What if we looked at it as an encrypted message that we can decode? The message is most definitely not written by a single writer (for the same reason that there is no supreme storyteller dictating history) but by many; the code is complex because there are multiple lines being written at the same time, intersecting without the guidance of a master plot; so the best we can do is try to isolate strands within the story. This has been the view of scientists who, at least since the times of Leibniz, have looked at nature as a "gigantic cryptogram, a gigantic series of coded messages" (Bronowski 1978, 48). Scientific understanding is all about trying to crack that code.

And yet, as Norbert Wiener, the father of cybernetics, pointed out, "Nature offers resistance to decoding, but it does not show ingenuity in finding new and undecipherable methods for jamming our communication with the outer world" (Wiener 1950, 34). Nature, in other words, does not play tricks and change policies just to confuse us; that, of course, is the prerogative of humans. Human communication is often distorted by misleading information and shifting encoding rules. Sifting information from misinformation, the signal from the noise, is what mathematicians and engineers did during World War II, a story now popularized by the *Imitation Game*, the 2014 movie on Alan Turing (starring the great Benedict Cumberbatch, who elsewhere plays the part of another master of decoding, Sherlock Holmes). On the other side of the Atlantic, a similar line of work was being led by Claude Shannon, a mathematician working at Bell Labs, the epicenter of much visionary research that was also immersed in the priorities of national defense. It was at this moment that the mathematical theory of communication is born.

The theory is, in fact, very different from how social scientists usually think about communication—mostly because it showed that you can decode a message without caring much for the meaning (Gleick 2011, 221). Much social research starts from the premise that conveying meaning is the fundamental problem of communication; but meaning is precisely what is often intentionally concealed, as in the encrypted messages that were being sent by Enigma, the cipher machine used by the German army. Appealing to meaning was not of much use in trying to decode those messages; this is why Turing's work and Shannon's theory were so revolutionary: they shifted how we think about communication to turn it into a game of encoding and decoding rules. Their work made explicit the process we take for granted when we speak in conversation, steps that do not come naturally to machines until they are instructed: encode a message so that it can be transmitted as a signal; find ways to eliminate the noise that distorts the signal during transmission; and decode the signal, dusting off the noise to recover the intended message. We automatically execute these steps as we speak to friends in a loud coffee shop; machines, however, need to be meticulously told how to communicate that way.

In Shannon's theory, which was first published in 1948 as a declassified version of his prior war work, messages are units of information that are not created but selected. This implies that the messages we send are choices we make, and choices have probabilities attached. In this view, language is governed by a set of probabilities: the words we use to finish a sentence are not random, they depend to a great extent on the words we used before; the letters we use to finish a word are not random either, this is why word prediction software generally makes good guesses and suggests endings as we type. The bottom line is: language has a structure, a structure that is preserved even when a message is encrypted. This was the key to the codebreaking efforts carried out during the forties—and the kernel that was to evolve into the technology that pervades our current communication networks.

Social life, we could argue, also has a structure that is often hidden, buried in noise. And in much the same way as probability can help reverse-engineer a cryptic code, it can also hand us a shovel to uncover the patterns that give meaning to the social world. As metaphors, "social organism" and "gigantic cryptogram" might seem equally gross simplifications. But the second analogy at least emphasizes the stochastic nature of social life, which means that its course is never fully random or fully deterministic: instead, it is a dynamic process that exhibits path dependence, where the present constrains the future but never fully shapes it; a process that results, to put it in the words of Hannah Arendt, from the "inherent tendency" of human action "to force open all limitations and cut across all boundaries"

(Arendt 1958, 190). What this means, for practical purposes, is that our depiction of the world is never complete; that we have to keep updating our judgments as new information comes in, in much the same way as cryptographers reallocated probabilities as new encrypted messages were intercepted. This is the way in which the signal can ultimately be separated from the noise (Silver 2012) and one of the main reasons why digital technologies are changing the way in which we can analyze the world compared to the telegraph era: we not only have more updates of social life as it unfolds; we also have the modeling techniques to adapt our knowledge to that constant flux of information.

The analogy with cryptography is also relevant because it helps make an important distinction that is not so clearly drawn when we think in terms of "social organisms" and their nervous systems: the distinction between uncovering meaning and doing something about it, once revealed. The mathematicians and engineers working in the decryption of war messages passed the intelligence on, when they were able to crack the code, to those who could make decisions on the basis of that information. The quality of their decoding had nothing to do with the quality of the decisions that followed—and, war being war, many were deplorable, triggering terrible consequences. But the lessons learned during the efforts to solve encrypted communication remain as a stepping-stone among the ashes of the conflict; they laid the road that was to lead to our current technologies and, arguably, to social life as we know it.

Today, commentators express fears that data science, and the new breed of researchers and technocrats orbiting Silicon Valley, interfere too much with decision making; this, they argue, threatens the right operation of democracy, because politics does not speak the same language as science (Morozov 2013). And the truth is that some algorithmic solutions to social problems fail miserably to accomplish their goals (O'Neil 2016). This book, however, stands by the claim that it is important to separate the functions of science from the functions of politics. This does not imply that the social sciences should not be normative or lead to action (or, most likely, reaction), but that the knowledge they produce should take precedence. Never before were the social sciences in a better position to decode the logic of social life and have a transformative impact through the design of technologies; but the decoding needs to go first: without it, there is no real understanding of the dynamics that drive social life. Understanding how networked technologies facilitate collective action, whether they make crowds smarter, or how they help anticipate natural disasters fall in the category of puzzles that need to be solved, problems to which this book pays attention in subsequent chapters. Policy implications will follow only if we decode the cryptogram—and this is not a matter for politics, but for research and data analysis.

1.3 Vast National Barometers

As important as analogies are for how we conceive the world, there is no doubt that better measurements help devise better theories—and this is the second theme cutting across all chapters in this book: that there is a true advance in understanding when we improve our instruments of measurement. The telegraph helped people discover the interconnected nature of meteorological phenomena: these, according to an 1848 commentator, were "no longer matters of superstition or of panic to the husbandman, the sailor or the shepherd" because the telegraph could now be used as "a vast national barometer" (Gleick 2011, 147). The craze for measurement that characterizes our days is, again, the most recent incarnation of an old impulse. Describing the first half of the nineteenth century, the historian Eric Hobsbawm writes: "It was the age of superlatives. The numerous new compendia of statistics in which this era of counting and calculation sought to record all aspects of the known world could conclude with justice that virtually every measurable quantity was greater (or smaller) than ever before" (Hobsbawm 2010 [1962], 359). Those were the times when industry and government intensified their data collection efforts; also when statistics (etymologically, the analysis of data about the state) grew to become the science of probability and uncertainty it is today.

The enlarged censuses and statistical compendia established social phenomena as an area of legitimate scientific enquiry. When Thomas R. Malthus elaborated the theory of overpopulation in his 1798 essay, he was turning something as private as fertility and sexual behavior into a matter of scientific and political interest. Scholars still debate whether there is a fatal fallacy in his theory, which predicts doom by the overpopulation of the earth—and seems to have everlasting influence in demographic thinking. But those same types of data also helped make visible the suffering and precarious living conditions of the dispossessed, fueling emerging social movements with facts that would help strengthen their cause. As Engels put it in his study of the working class in England, "A knowledge of proletarian conditions is absolutely necessary to be able to provide solid ground for socialist theories, on the one hand, and for judgments about their right to exist, on the other; and to put an end to all sentimental dreams and fancies pro and con." "Only in England," he continued, "has the necessary material been so completely collected and put on record by official enquiries as is essential for any in the least exhaustive presentation of the subject" (Engels 1987 [1892], preface to the first German edition). Data, then as now, was the best antidote to "sentimental dreams and fancies."

Likewise, much of the work that was done later by the British Fabian Society, including the work of the sociologist Beatrice Webb (one of the cofounders of the London School of Economics), relied on data gathered through surveys, which resulted in important indicators and poverty maps that challenged existing records. These maps described the realities of urban life, identifying poor areas and offering avenues for starting to think about how to improve living conditions. They followed the path opened by John Snow in his 1849 essay *On the Mode of Communication of Cholera*, a pioneering study on the social determinants of public health that used maps and statistics to show the connection of water quality and cholera cases. This attention to the urban environment was later picked up by the early Chicago school of sociology. The social sciences, in other words, emerged with the ultimate goal of improving collective well-being; but for that, the social world needed first to be characterized, and quantifiable data offered the most valuable resource.

The amount of data we can amass and process today is far larger than that collected in the nineteenth century—in fact, it has become another commonplace to claim that every day we create more information than in the entire previous history of humanity, or a variation of such a claim. However, a great deal of public discussion seems to be more concerned about the losses in privacy than about the gains in knowledge and how we can use that gain to improve the conditions of many. Privacy and its violation are important matters, which explains why so much attention is being paid to them: digital technologies, and their use for surveillance, create imbalances of information in favor of the powerful few, including not only corporations but also intrusive states (Schneier 2015). The way in which

those fears are articulated has also a resounding echo in history, with arguments that repeat many of the concerns surrounding older technologies.

When the telephone became the new disruptive technology, a commentator of the era said: "No matter to what extent a man may close his doors
and windows, and hermetically seal his key-holes and furnace-registers
with towels and blankets, whatever he may say, either to himself or a com-
panion, will be overheard" (Gleick 2011, 189–190). Voices, it transpires,
were the sound of private matters, and the telephone was opening a threat-
ening door to anonymous eavesdropping. According to the *New York Times*,
this door was indeed wide open: in 1877 two telephone men recounted
how they had heard "eloquent clergymen, melodious songs, midnight cats,
and 'other things which they did not venture to openly repeat,' including 'the confidential conversations of hundreds of husbands and wives'"
(Marvin 1988, 68). The telephone was redefining the boundaries of private and public in ways that many people found unsettling: "One common
complaint in the nineteenth century was that the telephone permitted
intrusion into the domestic circle by solicitors, purveyors of inferior music,
eaves-dropping operators, and even wire-transmitted germs" (Fischer 1994,
26). Our understanding of privacy today is, to a large extent, the result
of the renegotiations that took place as the electric wires extended their
stems.

Subsequent technological advances were not received more easily. When
the Kodak camera was introduced at the end of the nineteenth century,
bringing with it the now common term "snapshot," admirers were quick to
praise its ability to capture images spontaneously—the standard wet-plate
cameras of the time had, until then, made their subjects look stiff and eerie.
However, many thought that the new cameras posed unprecedented threats
to privacy. As one newspaper put it: "The sedate citizen can't indulge in any
hilariousness without the risk of being caught in the act and having his
photograph passed around among his Sunday School children" (Lohr 2015,
183). A few decades later, new fears arose with the emergence of the mainframe computer and the compilation by government and credit bureaus of
large databases with personal information: "Many people feared that the
new computerized databanks would be put in the service of an intrusive
corporate or government Big Brother" (Lohr 2015, 184). Once more, commentators reacted promptly to those fears, among them the prolific Vance
Packard, a leading social critic of the time, who wrote about the threats
of manipulative advertising and the dangers of computerized filing and

surveillance (Packard 1957, 1964; see also Horowitz 2000). Technologies change inexorably, but the reactions to them seem too human to evolve as fast—or to evolve at all.

The potential for mass, indiscriminate surveillance that our current communication technologies make possible has, surely, no precedents in history. But if we are to take history as a guide, we can only predict the recession of current criticisms, as new technologies settle with the dust of the conventional and the next big technological advancements arise. What will remain, once more, are the stepping-stones of added understanding that we lay down on the way. As cryptographer Bruce Schneier states, "there is enormous value in aggregating our data for medical research, improving education, and other tasks that benefit society. We need to figure out how to collectively get that value while minimizing the harms" (Schneier 2015, 8). We are, in a sense, at a crossroads similar to that facing the social scientists working in Victorian England: trying to find ways to use the newly available data for a good cause.

In what surely counts as another spin of the "eternal return," scientists today brand their work in very similar terms to those of their earlier colleagues. A recent account of the power of digital technologies to inform policymaking runs under the banner of "social physics," defined as a "quantitative social science" that "helps us tune communication networks so that we can reliably make better decisions" (Pentland 2014, 4). The key to this approach, which falls within the boundaries of an emerging field known as "computational social science," is the promotion of idea flow, which is shaped by the structure of communication through which people interact; digital technologies, the argument goes, are changing that structure for the better because they facilitate monitoring performance in real time, helping readjust the decision-making process as it evolves. The approach has found audiences in upscale policy arenas like the World Economic Forum, and in the United Nations through the Global Pulse initiative (Pentland 2014, chapter 11). This initiative envisions "a future in which big data is harnessed safely and responsibly as a public good" (http://www.unglobalpulse.org/about-new).

Such a defense of positive science in studying society and shaping governance also follows the trail of the nineteenth century. In 1872, Walter Bagehot, an English journalist (and editor in chief of the newspaper *The Economist*), published a book entitled *Physics and Politics*. The book—which exudes the prevailing social Darwinism of the era—defended liberal values and the superiority of "government by discussion": "Discussion," Bagehot claimed, "has incentives to progress peculiar to itself. It gives a premium to intelligence" (Bagehot 2007 [1872], 105). Before that, Adolphe Quételet used the expression "social physics" to talk about the statistical analysis of society (Quételet 1835), appropriating it from Auguste Comte, who as a result started using the term "sociology" (Comte 1830–1842). There is little doubt that, since then, we have improved considerably in our measurements, and the chapters that follow are a testament to that progress. But the grand vision of positivism, and the words of those who brandish it, have not changed much in the last two centuries.

1.4   The Unpredictability of Social Life

So, are our networks of communication helping us devise better measurements that lead to better theories and, if so, to better interventions? Yes, but with a limit—that imposed by the inherent unpredictability of human action, what Arendt called the "infinite improbability which occurs regularly." To put it in her words (loaded with gravitas):

> The life span of man running toward death would inevitably carry everything human to ruin and destruction if it were not for the faculty of interrupting it and beginning something new, a faculty which is inherent in action like an ever-present reminder that men, though they must die, are not born in order to die but in order to begin. (Arendt 1958, 246)

This declaration (which, obviously, also applied to women) is not that different from when Wiener, in his popular account of cybernetics, talked about "local and temporary islands of decreasing entropy in a world in which the entropy as a whole tends to increase"; these islands, he argued, are the key to progress (Wiener 1950, 36). And this is how the second law of thermodynamics tries to make existentialism look a bit more cheerful.

The bottom line is that human action (in the form of technological invention, policy, or intervention) is capable of triggering unanticipated reactions; this is another reason to keep our models of the world open, which offers the third and most important theme in the chapters that follow. The models we build to understand and intervene in the world should be capable of adapting to persistent feedback, to the ability of people to renew and invent—but also to the consequences that arise, unintended, from their interactions. Our constant adaptation to what irrupts as novel is what makes social systems so wonderfully open-ended, but also so difficult to govern. Unintended consequences are bad for prediction and control, but fortunately they are good for innovation and progress.

History gives us, again, a few examples of the unpredictability of social life. When the telegraph arose, many predicted the end of the newspapers—much as the digital media today are reputed to be causing the end of journalism (Zelizer 2015). The telegraph disrupted the normal operation of the news industry, which up to the 1830s "moved so slowly that there was no danger that one paper would steal another's story and be on sale at the same time" (Standage 2009 [1998], 146). News was often weeks old when it reached readers, especially foreign news. As newspapers became a more popular medium for mass communication, competition to get news first increased: being ahead of other newspapers meant selling more. So when the telegraph arrived to replace horses, carrier pigeons, and ships as the means through which news traveled, "the competition to see who could get the news first was, in effect, over. The winner would no longer be one of the newspapers; it would be the telegraph" (Standage 2009 [1998], 148). Many observers assumed that newspapers were doomed to disappear, relegated as they were to the role of commentators. As an American journalist put it: "the newspapers will become emphatically useless. Anticipated at every point by the lightning wings of the Telegraph, they can only deal in local 'items' or abstract speculations. Their power to create sensations, even in election campaigns, will be greatly lessened—as the infallible Telegraph will contradict their falsehoods as fast as they can publish them" (quoted in Gleick 2011, 145). We now know, of course, that these observers got it wrong.

Most voices predicting the end of newspapers failed to anticipate how the telegraph was triggering changes that would end up reconfiguring the industry. Prominent among these unanticipated effects was the emergence of news agencies like Associated Press in New York and Reuter in Europe, which allowed newspapers to cooperate in the creation of a network of reporters telegraphing news back from remote places (Standage 2009 [1998], 150). These new agencies helped newspapers expand their reach and coverage while minimizing the costs, an advancement that would not have been possible without the telegraph: "The relationship between the telegraph and the newspaper was symbiotic. Positive feedback loops amplified the effect. Because the telegraph was an information technology, it served as an agent of its own ascendency" (Gleick 2011, 145). Rather than burying the newspapers, the telegraph helped them rise to new heights.

Similarly, early commentators failed to anticipate how the telegraph would strengthen the power of the fourth estate. Diplomats, for instance, often felt sidelined by the telegraph in the exchange of information: "Traditionally, diplomats prefer slow, measured responses to events, but the telegraph encouraged instant reaction ... ; once the newspapers got hold of news, they would demand a statement from the government, which would then find its way into the hands of foreign governments via the media, circumventing conventional diplomatic channels" (Standage 2009 [1998], 158). Those in power probably did not anticipate the role that the telegraph would play in spreading the news of the revolutionary wave of 1848: "An entire continent waited, ready by now to pass the news of revolution almost instantly from city to city by means of the electric telegraph" (Hobsbawm 2010 [1962], 371). The spreading of the telegraph had been encouraged by military and commercial interests; but the effects of its expansion were difficult to contain within the safe borders of elitist aspirations.

This, of course, was not even the first time that new communication technologies triggered radical transformations as a byproduct of their original purpose. The printing press, for instance, helped initiate the Protestant Reformation in the early sixteenth century, which ended up shattering the foundations of the medieval order. In the words of a historian, "For the first time in human history a great reading public judged the validity of revolutionary ideas through a mass-medium which used the vernacular language together with the arts of the journalist and the cartoonist" (Eisenstein 2012, 164). Luther's theses spread so fast that they were known throughout Germany in two weeks, and throughout Europe in a month. The key to this fast dissemination was "the activities of the printers, translators, and distributors who acted as agents of the change" (ibid., 169). Without them, and the possibilities afforded by the press, the theses would not have traveled far from the church door to which they were, allegedly, originally nailed—this was the customary place for medieval publicity, a board that was considerably constrained in its ability to reach wide audiences.

Sometimes it is lack of imagination, or a blind fondness for the old ways, that prevents us from foreseeing the wider transformations that new technologies trigger; but more often the problem is not just lack of vision but the more inescapable fact that predicting effects is very difficult. As sociologist Duncan Watts put it, "when we think about the future, we imagine it to be a unique thread of events that simply hasn't been revealed to us yet. In reality no such thread exists—rather, the future is more like a bundle of possible threads, each of which is assigned some probability of being drawn, where the best we can manage is to estimate the probabilities of the different threads" (Watts 2011, 155). Because the past only offers an account of the things that happened, "not all the things that might have happened but didn't," we think the future is equally unambiguous. The problem is that such a projection does not factor in all the variables and alignment of circumstances that might tip the course of events one way or another—among them, the human ability to reclaim and repurpose technologies, and hence break expectations. History might spin in eternal recurrence, but, like a hurricane, it follows an erratic path.

1.5   Reasons and Passions

There is a fourth theme connecting the chapters in this book, and that is an implicit critique of what seems like a perennial opposition of the scientific and the humane—a dichotomy that often equates science with everything that is dry and evil, tempted by some Mephistopheles to surrender moral integrity in exchange for power. The modern Faust, we are often forced to conclude, works for Amazon, Google, and Facebook. In their attempt to quantify every aspect of human life, critics argue, these companies strip away what makes us human, all that is immune to quantification; or else they boil the fullness of the world down to the naked bones of numbers and algorithmic thinking. Algorithms, they claim, impose the rule of the technocrat; and this is bad because "technocratic thinking views pluralism as an enemy, not an ally—or, in geeks' own parlance, it's a bug, not a feature" (Morozov 2013, 137). According to these views, looming on the horizon is the dark dystopia portrayed in 2014 by Dave Eggers in *The Circle*, a novel that makes the reader look with dread at social media activity, a monster we feed gleefully to end up submitting to its boundless demands. "Could an algorithmic society," asks a commentator, "reduce us to no more than bundles of data, trundling through life, pushed and pulled this way and that?" (Handy 2015). We are willing to let technologies, it seems, squeeze us between digital rollers, even if we know we will come out as two-dimensional versions of ourselves, flat and flimsy like leaves falling in autumn.

The reality is that much of this discourse is highly misleading, both about the motivations that drive technological developments and about what algorithms can accomplish on their own. Algorithms are not the unrestrained Leviathan of our times—they respond to human skill and creativity pretty much like art does. And like art, the algorithms we produce can be good or bad. It would seem a big stretch to argue that art is conducive to fascism just because Marinetti declared that "art, in fact, can be nothing but violence, cruelty, and injustice," promising to "glorify war—the world's only hygiene—militarism, patriotism, the destructive gesture of freedom-bringers, beautiful ideas worth dying for, and scorn for woman" (Marinetti 1909). Art, surely, is not responsible for the delusions of megalomaniacs. But then the same applies to science, technological developments, and the algorithms on which they rely. It is one thing to adopt a critical stance toward technologies and the interests they serve; it is another to assume there is something intrinsically wrong with algorithms and the way they parse the world. Current discourse, in fact, often echoes the spirit expressed by Lamartine, politician and poet, following the defeat of the French Revolution: "All those mathematicians who then monopolized speech, and crushed us younger men under the insolent tyranny of their triumph, believed that they had forever exhausted in us that which they had withered and destroyed in themselves—the whole moral, divine, and melodious part of human thought. Nothing can picture, to those who did not experience it, the supreme bareness of this epoch. ... Mathematics were the chains of human thought. I breathe again, for they are broken" (Van Laun 1877, 279–280). Of course, we all know now that the Restoration brought a wave of obscurantism that imposed heavier chains on human thought.

Algorithms rely on symbols, as art and language do; they translate reality into a higher level of abstraction because that makes reality more manageable. The goal in this case is not to produce aesthetic reactions (although this depends on who you ask) but to produce the right outcomes. It is in defining those outcomes and in determining the purpose of the symbolic translation that imagination and creativity come in. Jeff Hammerbacher, one of the leading figures in the inauguration of data science as a science, declared in a 2011 interview: "The best minds of my generation are thinking about how to make people click ads. That sucks" (Lohr

2015, 84). What he meant is that there are other goals that those same skills can serve—many of them worthier of consideration, such as improving democratic accountability or designing better policy interventions. This book focuses attention on some of those applications, which offer the most interesting side of algorithmic thinking and connect with a long tradition in the social sciences in which data is used to examine the social world—and, ultimately, find ways to improve its governance. It is simply too easy to criticize algorithms for their pitfalls; it is far more exciting and important (and difficult) to try to improve them so that they do what we want them to do. They are, in the end, an extension of our ability to be creative.

A world driven by data and algorithms can indeed lead to unfairness and discrimination, intentional or not (O'Neil 2016; Steiner 2012). This does not mean we have to stop using data and algorithms as tools for decision making; it means that we have to start thinking seriously about how to design those technologies so that we take their societal consequences into account. This is a challenge that will not benefit from dichotomizing the scientific and humanistic views of the world. The human mind invented algorithms; they offer yet another language in our repertoire. This is a language that not everyone speaks fluently, much as not everyone can write poetry. It is easy to see why algorithmic decision making creates opaqueness: data-driven technologies are ubiquitous and are quickly outrunning public understanding. But this is, in reality, a communication problem. One solution to this lack of public understanding is to use the old storytelling technique to translate the inner workings of algorithms into a more common language, a language where assumptions and inferences, clues and logic, are made explicit; this approach has been called "algorithmic accountability" (Lohr 2015, 204). And this is, in a way, what psychologists have been doing with the inner workings of our own brain, which is very algorithmic in its operation but also hardwired with biases that easily mislead our judgments—errors of which we are usually not even aware (Kahneman 2011). The only way to overcome the limitations of algorithmic decision making is to understand how it operates and to feed that knowledge back into future iterations of design. This is where the learning happens, where we lay the stepping-stones that remain in place after the wave of the new crashes—the moment when fingers will, inevitably, start pointing elsewhere.

1.6   Book Outlook

This book offers an account of how far we have progressed in the approach that pioneering scientists took to analyzing the social world; it is also an account of how much there is yet to uncover. Progress, to quote mathematician and humanist Jacob Bronowski, is the exploration of our own error: "If we ask 'Why do we know more now than we knew ten thousand years ago, or even ten years ago?' the answer is that it is by this constant adventure of taking the closed system and pushing its frontiers imaginatively into the open spaces where we shall make mistakes" (Bronowski 1978, 113). The technological world in which we live today is full of similar reactions to the nineteenth century's technologies. Jules Verne's satire of the technocratic spirit of his age, captured in his 1863 novel *Paris in the Twentieth Century*, already depicted many of our current fears about automated machines and decision making. It does not matter how much technology changes: for some, the glass of technological innovation will always be half empty. This book pays attention to the other half, the half that is full.

The digital traces we leave online create new opportunities to decode social life and uncover the forces that drive social change—from massive mobilizations to tidal opinion change, from shifts in norms and conventions to the cascading effects of new behavior. As the brief historical overview provided in this chapter suggests, communication has always created the connections that link human actions into a massive invisible web. This interdependence is the key to the unpredictability of social life, and to its unintended consequences. But today we can grasp those effects better because we have at our disposal computational and theoretical developments that were not available in the nineteenth century. Though their communication revolution might look similar to ours in hindsight, today we are more skillful, creative, and versatile in using the data that communication technologies generate.

Chapter 2 gives a more theoretical context to many of the ideas introduced here, especially the unpredictability of social life as it relates to interdependence and unintended effects. Social scientists have long considered the unintended consequences of human action, and puzzled over the mechanisms that make individual behavior activate seemingly autonomous collective dynamics—those operating without designer or director. Today, digital technologies are the conduits for many of the chain reactions that derive into that kind of cumulative effect. Content that goes viral, for instance, usually starts as private communication, initially generated without a large audience in mind. In a similar fashion, political protests often start with a set of goals that end up escalating beyond those originally envisioned. Unintended consequences can also take the form of perverse effects, as when rumors and misinformation spread. New communication technologies generate data that helps us reverse-engineer the feedback mechanisms that make these unintended consequences emerge. If governance and policymaking have a lesson to learn from this dimension of social life, it is that interventions often trigger responses that divert the intended course of action. And there is no way to plan for that, other than to be responsive to change.

Chapter 3 focuses attention on how communication generates social dynamics in the aggregate, including episodes of what was classically referred to as "collective effervescence" or what we now call, with a marketing slant, "buzz." Digital technologies are helping us understand how communication patterns fluctuate over time, how we can best characterize those dynamics, and how we can measure irregularities and identify significant spikes. The amount of time that lapses between the messages we send and their reception (i.e., the amount of time it takes for information to flow) is not constant: it shrinks and expands, with exceptional moments when communication rates accelerate and create the peaks that we associate with trending topics or buzz. Looked at from the aggregate, temporal patterns of communication reveal shifts in the allocation of public attention. This gives us new insights into what attracts attention, what drives it away, what underlies the formation of audiences, and how long communities of interest last. As with the telegraph, the rhythm of communication can help measure the pulse of nations—the difference is that now the rhythm runs much faster, with implications for how social influence unfolds. The speed and reach of communication has moved to a different scale; and given the way in which interdependence operates, that change of scale leads to a change of outcomes—including the ability to react faster to the unintended consequences of human action.

Chapter 4 moves from the aggregate to the local to delve into the mechanisms that activate dynamics of social influence, including how communication technologies are shaping contagion effects. The old metaphors comparing society to a living organism inevitably led to biological ideas of contagion: social change was seen as a process in which ideas and behavior spread by means of exposure. The telegraph and the telephone created bonds that detached contact from physical space, but the mechanisms—exposure and imitation—remained the same. Digital technologies have kept the metaphor alive, but one of the strongest empirical regularities uncovered by the analysis of digital data is that large-scale contagion is very uncommon. The chain reactions that make information travel from person to person and reach a large number of people are the exception, not the rule; the vast majority of messages or behaviors fall into oblivion before they can activate chain reactions of any kind. As rare as cascades are, however, there are very salient examples in which information and behavior run, to put it in the words of another common metaphor, "like wildfire." This chapter considers the mechanisms that underlie those episodes of large-scale diffusion and whether the fire can be traced back to a single spark or to many flickering flames. The paths that social influence follows, this chapter argues, are not erratic, but they are also not easy to foretell.

The dynamics that take place between the level of individual actors (exposure, imitation) and the level of aggregated collectives (trending topics, opinion shifts) are considered in chapter 5. This, the book argues, is the level of analysis where most theoretical advances have taken place since the emergence of digital technologies—and that sets the social science we can conduct today clearly apart from the first social scientists' attempts to decode the social world. The theory of networks offers the language to make this level of analysis operational: it describes interdependence beyond the horizons of individual actors and their groups of reference. Networks help measure social distance, and how we navigate that distance, in powerful new ways. Network theory also offers a rich explanatory tool to account for the sort of dynamics that are unplanned and unintended, like the large-scale coordination of spontaneous actions. There are many policy implications that derive from the analysis of large communication networks. The chapter pays special attention to those that rely on network structure to successfully diffuse information.

Chapter 6 looks at the constraints that space imposes on communication, and at how communication in turn reshapes those constraints. Early social scientists were concerned with how the growth of cities was transforming communication dynamics and the social life they sustain. Digital technologies have eroded the constraints of geography, but space is still a relevant factor in understanding the causes and effects of communication: there are still many geographical boundaries that shape our choices of who we interact with. At the same time, communication data is being used to shed light on how spatial partitions are not always the most informative way to analyze collective behavior, from mobility patterns to the diffusion of information. Understanding the constraints that space imposes on communication, and how communication often challenges those constraints, gives us, this chapter argues, a starting point to devise strategies for intervention—much in the same way as understanding the realities of urban life in the London of John Snow helped improve public health and living conditions.

A broader discussion of the policy implications of digital research is offered in chapter 7. Normative models of how we envision the societies we want (i.e., environmentally friendly, safer, or more protective of private life) depend on how people respond to changing norms and adapt their opinions and behavior accordingly. In other words, regulators and policymakers need a social context that responds favorably to the changes they want to promote. This chapter recapitulates the discussion of prior chapters to assess how digital technologies are changing our conception of governance; it also considers whether they put us in a better position to understand the forces that shape decision making—and, by extension, social change. One prominent advantage is that digital data enriches the layers of evidence on which decision making can be rooted. Although algorithms will never be a substitute for human decision making (among other things, because they are written by humans), they offer an important aid in parsing digital information and guiding the decisions we can make on the basis of that data. This chapter will explore why and how, paying especial attention to the consequences for how we understand privacy and transparency.

The final chapter offers an evaluation of the questions that remain open today—and that will likely remain open for many years to come. The goal is to offer a sober summary of the advantages we have gained by applying data science to the examination of social questions, but also to acknowledge the limitations of this approach and discuss how to best channel efforts to solve those limitations. Communication technologies are changing the way in which we represent the social world and act on it, but they are also changing the way in which we organize knowledge. Amid these transformations, social theory still provides a unique compass to navigate the sea of data that surrounds us; but only if we know how to exploit these new data resources, the chapter concludes, will theory building allow us to reach new shores.

Overall, the book aims to evaluate how far we have moved since social research emerged to make sense of the ugly world that came out of the industrial revolution. The distance traveled is not measured in the linear way in which we connect two points on a map; in this case there is no clear destination. But there is a sense of progression in the realization that we can now read aspects of social life that seemed encrypted before—especially as they relate to the unintended effects of communication. Most importantly, there is a sense of advancement in our ability to point to new problems that we did not even know existed. Data is most interesting, and most likely to spur improvement, when it is used to quantify how much we do not know. For that reason, the book brings together the spirit of data science, in its quest to yield insights from large volumes of data, and the theoretical roots of communication, understood broadly as the study of interdependence and influence in social life. To determine how much we do not know about the social world, we need to engage with the data and the algorithms that allow us to parse all the information we generate by being social; and we need to look at that data through the lens of theories that can capture the complexity of social life. The following chapter starts by delimiting the scope of those theories—and the sort of questions they allow us to ask.

2   Old Puzzles, New Evidence

The social world abounds in paradoxes. One of the most prominent (and mind-bending) is the Liar's Paradox, a puzzle created by self-reference or our ability to make statements that refer to themselves. If a person says "I am a liar," we are forced to conclude that the sentence is both true and false: a liar that tells the truth is not a liar; but then he is deceiving us, which confirms he is a liar after all, which in turn means he is telling us the truth, and so on. This circularity creates a prison for the mind, challenging our most entrenched intuitions of what truth and knowledge mean. The paradox presents an epistemological problem that has attracted constant attention over the centuries and has stirred many controversies in the attempts to solve it (Sainsbury 2008). As unnerving as the puzzle might be, however, its persistence has not been futile: it has encouraged philosophers and mathematicians to develop formal languages that do not fall into the contradictions of everyday talk. These formal languages, in fact, offer the encoding rules that make our current communication technologies possible—they are the languages that allow our computers to speak in their logically flawless way.

Of course, everyday talk still articulates our world: without natural language, there is no human communication; and without communication, there is no social life—a realm where paradoxes cannot just be eliminated through formalism. Social life, actually, is shaped by another version of the self-reference problem, what sociologists call "reflexivity" or the loop that links social reality with the theories we devise to explain it: by trying to understand the way in which society operates, we change our beliefs and therefore our behavior, ultimately invalidating the theory that started the loop. To imagine how reflexivity works, think about elections and the impact that polls and forecasts have on voting behavior: if candidates or parties are portrayed in the media as likely winners, more people might decide to vote for them, starting what is known as the "bandwagon effect"; conversely, voters might also mobilize to increase support for the competing candidate, the one who is expected to lose, triggering a phenomenon fittingly called the "underdog effect" (Mutz 1998). Either way, these two scenarios portray a situation in which public opinion feeds on itself—like a pair of Escher's hands drawing each other into existence.

The reflexivity problem often takes the form of the observer effect, which refers to the fact that people tend to modify their behavior if they know they are being watched. In a famous study conducted in the 1920s and 1930s in a factory outside of Chicago, researchers manipulated the levels of lighting to test its impact on the productivity of workers. Productivity increased, but it was not because of the lighting: knowing they were being observed, workers wanted to make a good impression on researchers and managers, so they worked more intently (Roethlisberger et al. 1939; see also Franke and Kaul 1978). Since then, our measurement tools and experimental techniques have improved considerably, but we still often fall into the trap of the observer effect. In fact, digital technologies have created a new version of the reflexivity problem by allowing us to modify our behavior as we observe it through the screens of our devices, the monitoring windows of measurement instruments that never go offline.

In 2008, for instance, Google launched a project known as Flu Trends that analyzed search queries to estimate the prevalence of flu symptoms in the population. The idea was that by using "the collective intelligence of millions of users," search logs could provide "one of the most timely, broad-reaching influenza monitoring systems available" (Ginsberg et al. 2009, 1014). In 2013, however, Flu Trends was reported to drastically overestimate peak flu levels, making predictions that almost doubled official data. One of the reasons for the miscalculation was the flawed assumption that search behavior is driven by external events, like having flu symptoms, when in fact it is also driven endogenously by Google itself and the way in which it recommends search terms to users (Lazer et al. 2014). By trying to anticipate the information users need, Google ends up shaping search patterns: their recommendations introduce an amplifying effect that distorts the information revealed by search terms about motivations. Observing the phenomenon, in other words, changes the phenomenon itself.

The social world is thus unique because it responds to human action and to the theories we use to explain those actions; the natural world, on the other hand, is not responsive in that sense because its workings are simply immune to our stories: no comet ever changed its orbit because of human prophecies; the earth never stopped spinning around the sun, regardless of centuries of religious storytelling; and the continents keep on drifting across the ocean bed even when no one is really noticing. The key to social life is that when we change the way we think, we change our behavior; and when a high enough number of us change behavior, the social system starts operating differently—even if that was not the original plan for any individual involved. And here is where we find another prominent paradox: as we pursue our own myopic interests, we often trigger consequences that we did not intend or even envision.

This paradox has attracted a great deal of attention from social scientists and their precursors: it is what Bernard Mandeville had in mind when, back in the early eighteenth century, he talked about private vices leading to public benefits (Mandeville 1988 [1714]); what Adam Ferguson highlighted fifty years later as he observed that social phenomena are "indeed the result of human action but not the execution of any human design" (Ferguson 1767, 205); and what Adam Smith famously called, around the same time, the "invisible hand" (Smith 1759, IV.I.10), a metaphor that came to substitute for old ideas of Providence and divine fate—even if it still relied on omnipotence (it is difficult not to imagine, reading Smith, a Michelangelo hand playfully pulling the strings of society). Even Aristophanes, the ancient Athenian playwright, believed that a special providence watched over human affairs so that "all our foolish plans and vain conceits are overruled to work the public good" (Hayek 1966, 130). We now think of the invisible hand as quintessential to the liberal conception of markets, but the phenomenon of unintended consequences is ubiquitous. And rather than a hand, what stir these consequences are networks of interaction, the streams of interdependence that underlie, like groundwater, the surface of social life.

2.1 The Law of Unintended Consequences

The paradox of unintended consequences is that they result from intentional actions: How can individuals bring about facts that fall far from their

original plans? How can we explain the emergence of social phenomena that are not intended or designed? And how can we control or regulate those unintended consequences, when there is no responsible actor
to point at? The answers to these questions are essential, because social
change is often driven by the unanticipated effects of human action: there
is no one prescient instigator, just an accidental alignment of many actors
(and their circumstances) pursuing their own goals; and so if we want to
understand the causes and consequences of social change, to encourage or
harness it, it is important to uncover the forces that make change happen.
"Society," claimed Durkheim back in 1895, "is not the mere sum of individuals"; instead, "the system formed by their association represents a specific
reality which has its own characteristics" (Durkheim 1982 [1895], 129). It
is in determining the characteristics of that reality, and the nature of the
association between individuals, that digital technologies are helping us
decode the puzzle of unintended consequences.

The emergence of the World Wide Web is itself probably one of the most
influential manifestations of unintended effects. Originally conceived as
a repository of scientific documents (Berners-Lee and Fischetti 2000), the
Web soon became an ecosystem with its own rules, evolving with "no central node, no command hub" (Isaacson 2014, 411), to attain a coverage
and versatility far beyond the horizons envisioned by its inventor. In the
original proposal to fund his project, Berners-Lee wrote: "We should work
toward a universal linked information system, in which generality and
portability are more important than fancy graphic techniques and complex extra facilities" (Berners-Lee and Fischetti 2000, 227). It was difficult,
back then, to anticipate that "fancy graphic techniques" and "complex
extra facilities" would be what the Web is all about today—as difficult as
anticipating that the Web would drastically shift the political economy of
information. The basic architecture of the Web relied on voluntary contributions and the decentralized decisions of many users to create links. Soon,
actors like Google capitalized on that information to improve search results
using the ranking implicit in the structure of hyperlinks (Brin and Page
1998); this idea allowed Google to quickly become the corporate giant it
is today. However, no single web manager adding links to their pages had
the intention of granting such a resource to any one corporation; creating a
collective wisdom that could be monetized is one of the many unintended
consequences that followed the invention of the Web.

This inability to foresee the course of social events is inescapable. As Karl Popper eloquently explained in his book *The Poverty of Historicism*, "the course of human history is strongly influenced by the growth of human knowledge"; to the extent that we cannot predict the future growth of our knowledge, "we cannot, therefore, predict the future course of human history" (Popper 2002 [1957], xi). His book was an explicit attack on early social theories and their more contemporary sequels; as chapter 1 explained, the first social scientists were strongly influenced by evolutionary analogies: society was seen as an organism that evolved through stages, and those stages where inexorable. "Even when a society has begun to track down the natural laws of its movement," wrote Karl Marx, "it can neither leap over the natural phases of its development nor remove them by decree" (Marx 1992 [1867], 92). No one would seriously claim today that there are tendencies in social life that work "with iron necessity towards inevitable results" (ibid., 91); but recent technological developments, and in particular Internet technologies, have inspired similar claims of inevitability (Howard 2015; Zittrain 2008). Intertwined as technological developments are with the state of our knowledge, however, it is difficult to foresee how they will unfold. As Popper put it, "we cannot anticipate today what we shall know only tomorrow."

There is nothing more serendipitous than the progress of knowledge and its translation into the technologies that we now take for granted. As the Web grew exponentially during the 1990s, it became necessary to facilitate access to all the information it contained and help users find whatever content they needed. The first solution was to compile directories using human editors that would classify websites in categories such as business, education, or entertainment; Yahoo! was born as one such directory. Those in charge of designing directories failed to realize, though, that most users did not want to navigate the Web by exploring; instead, they wanted to seek specific information. According to an editor in chief of the Yahoo! portal, "the shift from exploration and discovery to the intent-based search of today was inconceivable" (Isaacson 2014, 442). What now seems like an obvious solution back then still had to be revealed.

The Web was conceived as a repository of information, and so it was first analyzed as one: the maps of that ever-expanding territory relied on categories and classifications. But the Web is also a collaboration system, as science is, and the first to realize that this analogy could open an alternative way to map the Web was Larry Page, cofounder of Google. The key was to assume that links, like citations to scientific papers, are a good proxy for content relevance. This approach was "a melding of machine and human intelligence" because the algorithms "relied on the billions of human judgements made by people when they created links from their own websites" (Isaacson 2014, 459). The rest, as they say, is history—which, of course, we can only tell with the benefit of hindsight.

Since then, search algorithms have grown more sophisticated, mostly because now they incorporate other technological advances that allow factoring in contextual information (e.g., geolocation or search history). The algorithms have grown so complex, in fact, that they trigger their own version of unintended consequences, as the Flu Trends example discussed above illustrates. Technologies, in this sense, offer another breeding ground for social paradoxes—but only because technologies themselves are social; that is, they create another space for human interaction.

The process through which unintended consequences arise in social life was systematically examined for the first time by Robert Merton in a 1936 essay titled "The Unanticipated Consequences of Purposive Social Action." The two most important factors leading to unsuccessful prediction and planning, he explained, are ignorance and error. Error may arise during any phase of purposive action: "we may err in our appraisal of the present situation, in our inference from this to the future objective situation, in our selection of a course of action, or finally in the execution of the action chosen" (Merton 1936, 901). Ignorance, on the other hand, can derive from lack of adequate knowledge but also from "the interplay of forces and circumstances which are so complex and numerous that prediction of them is quite beyond reach" (ibid., 900). This type of ignorance comes out of the intrinsic complexity of the world; it is not subjective lack of knowledge, but an objective attribute of social life. And an entire science has evolved, since Merton's days, to make sense of that inherent uncertainty.

Complexity is the science of systems in which many interacting parts bring about spontaneous order, with no one being in charge or consciously planning anything. It is how the metaphor of an "invisible hand" gets translated into a manageable research program (Waldrop 1992). In systems that are complex, the slightest vagueness about initial conditions grows inexorably, as illustrated by another metaphor popularly known as the Butterfly Effect: the idea is that, in trying to predict the path of a tornado, even minor perturbations like the flap of a butterfly's wings in some other part of the world might trigger a chain reaction that will deviate the tornado's course (Gleick 1988, 20). This means that, no matter how much effort we put into foreseeing events, "after a while, [our] predictions are nonsense" (Waldrop 1992, 128). Small happenings introduce errors in our projections that get amplified until they break the mold of the prediction. This fact is particularly harmful when we assume that past experience is a good guide to future expectations: chances are that the current conditions are different, if only slightly; and these differences will get amplified to become outcomes we cannot anticipate.

In the social world, unpredictability is the key to social change. We tend to think of change as the outcome of clashes of interests or zero-sum games where one actor's gain is another actor's loss. And, true, a great deal of social change results from an intentional confrontation with a status quo that is considered unfair (Hirschman 1982; Hobsbawm 2010 [1962]; McAdam 1982; McAdam, Tarrow, and Tilly 2001). But social change also results from localized events inducing "interminable chain reactions" that end up generating the opposite of what was originally intended (Boudon 1982, 11). This phenomenon was illustrated by the now-classic segregation model introduced by Schelling in 1969. The idea of this model, which replicated housing mobility patterns, was to show that even when individuals are not explicitly pursuing the creation of segregated neighborhoods, they might still trigger this aggregate result with their decisions to move to a different location. The reason for that result is that each individual move changes the perception of those that stay behind, who consequently might decide to move as well, which will in turn affect the perception of the other neighbors, and so on (Schelling 1969). This model is just an illustration of what happens in situations in which people's behavior reacts to the behavior of other people. These scenarios, as chapter 4 will explain in more detail, "don't permit any simple summation or extrapolation to the aggregates" (Schelling 1978, 14). What this means is that the patterns we can see at the societal level (the whole that we can only assess from a bird's-eye view) do not necessarily disclose much information about the mechanisms that brought them into existence.

Many patterns observed through the use of digital technologies follow this same logic. Increased ideological polarization, for instance, is frequently denounced as one of the most perverse effects of online communication

(Sunstein 2017). Yet no single individual can bring about or prevent patterns of ideological segregation that depend on what many other individuals are simultaneously doing. True, new technologies allow selective exposure and the filtering of personalized content at unprecedented levels (Pariser 2011); but the fact is that people have always made discriminating choices: "If job vacancies are filled by word of mouth or apartments go to people who have acquaintances in the building, or if boys can marry only girls they know and can know only girls who speak their language, a biased communication system will preserve and enhance the prevailing homogeneities" (Schelling 1978, 147). Whether digital technologies should be designed to make the sorting less biased is an important topic for discussion; but sorting has always shaped human dynamics and introduced amplifying effects for which no single actor is responsible. Technological solutions could override the consequences triggered by the choices we make; trying to regulate these unintended consequences, however, requires understanding first what lies within the black box of the social paradox.

The claim that social change has perverse effects has, of course, also been used ideologically, without the support of much empirical evidence. As Hirschman explains in his book *The Rhetoric of Reaction*, "the perversity claim would probably be pronounced the winner as the single most popular and effective weapon in the annals of reactionary rhetoric" (Hirschman 1991, 139). Throughout the last two hundred years, those opposing historical struggles for civil, political, and social rights (from the French Revolution, to universal suffrage, to the welfare state) have claimed that any attempt to change things can only backfire and exacerbate the condition to be remedied. Ironically, even if the concept of unintended consequences introduced uncertainty and open-endedness into social thought, "the purveyors of the perverse effect retreat to viewing the social universe as once again wholly predictable" (ibid., 36). It is this sort of predictability that is often implied in recent reactions to the evolution of digital technologies, which depict a future where the Internet becomes a victim of its own success (bringing us down with it) but that we can still somehow derail: if we pay enough attention today, "we can stop that future" (Zittrain 2008, x); if we don't, this might be our "last best chance for an open society" (Howard 2015, xvii). As visionary as these claims might be, the fact remains that the future is yet to be written, in great part because it results from the creative force of unintended consequences.

2.2   Self-Fulfilling and Self-Defeating Prophecies

When fears become a reality, we talk about self-fulfilling prophecies; when the fear of some consequence drives us to find solutions before the problem occurs, we talk about self-defeating prophecies. The underdog effect introduced earlier is a version of this sort of prophetic thinking; so is a situation in which constituents, believing their candidate will win, decide not to vote, thus overturning the prophecy. As Merton put it, "the empirical observation is incontestable: activities oriented toward certain values release processes which so react as to change the very scale of values which precipitated them" (Merton 1936, 903). When predictions are made, inevitably they change the course of developments. This, in fact, is a very old idea, going back to Greek mythology and the legend of Oedipus, who killed his father as a direct result of the prophecy that had caused the father to abandon him in the first place (Popper 2002 [1957], 11). "The interaction between the scientist's pronouncements and social life," it follows, "almost invariably creates situations in which we have not only to consider the truth of such pronouncements, but also their actual influence on future developments" (ibid., 14). Prophecies are like a snake that bites its own tail.

For self-fulfilling prophecies to exist, the prophecy's definition of a situation has to be false at first but is made true with the adjusted behavior that follows the false definition. A classic example involves a bank that becomes insolvent because a fabricated rumor spreads and everyone starts withdrawing their money (Merton 1948). A more current example would involve a viral marketing campaign launching a product destined to attract everyone's attention; only when the product does go viral (which does not necessarily happen often; Berger 2013) does the definition of the campaign become real. False definitions turn true because "we respond not only to the objective features of a situation, but also, and at times primarily, to the meaning this situation has for us" (Merton 1948, 194). Objective facts, in other words, matter less than subjective perceptions. Ideological polarization results from our thinking that we do not have anything in common with others assumed to think differently from us, so the definition becomes real: we end up creating and inhabiting our own echo chambers (Sunstein 2017). Prejudices are an important driver of selective exposure, and they are one of the most prevalent forms of self-fulfilling prophecies: "what people think of us is bound to some degree to fashion what we are" and "the way we perceive qualities in others cannot help but have an effect on what qualities others will display" (Allport 1979, 159). This happens regardless of whether interactions take place online or offline, as long as those interactions function like a hall of mirrors.

The idea of self-fulfilling prophecies implies that "certain expectations are of such character that they induce the kind of behavior that will cause the expectations to be fulfilled" (Schelling 1978, 115). Often this activates a vicious circle, as when we label people in such a way that they become conditioned and are forced to meet our expectations: "if a particular minority is considered incapable of holding responsible positions, they will not be hired for responsible positions; they will have no opportunity for experience in responsible positions; and, lacking any such experience, they may indeed be incapable" (ibid., 116). Digital technologies and algorithmic profiling are creating new tools to enforce self-fulfilling prophecies. Predictive policing, for instance, uses digital records (and the breadcrumbs we unwarily leave online while using portable technologies) to identify potential suspects and to produce "models to decide where and when to patrol" (Mayer-Schoenberger and Cukier 2013; O'Neil 2016). Once an individual or group is classified as potentially deviant, the labeling is likely to shape their behavior in a confirmatory way, as sociologists researching stigma and crime have long denounced (Becker 1963; Goffman 1963)—and as Charles Dickens already portrayed in his 1844 novel *The Chimes*.

Profiling for marketing purposes might also reinforce social discrimination: "if you consistently get ads for low-priced cars, regional vacations, fast-food restaurants, and other products that reflect a lower-class status, your sense of the world's opportunities might be narrower than that of someone who is feted with ads for national or international trips and luxury products" (Turow 2012, 6). Research conducted in 2013 showed that algorithmic searches created what is known as "discrimination by statistical inference": when names predominantly assigned to black babies were the subject of online searches, the ads delivered by Google were far more likely to suggest an arrest record ("Trevor Jones, Arrested?") than when the names used were predominantly white (Lohr 2015, 192–193). Today, and partly as a result of this research, Google no longer suggests ads when searches involve names of people; human judgment, this example shows, is still the gold standard to assess the value of data correlations.

As bad as algorithms might look when they reinforce self-fulfilling prophecies, the reality is that they are perpetuating a very old problem. "Our politicians," claimed Immanuel Kant in 1784, "are just as successful in their prophecies. One must take men as they are, they tell us, and not as the world's uninformed pedants or good-natured dreamers fancy that they ought to be. But 'as they are' ought to read 'as we have made them by unjust coercion, by treacherous designs which the government is in a good position to carry out.' ... In this way, the prophecy of the supposedly clever statesmen is fulfilled" (Kant 2013 [1784], 68). Breaking this cycle involves uncovering the perverse, self-fulfilling effects of discriminatory labels and rewriting the definition that sets the cycle in motion. This is a social rather than a technological decision; and digital data can be just as good at discovering profiling practices as at allowing them: they can help document the extent to which prejudices distort reality, and be used to uncover inequalities or unfair discrimination. Chapter 7 returns to this question.

Self-fulfilling prophecies can, of course, also activate a benign circle, as when we come up with new norms and conventions, design institutions that allow coordination, and make collective action easier to sustain. Most social life relies, in fact, on the products of successful prophecies: the institutions that we take for granted, like money or signaling systems, exist only because we agree that they exist (Searle 1995). Conventions require mutually reinforcing expectations to be of any value, although the value does not depend on any intrinsic property of the convention: it does not matter whether we drive on the left or the right side of the road, as long as we all agree on which side. Conventions are therefore a crucial component of social life because they facilitate interaction and communication (Bicchieri 2005). Today many of these conventions take the form of technological standards.

A standard usually emerges from coordination dynamics that are very similar to the bandwagon effect in voting behavior: once a high enough number of people start using a new technology, network effects will amplify its value and consolidate its predominance. When similar technologies compete, insignificant differences in initial adoption rates are quickly magnified: "an early lead gained by accident can generate unexpectedly large differences in final outcomes" (Grewal 2008, 38). When a large enough number of people define a situation as real (i.e., believing that technology A is superior to technology B), the situation becomes real, regardless of whether the original definition was in fact accurate. Because of this, the diffusion of technology famously gets trapped in suboptimal equilibria—think about the still prevalent QWERTY keyboard and how far we are from the constraints of mechanical typewriters (Stamp 2013). The QWERTY arrangement remains the standard, even though alternative ones have since been proposed to make typing more efficient. The path dependence of technological evolution, and the emergence of dominating standards, are some of the most visible legacies of prophecies that come true.

Ultimately, as Merton put it, "history creates its own test of the theory of self-fulfilling prophecies" (Merton 1948, 197). Meanwhile, however, the theory confronts us with a more urgent question: if our prophecies create social reality, how do we escape the circularity? Doesn't this logic make us fall into a trap similar to the Liar's Paradox? The answer, fortunately, is no. As anyone working in marketing or public intervention campaigns knows, it is not enough to define a situation as real to make it real—there has to be the right resonance, the appropriate chain reaction, and this is a social fact that does not depend on what goes on in the mind of any particular individual. Self-fulfilling prophecies rely on domino effects that escape the control of subjective perceptions and thus break the circularity of social constructivism.

Positive feedback plays a fundamental role in the fulfillment of prophecies: attaining a critical mass of people to bring down a bank requires the rumor of insolvency spreading in a population; pushing a product beyond the viral threshold requires the many hands that the campaign cannot buy; and allowing an online platform to become the next big hit depends on having a large enough number of people willing to switch platforms. All these processes are based on individual decisions, but those decisions are not independent: they are connected by communication channels that allow small initial moves (the first lie about a bank, the first few people buying a new product or joining a new platform) to be noticed, spread, and turned into social facts. Self-fulfilling prophecies are the stories that set these dynamics in motion; but positive feedback is the amplifier that makes those stories come true—and this is the one element in the puzzle that digital technologies are helping us decode with better measurement tools.

2.3   Cumulative Effects

The Web started as a small collection of information islands connected through links that made mental associations public and clickable. Soon the islands grew to become continents formed by millions of pages where links laid down a complex system of roads directing users' attention. Search engines started crawling that space and the first maps of the Web were drawn, revealing a very unequal structure where a few sites concentrated most of the attention, as conferred through links (Adamic and Huberman 2000; Albert, Jeong, and Barabási 1999; Barabási, Albert, and Jeong 2000; Broder et al. 2000; Huberman and Adamic 1999; see also Huberman 2001). This stratification was not very different from what researchers had long revealed about the structure of science, which is also characterized by a very unequal distribution of visibility: a few scientists tend to accumulate most of the citations in any given field (Merton 1968). It is this similarity that inspired the creation of Google, the first search engine that exploited the distribution of links to yield better results to queries. The analogy involved making two assumptions: first, that each link was equivalent to a vote of confidence; and second, that thousands of people could not be wrong in their agreement to vote for the same information resources (Brin and Page 1998). These assumptions improved the quality of search results, but do they also help us understand the emergence of the largest information network in history?

If someone completely oblivious to the history of the Web were to look at one of its maps, she would be tempted to think that such a system was designed according to some plan; perhaps she would even think that the stratification was built into the system willingly, to improve, for instance, efficiency in the information search process. But, as with Schelling's segregation model, the overall patterns can be very misleading about the intentions that brought them into existence. Of course, we know that there is no obvious way to centralize decisions on the Web: even when Google tries to delete content (most probably under the requirement of European courts; Schechner 2014), millions of servers around the world may still contain copies of that content—servers that are out of reach for any one single actor, even mighty Google. So the question remains: What gives rise to the structure of the Web, which is the unintended outcome of many intentional decisions? One of the simplest models to explain its emergence relies

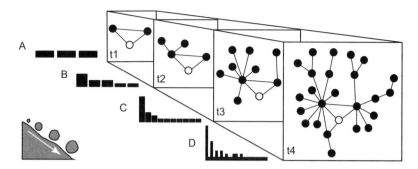

Figure 2.1
Illustration of cumulative effects in networks

on a mechanism known as preferential attachment (Barabási and Albert 1999). This mechanism offers a way to encode positive feedback and reconstruct the unintended effects of cumulative advantage.

To illustrate how this mechanism operates, we can build a network from scratch and simulate its growth. Let's assume that, at the very beginning, there are only three websites online, as depicted in the slice *t1* in figure 2.1 These websites have the exact same number of links: each connects to two other sites, so they are identical in their centrality, as the histogram in panel A indicates. At some point down the line, for whatever reason, one of the sites accumulates two more connections: perhaps random conversations make other people know of its existence or perhaps the contents are genuinely better than in the other two sites. Whatever the reason, the idea behind the preferential attachment mechanism is that this small initial variation will be amplified over time: as new nodes enter the network (i.e., as new sites are published), they will tend to connect to the better-connected sites, which also tend to be the oldest. The mechanism, in other words, assumes that the growth of the network is not random but shaped by what happened in the past.

The process is not deterministic: some new sites will still link to less central sites (because, perhaps, that is where the most relevant content is); but over time the propensity to link to the most visible sites, i.e., the sites that are known to most people, will translate into the substantially more heterogeneous structure that appears at the end of the process: nodes are now decidedly more unequal in their connectivity, as the histogram in panel D shows. And this happens regardless of the initial conditions: even though the three sites were at first identical, one of the sites, represented by the white node, ends up being significantly less popular and central. The nodes in this network, in other words, increase in prominence like snowballs rolling down a slope: the initial push pretty much determines their growth.

This preferential attachment mechanism is enough to reproduce, in a modeling context, the observed structure of the Web (Barabási and Albert 1999). Of course there are other mechanisms that also trigger this rich-get-richer phenomenon—mechanisms that are, in fact, more aligned with how things work in social life. One alternative approach, for instance, models agency more explicitly by assuming that new nodes will connect with existing nodes as a function of popularity but also of similarity, which captures the tendency to connect with others who share similar characteristics, e.g., language (Papadopoulos et al. 2012). This more refined specification of preferential attachment keeps, however, the same crucial element at its core: a positive feedback mechanism that reinforces initial advantage. Positive feedback is what creates inequality over time, the unintended consequence of many parallel choices to link, or not, to a given site (as unintended, by the way, as creating a network that is more robust and easier to navigate, properties to which chapter 5 will return). Positive feedback creates reinforcement; and reinforcement, to continue the metaphor, acts like the slope allowing the snowball to grow.

The path-dependence dynamics captured by preferential attachment are also similar to those shaping science: as new research is published, it tends to cite previous work that is already visible, and this reinforces the prestige of a few scientists who soon become outliers in their visibility. One consequence of this is that "eminent scientists get disproportionately great credit for their contributions to science while relatively unknown scientists tend to get disproportionately little credit for comparable contributions" (Merton 1968, 57). When success breeds success, cumulative effects amplify any initial advantage, however random it may be; this is why early career development is so important in most academic trajectories: it is the stage where support for research will have the most lasting influence (Petersen et al. 2011). Likewise, links on the Web are votes of confidence that signal endorsement or trust. Early endorsement creates the initial advantage that gets amplified; the value of links, however, gets progressively biased as rich-get-richer dynamics unfold. These are the dynamics that explain why a few popular items in social media (memes, news, tweets) tend to crowd out all the others, irrespective of how they compare in quality (often, in spite of it).

Like all paradoxes, the process of cumulative advantage contradicts itself by having both good and bad consequences. The main perverse effect is that the accumulation of prestige generates inequality, shaping success and life trajectories in ways that are disproportionate to actual merit (DiPrete and Eirich 2006). Cumulative effects, however, also generate positive outcomes, like increasing the visibility of new ideas and improving the efficiency of their dissemination. When information abounds, coming up with good filtering methods is key to identifying good content. This is as true in science as in the world of online technologies. As Merton put it, "confronted with the growing task of identifying significant work published in their field, scientists search for cues to what they should attend to" (Merton 1968, 59). New contributions or discoveries sink into oblivion if they are not communicated effectively, and a rich-get-richer system narrows down the number of voices to tune into by giving more credibility to a few. Even paradigmatic shifts, triggered by what Thomas Kuhn called anomalies in research, require an effective communication to take hold (Kuhn 1962). New paradigms, in fact, soon generate the same inequality in the distribution of visibility as the paradigms they replaced, with a few scientists accumulating most of the citations—and most of the prestige.

The distribution of visibility online is equally skewed, but there are two competing forces in how digital technologies shape cumulative effects. On the one hand, search engines reinforce rich-get-richer dynamics by giving more visibility to content that is already visible; in this sense, they activate a higher-order feedback mechanism that amplifies that triggered by people when they link or like (Easley and Kleinberg 2010, 489). On the other hand, recommender systems direct attention to less popular content if it matches the interests revealed by the user (Anderson 2007, 55); this is the reason why relatively obscure content can surface from the shadows and become a big hit. Digital technologies add more complexity to the already complex social world, creating an architecture that reinforces asymmetries but also flattens old media hierarchies, allowing information to spread fast and giving visibility to otherwise unpopular content. Either way, for better or worse, there is no single actor that is responsible for the consequences of those complex interactions, and there is no linear story that can join individual decisions the way frames are spliced in film: this is a story that has no writer, director, or preconceived narrative thread. There are, however, prompts cueing actors to behave in a particular way; these prompts speak when actors let the decisions of others influence their own behavior.

To understand how influence triggers positive feedback and cumulative effects, we need to look at the history of a social system; that is, at how the interactions that sustain the system evolve over time. We can simulate that history and then see if the results match observed data: this is what preferential attachment and related models do in their attempt to reproduce inequality in networks. Alternatively, we can use digital technologies to directly observe those histories as they unfold: this is what recent online experiments have done in their attempt to uncover the logic of cumulative effects and self-fulfilling prophecies. The key to these experiments is randomization, or the assignment of people to parallel worlds that evolve separately and under slightly different conditions (Watts 2011, 76). We cannot rerun the course of history to test counterfactuals: we cannot go back in time, invent a different Web, and launch it in parallel to the Web we know to see how different the present would look after that alternative course of events. But we can use the Web we have to create small microcosms that evolve independently of each other and see how dissimilar they grow.

Digital technologies allow running experiments in both artificial and natural environments. One of the firsts attempts to uncover the mechanisms of popularity and inequality involved creating an artificial cultural market (in the form of a website) where users could listen to, rate, and download songs by unknown bands (Salganik, Dodds, and Watts 2006). Participants entering the site were randomly assigned to two experimental conditions: in one, they decided who to listen to and how to rate songs using only the name of the bands and the song titles; in the other, they could also see how many times a song had been downloaded by previous participants. Participants assigned to this social influence condition were further sent to eight independent worlds where downloads accumulated only from participants in that same world. The experiment used the independent condition to determine the quality of songs: their success in this condition relied only on their intrinsic characteristics. What the results showed is that the success of songs varied drastically across histories: on average, the best songs did well and the worst songs did poorly, but songs of any quality experienced a wide range of outcomes across worlds; in other words, the feedback mechanism introduced in the form of social influence increased the unpredictability of success.

More recent experiments also show evidence that positive feedback operating on a small initial advantage increases inequality and rich-get-richer effects (van de Rijt et al. 2014). In this instance, the experiments take place in natural online environments representing different types of reward systems: a crowdfunding website (kickstarter.com); a consumer reviews platform (epinions.com); a crowdsourced encyclopedia (wikipedia.org); and a petitions website (change.org). Reward in these systems takes different shapes: it is measured as financial gain, endorsement, social status, or social support, respectively; but in all of them arbitrary initial endowments—the experimental interventions in the form of random donations, positive ratings, editing awards, and signatures—create lasting disparities in individual success. The experiments show, in other words, that past and future rewards are linked and that positive feedback has self-fulfilling effects regardless of the social environment. However, the results also show that opportunities for manipulation are offset by the decreasing marginal returns of increasing endowments. What this means is that larger initial advantages (i.e., higher donations) fail to produce much further differentiation. This suggests that cumulative advantage shapes the collective dynamics that create inequality but within the limits drawn by actual merit.

All these experiments depict how social paradoxes arise in the tumult of daily interactions; they also demonstrate why meaning is often not relevant to decode the logic of social life. Aggregate patterns—to recover the metaphor introduced in chapter 1—are like encrypted messages: the meaning that brought them into existence is less relevant than the probabilistic structure they hide. The reason, paraphrasing Ferguson once more, is that social phenomena result from human action, not from human design: intentions or meaning matter less than the way in which actions intertwine to create path dependence, probability trails that fork and extend beyond the control of any one actor. Digital technologies have opened a way to decode the snowballing effects that shape collective dynamics; they have also made it more patent than ever that structures of power often derive as the unforeseen consequence of our myopic actions, emerging from the myriad choices we make in our daily routines. The assumption behind the invisible hand metaphor was that the unintended effects of human action always worked for the public good; we now know that this is not necessarily true.

2.4 The Power of Communication

When we think about communication as a tool of power, we metaphorically think about it as a chisel that shapes people's minds to favor political or economic interests. The role that mass media play in engineering consent and manipulating the habits and opinions of the public has been a focus of attention since, at least, the 1920s (Bernays 1928; Lippmann 1922). Since then, media organizations and the public relations industry have, if anything, strengthened their role in the enforcement of self-fulfilling prophecies and the manipulation of public views (Herman and Chomsky 1988). But propaganda studies or a political economy approach to communication do not help us understand an important dimension of power. This dimension cannot be decoded in the terminology of conflicting interests and media bias; it arises, instead, from the way in which communication enforces interdependence: "Injustices, inequalities and conflicts are not necessarily produced by domination; the interdependence of social agents, and the impossibility of defining an optimal organization of that interdependence, may also be held responsible" (Boudon 1982, 12). This is the one aspect of social life that, because of its complexity, resists manufacturing and manipulation.

No one is responsible for the inequality that arises from feedback effects, especially as they amplify random initial advantages. Much in the same way, in a world that communicates with networked technologies, asymmetries inevitably grow out of individual free choices: we decide to use one search engine rather than another; we decide to spend more time in one social media platform and less in competing ones; and, ultimately, all these choices create a state of affairs in which some technologies end up dominating, constraining the range of alternatives and our ability to decide (Grewal 2008). Positive feedback generates the sort of network externalities that consolidate some technologies as dominant: when the value of technologies depends on how many other people use them, the decisions to adopt are not independent; and, as in the music experiment, asymmetries soon ensue when we pay attention to the actions of other people. Following the logic of self-fulfilling prophecies, the consequence is that "social actors are trapped in a web of their own making; they reify social reality, failing to realize that they are responsible for creating it" (Biggs 2010, 311). And this leads us to ask the following question: How do we regulate the perverse effects of our interactions while preserving the positive consequences?

Crowd intelligence and herd behavior offer an example of the tightrope social paradoxes make us walk. Both result from aggregating distributed information, but if the first improves our decisions, the second biases our choices—and we can easily go from one to the other without much notice. Herding occurs when people act based on inferences drawn from what other people have done before, like choosing a restaurant just because there are more people sitting inside and we assume it has better food (Easley and Kleinberg 2010, 427). Of course, if that was the logic followed by everybody in that restaurant, chances are that the food is not particularly good (in the same way that the total downloads of songs in the experiment were not an accurate estimate of their intrinsic quality). Collaborative filtering, rating systems, and crowdsourcing, on the other hand, help aggregate the bits of knowledge contained in the heads of many people, offering services and information that no single individual could produce on their own (Benkler 2006; Surowiecki 2004). The Web is one such example of collective intelligence, the unintended consequence of many actions that turned out to work for the public good. But there is a thin line separating collective intelligence and herding (Muchnik, Aral, and Taylor 2013). Being able to draw that line has important consequences for how we understand inequality and power in this digital age.

Some of the unintended effects of interdependence are good and should be encouraged, as when they boost participation in civic events (Margetts et al. 2015); some others, like network effects that give too much control to any one single company, should be regulated and restrained. Social influence lies at the core of dynamics that lead to collective action or market dominance; in one case, however, it creates opportunities for action, while in the other it narrows down the decision space. Likewise, social influence can help spread important information or instill norms that are beneficial, but it can also disseminate misleading news and false rumors. The power of communication develops in our daily interactions, even if we are not aware or in control; and it acts without a purpose, with both beneficial and perverse effects.

Many social institutions, like signaling systems or road conventions, arose to regulate perverse effects, e.g., the accidents that would result from uncoordinated traffic. Digital technologies offer new tools to complement that type of regulation. Recommender systems, for instance, can be adapted to discount the bias introduced by herding. Digital data can also help us harness unintended consequences by reducing the ignorance and error that affect many of our predictions. As Merton put it, "the self-fulfilling prophecy, whereby fears are translated into reality, operates only in the absence of deliberative institutional control"; it is only through research and interventions that "the tragic circle of fear, social disaster, reinforced fear can be broken" (Merton 1948, 210). Though Merton's message was directed at ethnic prejudice, his words could also aptly describe recent reactions to technological developments said to endanger social life as we know it (Carr 2010; Turkle 2011). Technologies can backfire in their operation—but only because they are as open-ended as the social environment in which they thrive.

2.5   Why Focus on the Unintended?

Unintended consequences trick us into making flawed assumptions about individuals based on the aggregates they form. Today, digital technologies channel many of the chain reactions that lead to those cumulative effects, adding additional layers of complexity to social processes that were already complex. There are, overall, two types of unintended consequences. There are those that lie at the heart of innovation, as when we repurpose technologies for ends that were not imagined by their inventors, be they the engineers behind the telegraph or the coders that added the first links to an incipient Web. These unintended consequences add value to the original goals, and stand as an important force in dynamics of progress and change. But then there are the backfiring effects that turn well-intentioned actions into perverse outcomes. Data science, this book argues, is most useful in uncovering these effects and identifying the triggers so that perverse consequences can be tamed. For that, data science makes use of one of the byproducts that derive from our use of technologies: the digital trails that we generate without intending to solve any social paradoxes but that we can still use for that purpose. Decoding the logic of unintended effects is important to design better policies and actions, and to monitor our interventions in the world.

Digital technologies are allowing us to crack the logic of complex dynamics by granting access to richer data and providing the tools to parse that information. But they are also illuminating why communication has power is subtle ways, why it drives social change without anyone being in charge, and ultimately how to regulate this blind process so that it works in favor of the public good. First, however, we need to understand the logic that underlies the workings of decentralized communication. This chapter has paid attention to the nature of social paradoxes, and to what creates the dissonance between individual motives and collective dynamics. The next three chapters consider in more detail the three levels of analysis that are involved in the process of bringing about unintended consequences: the aggregate patterns that emerge from social interactions; the individual mechanisms that activate dynamics of social influence; and the role that networks play in turning individual actions into collective outcomes. The following chapter starts by paying attention to the whole that is more than the sum, and how we can best characterize its patterns and flows.

3 The Effervescence of Collective Behavior

In 1898, the Paris newspaper *L'Aurore* published on its front page an open letter in which Émile Zola accused the French army—the most untouchable institution at the time—of corruption and fraud. The letter was published at the height of the Dreyfus affair, which started when Alfred Dreyfus (artillery officer, also French Jew) was unjustly accused of selling military secrets to Germany. "I accuse the War Office," wrote Zola, "of having conducted an abominable campaign in the press ... in order to cover up its misdeeds and lead public opinion astray" (Zola 1998, 52). What started as a miscarriage of justice soon escalated into one of the largest political scandals ever to shake France (Read 2012), a fateful episode seen by many as a precursor of the organized antisemitism that was to break out in Europe just a few decades later (Arendt 1973). Public opinion was radically divided between those who believed in Dreyfus's innocence and those who believed he was a traitor. A cartoon of the time shows a dinner gathering that starts with the pronouncement "First of all: let us not speak about the Dreyfus affair!" and, of course, ends up badly (amid stabbing forks and broken bottles) because in the end they did discuss it (van Ginneken 1992, 216). The divisions stirred by the affair ran across all sectors and classes of French society, revealing deeply entrenched attitudes toward national identity, patriotism, and racial prejudice. But what makes these events so unique is that newspapers, which had started to emerge in their modern mass circulation form in the last quarter of the nineteenth century, became for the first time prominent makers of public opinion.

The rise of the newspaper industry was encouraged by the alignment of several factors, including growing literacy, the absence of censorship, volatile politics, and laxer libel laws (Read 2012, 33). The press was one of the main instigators of the antagonism that defined the affair. *L'Aurore* sold around 200,000 copies each day (many more on the day of Zola's letter); its rival newspaper, *La Libre Parole*, which emerged to promote antisemitism, sold as many as 500,000 copies each day (ibid., 238). In fact, *La Libre Parole* was "transformed overnight from a small and politically insignificant sheet into one of the most influential papers in the country" (Arendt 1973, 96)—it had, after all, scooped the news of Dreyfus's arrest. The press helped both sides of the affair to spread their reasons and (most frequently) passions, so much so that statesmen compared the agitation to a national "nervous breakdown" (van Ginneken 1992, 214). The affair was explosive because of the way the story was told. Its outbreak coincided with the rise of the "intellectual," a term that was actually coined in its present-day sense during these events (ibid., 212–214). Opinion leaders used the press to organize and mobilize. It wasn't only Zola who tried to stir the public with his appeals to reason; the anti-Dreyfusard league also extended a web of influence through the press. One of the threads led straight from the army to the *Libre Parole*, "which, directly or indirectly, through its articles or the personal intervention of its editors, mobilized students, monarchists, adventurers, and plain gangsters and pushed them into the streets" (Arendt 1973, 110). After his letter was published, Zola was repeatedly attacked by mobs that were energized by the messages coming out of the presses.

And so it was around these convulsive years that social science started to emerge as a discipline with an institutional representation and a recognized identity. The largest social science teaching institution in the country, the Collège Libre des Sciences Sociales, was established in 1895 under the leadership and fundraising efforts of Jeanne Weill (Clark 1973, 156). The world was changing fast, and social issues were becoming a priority in many intellectual circles. Even if social science was in fashion, however, the university system was still reluctant to incorporate it into the curriculum, so satellite institutions and colleges had to emerge to create that missing space for scholarly discussion. Weill (who published under the male pseudonym of Dick May) wrote prolifically about the importance of teaching social science, which she took to include "all that constitutes or determines the circumstance, rights, and duties of those living, or destined to live, in society" (May 1896, 1). Lectures at the Collège attracted hundreds of students coming from a variety of institutions, including the Sorbonne. Those students had to be motivated largely by the materials discussed, "for there were no examinations, prizes, degrees, or awaiting careers" (Clark 1973, 157). It was in this environment that Émile Durkheim and Gabriel Tarde engaged in the intellectual debate that was to shape the social sciences as we understand them today. Their disagreement gave rise to the field of research known today as collective behavior, which survived for many years in the shadows of more mainstream approaches to the analysis of social life. More than a century later, digital data is finally turning collective behavior into the prominent (and burgeoning) research domain it failed to be for a long time.

Both Durkheim and Tarde had been interested spectators of the Dreyfus affair: they were part of the group of intellectuals that signed pro-Dreyfus manifestos following Zola's letter (Clark 1969; Clark 1973; Katz, Ali, and Kim 2014). But it was Tarde's ideas that were most clearly shaped by the affair and what it represented. The events made him realize that the press was a powerful mobilizer, capable of shaping views and spurring action (Katz, Ali, and Kim 2014, 17). The older Tarde was ideologically more conservative than Durkheim; yet he ended up being a theorist of social change as a result, in part, of what the Dreyfus case revealed about the impact communication could have on opinions and behavior. The more liberal Durkheim, on the other hand, was (paradoxically) more concerned with social order and consensus, partly because he was also more aligned with the ideology of the Third Republic and the notions of patriotism and national identity that were so prominent at the time (Clark 1969, 10; van Ginneken 1992, 197). At the heart of their disagreement there was a difference concerning what counted as a social fact—the unit of analysis that was to give sociology its unique niche in the pantheon of knowledge—and how social facts could be measured. For Durkheim, social facts were equivalent to social structure (which census data had been approximating for a few decades already); for Tarde, social facts arose from collective dynamics triggered by interpersonal interaction and communication (easy to observe but difficult to measure with the tools available at the time). The debate, by all accounts, was won by Durkheim: he had, after all, managed to enter the Sorbonne in 1902, gaining the institutional support and the networks that were precluded to those outside of the university system. In hindsight, however, Tarde's ideas seem the more powerful (and visionary) of the two.

3.1   The Nature of Social Facts

The debate between Tarde and Durkheim developed in journals during the 1890s but intensified between 1902 and 1904, when both of them were in Paris. Durkheim had defined a social fact as "any way of acting, whether fixed or not, capable of exerting over the individual an external constraint"; a social fact, he continued, has "an existence of its own, independent of its individual manifestations" (Durkheim 1982 [1895], 59). His study on suicide offered a prominent example of what he meant by "external constraint." Statistical and census data, which had been collected since Napoleonic days in an effort to unify administrative procedures, showed that regional differences in number of suicides remained constant over time, and that there were discernible regularities across demographic groups, e.g., rates were higher among men than women, or among Protestants than Catholics. What this suggested, he argued, is that the act of suicide shouldn't be considered a phenomenon resulting from individual predispositions but, instead, should be seen as the consequence of group processes captured by social structure (van Ginneken 1992, 196). For Tarde, who was closer to Anglo-Saxon individualism than to the collectivism that dominated France, social influence was instead the quintessential social fact (ibid., 198). Social facts could only start with individuals and their interactions, not from some external—and mysterious—force. Unfortunately, he had little access to data that could help sustain his intuitions; all he could rely on were impressionistic observations drawn from what he saw happening in a convulsive France.

    In one of their debates, the key to their discrepancy was summed up with one question: "Does Mr. Durkheim think that social reality is anything other than individuals and individual acts or facts?" To this question, Tarde replied: "If you believe that, I understand your method, which is pure ontology. Between us is the debate between nominalism and scholastic realism. I am a nominalist. There can only be individual actions and interactions. The rest is only a metaphysical entity, mysticism" (Tarde 1969, 140). The debate boiled down to "the age-old discussion over the relation between continuity and change, the whole and the parts" (van Ginneken 1992, 202–203). For Tarde, social action could not derive from the constraints of external impositions, with their deterministic grasp; it derived, instead, from spontaneous imitation, a word he used to talk about social influence.

Influence, for Tarde, was a source of socialization but also of innovation and change. Following the recurrent metaphor of society as an organism, he also used the term "contagion" to refer to the collective dynamics that arose from social influence. Like many of his contemporaries, "Tarde saw in biological processes of contagion a model that offered analogies with processes of social change" (Boudon 1982, 12–13). This is most clearly revealed in his *Laws of Imitation* (1890), where he talks about diffusion and how ideas spread through the population.

"Invention and imitation," Tarde claimed, "are the elementary social acts"; they were also, to his mind, the key to progress, which he defined as "a kind of collective thinking ... made possible, thanks to imitation, by the solidarity of the brains of numerous scholars and inventors" (Tarde 1969, 178–179). In this conception of influence, Tarde was inspired by Walter Bagehot, introduced in chapter 1 as one of the early exponents of "social physics": his book *Physics and Politics* had an entire chapter on the role of imitation in nation building, and had been translated into French in 1877, with several reprints in subsequent years (van Ginneken 1992, 198). "No one needs to have this explained," wrote Bagehot, "we all know how a kind of subtle influence makes us imitate or try to imitate the manner of those around us" (Bagehot 2007 [1872], 65). According to Tarde's account, innovation occurs when people resist imitation; but for innovations to spread, imitation still needs to be a driving force in society. This is one example of why Tarde's ideas are so visionary: today's instantiation of social physics still sees "social learning and social pressure as primary forces that drive the evolution of culture and govern much of the hyperconnected world" (Pentland 2014, x). The "solidarity of the brains" that Tarde praised has also much in common with current notions of collective intelligence (Surowiecki 2004). In both accounts, progress is defined as the ability of groups to find solutions to problems no individual could solve as successfully on their own.

The technological changes that irrupted in the course of the nineteenth century (e.g., the railroad, the telegraph) were, according to Tarde, the key to understanding the emergence of the public and opinion dynamics (van Ginneken 1992, 220). Communication technologies had multiplied interactions "beyond all expectation," with the consequence that the "action of imitation" had become "very powerful, very rapid, and very far-reaching" (Tarde 1969, 181). It is difficult, reading this, not to draw parallels once more with what many authors write today about the digital revolution. "The pace of communication," it has been recently claimed, "has accelerated and intensified. All of this connectivity means that news and updates about people and institutions cascade through the Internet" (Rainie and Wellman 2012, 228); it follows, claim others, that "online networks provide new avenues for influence and social contagion" (Christakis and Fowler 2009, 285). It would be hard to find someone today who does not agree with those statements. And yet, as novel as these transformations might seem, the consequences of an increased connectivity were already being envisioned by Tarde in the last decades of the nineteenth century. New avenues for social influence have since been paved (and many more are in the making); but, crucially, the operating mechanisms that activate streams of influence were already singled out by social scientists trying to make sense of a much older revolution.

Of course it was very difficult back then to decode the dynamics of change unleashed by social influence: there was no obvious data, or modeling approach, with which to analyze communication dynamics in any systematic way. The Dreyfus affair had revealed the significance of a new phenomenon: the ebbs and flows of collective attention, and its repercussions for political action, including institutional reform. But like a monster inhabiting the depths of a lake, only a part of that beast could be seen emerging from dark, murky waters, and the best that observers could do was to capture the surface with a broad brush. This is another reason why Durkheim's ideas ended up having a much stronger repercussion: his research wisely exploited the best data that was available at the time, which took the form of large-scale statistics and census records (some of them collected by the same department that Tarde was directing at the Ministry of Justice). Tarde, on the other hand, was trying to cast light on what was still invisible, so he could only resort to metaphors—always imprecise to the scientific mind. For Tarde, society was like "one large irrigation system: with currents, undercurrents, and countercurrents in constant flux" (van Ginneken 1992, 200). And just as drops falling into the water make rippling circles merge, so does influence, in Tarde's account, create patterns that bring individuals together while increasing the volume and speed of opinion flows.

Those currents "in constant flux" were difficult to map and analyze: no census could account for the dynamics because, to begin with, censuses were not meant to map that sort of change. The focus on the data resources that were available in those days imposed, in fact, important limitations on social thought, the most prominent being that census data disregarded the mechanisms that generated the observed patterns. "For Durkheim," to use one more analogy, "a tsunami just blows in from the sea, ready-made; Tarde wants to know how it was assembled" (Katz, Ali, and Kim 2014, 8). This was probably the largest difference between the two thinkers, and the reason why Durkheim managed to create a school while Tarde's ideas languished: there was no clear evidence that could help him illuminate the question of assemblage. All he could do was to describe intuitions and what common sense told him about the phenomena he observed—observations that were mediated, in great measure, by the same press that was shaping that reality. (The recourse to common sense, some would argue, has in fact not ceased being important for observers of the social, with all the traps it entails; see Watts 2011, 2014). The Durkheim-Tarde debate, in the end, reflected the limitations of their science—and the nature of academic politics, which had to find a winner nonetheless.

And yet, as much as their views differed in important respects (and as much as they further exaggerated their differences for the sake of public debate), Durkheim and Tarde converged in one important, if often disregarded, aspect: their assessment of what makes collective dynamics so puzzling and interesting. In 1892 Tarde put it this way: "By virtue of what miracle do so many people—once dispersed and indifferent to one another—develop solidarity, aggregate into a magnetic chain, shout the same cries, run together, act concertedly? By the virtue of sympathy, the source of imitation" (quoted in van Ginneken 1992, 193). This notion of a "magnetic chain" is not very different from the idea of "collective effervescence" that Durkheim introduced in his *Elementary Forms of Religious Life*, first published in 1912:

Within a crowd moved by a common passion, we become susceptible to feelings and actions of which we are incapable on our own. ... Under the influence of some great collective upheaval, social interactions become more frequent and more active. Individuals seek each other out and assemble more often. The result is a general effervescence characteristic of revolutionary or creative epochs. (Durkheim 2001 [1912], 157–158)

Durkheim's characterization of collective effervescence and Tarde's theory of social imitation are the early precursors to the field of research today known as collective behavior. This branch of social inquiry analyzes dynamics that are irreducible to more static structures, "such as class, ethnicity or bureaucracy" (Katz, Ali, and Kim 2014, 6), and it emerged with some force when Tarde's ideas were transported across the Atlantic to settle the foundations of the early Chicago school. Robert Park and Herbert Blumer led the way in the consolidation of those ideas (Clark 1969, 68; van Ginneken 1992, 228), a legacy that was perpetuated by some of their students under the by then recognized labels of *Collective Behavior* (Turner and Killian 1957) and *Collective Dynamics* (Lang and Lang 1961). Interactions, communication, mass media, and opinion change were central to their theorization—as was the idea of interpersonal influence, to which the Columbia school, with Lazarsfeld at the helm, also paid systematic attention (Katz and Lazarsfeld 1955; Lazarsfeld, Berelson, and Gaudet 1948). Today, digital technologies have placed the analysis of spontaneous and unstructured social action (with its long theoretical lineage) back at the heart of social inquiry, enabling a research agenda that has come to be known as computational social science (Lazer et al 2009). Insights are now coming not just from the social sciences (with their historical boundaries) but from the many attempts to analyze the available evidence with new tools—new, at least, to how the proponents of collective behavior research traditionally pursued their work.

Digital technologies have made measurable what, back in the nineteenth century, was very difficult to grasp—and remained difficult for many of the decades that followed. The traces we leave online are providing the empirical piece that was missing in Tarde's conception of communication as the quintessential social fact, and of interpersonal influence as the main driver of social change. These are the two pillars on which collective behavior research stands. Recent research is pushing our understanding of communication and social influence to frontiers that are new and exciting. Digital data, for instance, is revealing interesting patterns in the aggregate dynamics of interpersonal communication and helping us reconstruct the pathways of influence that drive collective phenomena (e.g., the irruption of trending topics or large-scale coordination in the form of protests or social mobilization). These pathways of influence are the diffusion streams that, for long, could only receive metaphorical treatment. The following chapter will dive into the mechanisms that activate those dynamics at the individual level; the remainder of this chapter will consider in more detail the temporal signatures that characterize the emergence (or sudden explosion) of collective attention.

3.2   The Rhythms of Communication

The closest Tarde ever got to finding measures for his ideas on communication and interpersonal influence was when he suggested compiling "statistics of conversation." As he put it in 1901:

> The average walking speed of pedestrians in various capitals of the world has been measured, and the statistics that were published showed rather large differences in speeds, as well as steadiness, from one to the next. I am persuaded that, if it were considered worthwhile, it would be possible to measure the speed of conversation in each city as well ... the study could develop into a sort of social psycho-physics. The elements, for the moment, are lacking. (Tarde 1969, 45)

A few years earlier, in 1899, just after Zola had returned from exile and Alfred Dreyfus received a pardon from the President, Tarde had published an article in which he discussed the importance of informal communication (the manuscript shows the handwritten comment: "Maybe add some pages on the Affair???," but in the end he opted not to add those pages; van Ginneken 1992, 220). In the article, Tarde gives a few statistics on how much the volume of interpersonal correspondence—including postal letters and telegrams—had grown in France during the nineteenth century. He takes the sharp increase in correspondence as evidence of strengthening interpersonal influence: conversation, in the end, was for him "the strongest agent of imitation, of the propagation of sentiments, ideas, and modes of action" (Tarde 1969, 308). And yet, once again, the elements were lacking:

> Letters have just about the same format, the same type of envelope and seal, the same type of address. ... We know their number, but not even their length. It would be interesting to find out, at least, if as they become more numerous they become shorter, which seems likely, and more prosaic as well. And if statistics existed for conversations, which would be just as legitimate, one would wish, likewise, to know their length, which in our busy century could be in inverse relationship to their frequency. The cities in which it rains the most, in which the most water falls from the sky—please excuse the analogy—are quite often those where it rains the least often. It would be especially interesting to know the innermost substantive transformations of letters as well as of conversations, and here statistics give us no information at all. (Tarde 1969, 316)

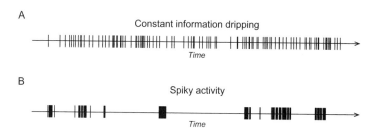

Figure 3.1
Temporal profiles of communication

Today, those statistics are finally available, and they offer important insights on the speed and rhythms of conversation—important for the reasons that Tarde intuited: if communication is the main channel through which influence flows, then the rate at which it happens, and its timing, matter greatly for understanding the effects of informal talk.

Digital technologies generate the activity logs that allow us to reconstruct the pace of interpersonal communication—at least as it evolves online. The analysis of those conversations reveals that informal talk has a very characteristic temporal profile: the same lapse of time can accommodate significantly different amounts of activity beyond the usual circadian cycles; and this suggests that communication is driven by temporal correlations that generate activity spikes. It is during those spikes that opportunities for influence are heightened. Figure 3.1 illustrates the idea. Communication events (e.g., the number of messages generated as a response to previous correspondence, or the number of phone calls made) do not follow the uniform pattern depicted in panel A. This scenario captures dynamics in which every temporal window (say, consecutive days) can be characterized by a similar volume of communication and messages follow each other with similar waiting times, suggesting that information is constantly dripping with comparable intensity. By contrast, the analysis of digital data reveals that activity levels and delay times are closer to the dynamics depicted in panel B: interpersonal communication is characterized by sudden rises in the volume and intensity of the interaction. In this scenario, there are long periods of low or nonexistent communication (which generate spikes in the delay times that separate communication events) and then brief periods of intense activity (which generate bursts in volume or communication bandwidth). Patterns like these were first identified in the analysis of email communication (Barabási 2005; Johansen 2004), but they have also been observed in the sort of letter writing that Tarde had in mind (Malmgren et al. 2009; Oliveira and Barabási 2005; Vazquez et al. 2006) as well as in phone conversations (Candia et al. 2008).

This data offers a good approximation to the "statistics of conversation" that Tarde wanted to compile; it also helps test his suspicion that the frequency of communication might be detrimental to its length and substance. What research shows is that the response time and the length of the messages do not correlate; that is, higher frequency of communication is not necessarily a synonym of less substance (Barabási 2005; Oliveira and Barabási 2005). Longer response times, however, do exacerbate delays, shaping the overall patterns of information exchange. These patterns pose two questions: What generates activity spikes, and why are they important? At the individual level, different mechanisms have been proposed to explain the intermittent rhythms of communication: they range from the need to set priorities under time constraints, which generate queues and delays (Vazquez et al. 2006), to more prosaic mechanisms of personal preference coupled with periodic cycles (Malmgren et al. 2008). Whichever the mechanism, the result is cascading and correlation in communication patterns: when we send one message (or when we make a phone call), we are more likely to engage in further correspondence (or initiate further calls), hence the spiky nature of the temporal trail. And this matters because if social influence is channeled by communication, then the strength of the influence will be intensified in specific periods—the timing of which cannot be easily anticipated.

Spikes in communication generate capacity issues: there is only so much attention one can pay to correspondence or informal conversation. But, most importantly, they also introduce further dependencies: every message, in the end, involves at least two people who have to adjust their rhythms to continue the conversation. Tarde suggested that conversation was a strong agent of social influence: informal talk was, to him, the main propagator of ideas, "the little invisible spring that flows, albeit irregularly, at all times and in all places" (Tarde 1969, 58). The events surrounding the Dreyfus affair, and the deluge of public discussions around it, were after all an important source of inspiration for his thinking. But the temporal dependencies of conversation dug up from digital data help us take Tarde's intuitions much further: we can now examine the feedback loops that make public talk spiral out to reach visible heights, the moment when individual patterns of communication converge to generate global spikes in the allocation of attention. We now call these spikes trending topics or buzz—exactly what the Dreyfus case would have been if nineteenth-century letters had displayed hashtags instead of postage stamps.

3.3   The Dynamics of Collective Attention

If the Dreyfus affair shows anything, it is that the members of the public fed on each other's reactions—but also that newspapers triggered many of those public outbursts. Whether ideas propagate through interpersonal networks or are inserted through external means is a question that has been at the heart of social thought since the late 1800s. Tarde wrote: "We shall never know and can never imagine to what degree newspapers have transformed, both enriched and leveled, unified in space and diversified in time, the conversations of individuals, even those who do not read papers but who, talking to those who do, are forced to follow the groove of their borrowed thoughts. One pen," he concluded, "suffices to set off a million tongues" (Tarde 1969, 304). These ideas anticipated the hypothesis of the two-step flow of communication popularized half a century later by Lazarsfeld and his team (Katz and Lazarsfeld 1955; Lazarsfeld, Berelson, and Gaudet 1948). The hypothesis stated that mass media did not have as strong an effect on individuals as commonly assumed: their influence was instead mediated by interpersonal communication and, in particular, by opinion leaders diffusing information and their own take on the news.

As originally formulated, though, the two-step flow theory was undermined by the nature of the data analyzed, which did not allow a comparison of leaders with their respective followers, "but only of leaders and non-leaders in general" (Katz 1957, 64). However, the theory transplanted Tarde's ideas, which were nourished by "the *mondain* Parisian conversationalists of Proustian salons," to the more prosaic world of "middle-class Ohio housewives" (Clark 1969, 57–58). And, in this instantiation, the theory got closer to finding an answer to the question of what makes communication an important agent of change. For starters, Lazarsfeld's studies helped identify ways to measure the complexity of the pathways through which influence spreads; interpersonal influence, after all, "comes in chains longer than two," since those serving as opinion leaders are often influenced themselves by other people (Katz 2006, xxiv). A few decades later, digital technologies have shifted attention again, this time from middle-class housewives to social media users. And this latest empirical shift is allowing us to map the chains of influence in a more precise way. The underlying question, however, remains very similar to Tarde's speculation: Does one pen suffice to set off a million tongues—or, rather, can one tweet set off a million typing fingers?

The short answer is yes, but only rarely. Research has suggested that in the vast majority of cases messages in social media sink into oblivion, stirring not much of a reaction in their audience; at most, they get retweeted a few times, but the chain does not go far or is soon broken (Goel, Watts, and Goldstein 2012). Even when certain discussion topics attract the attention of many people, it is not because of an exponential snowballing started by one broadcasting actor—or not necessarily. Instead, topics may become big following very different diffusion pathways (Goel et al. 2016). Sometimes the chain reaction is wide but shallow, sometimes it is deep but narrow; and overall, diffusion events look as different as the silhouettes of trees in a forest. When a topic gains traction and irrupts as one of the singular peaks in the uniform sea of collective attention, there is rarely one big opinion leader letting her influence fan out widely; chances are that many individuals contributed to create fragile chains perpetuating the flow. Prior analyses of chain letter data based on email transmission (ancient times in the history of the Internet) show similar patterns (Liben-Nowell and Kleinberg 2008). What this evidence suggests, overall, is that social influence creates diffusion paths that are fragile—a snapped link, and the chain stops.

Raising awareness on a large scale is therefore not common or easy. Successful diffusion events are as much outliers as the spikes of activity observed in personal communication—and as the Dreyfus affair is in the chronicles of modern history. And yet they do happen. How do the little drops of individual attention converge to increase the volume and the speed of opinion currents, to the point that they can no longer be ignored? The answer to this question requires analyzing the dynamics of collective attention. These dynamics can be characterized by their temporal signature, and by the fact that they might require different scales to help us see relevant patterns—much in the same way as zoom lenses need to be adjusted to follow framed action as it unfolds. If we zoom in too much (by analyzing activity on, say, a scale of minutes as opposed to hours), we may lose sight of any meaningful patterns; if we zoom out too much (if we use a scale of days as opposed to hours), we might be unable to identify significant change. Digital data is helping differentiate collective phenomena in terms of these temporal dynamics; and, at the same time, it is also helping reveal whether the buzz is driven by informal talk or by the injections of mainstream media.

Research on social media suggests that collective attention falls into one of three broad categories: it can be constant, periodic, or (more interestingly) concentrated around isolated peaks (Lehmann et al. 2012). This raises a set of questions: What drives that sharp and sudden escalation in the attention of many? Are people converging from the bottom up, responding to chain reactions and diffusion streams—which, as fragile as they are, can still bring many people to pay attention? Or is it just mass media making audiences respond like water to dropped stones? The key to answering these questions is in the analysis of the temporal patterns that precede and follow attention peaks. Activity might concentrate mostly before the peak (in which case the momentum builds up progressively); or the peak might in fact start suddenly (in which case activity trails down after). The second scenario most clearly reveals the imprint of mass media, the exogenous source that triggers a sudden surge in collective attention (ibid., 254). The first scenario, on the other hand, is more aligned with collective dynamics that emerge spontaneously—not necessarily isolated from events happening in the larger context but driven, mostly, by informal talk.

Of course, many empirical scenarios fall in between those two poles: collective attention is not fully driven by endogenous forces (e.g., social influence, contagion) or fully driven by exogenous factors (e.g., mass media); it responds, instead, to a combination of the two. And this is where social media are providing further evidence in support of the two-step flow of information. Research has shown that only a fraction of all information generated in online networks goes to ordinary users directly from the media; the rest comes to them through a subset of users who play the role of opinion leaders: they are exposed to more media content, and it is through them that news reach most of the population online (Wu et al. 2011). Digital data has allowed us, for the first time, to go from the general idea of the two-step flow of information to measuring the actual fraction of all information that originates in the media and that travels, directly or indirectly, to people.

In a different study, researchers looked at the "effective shelf-life" of articles posted on a news media site, a term they defined as the time span during which articles receive most of their visits (Castillo et al.

2014). What they found is that for the majority of news (about 80%) traffic decreases monotonically during the first 12 hours of being posted. What this means is that news grows old fast and audiences move on quickly to the next new topic. However, the remaining 20% shows an interesting pattern: for about half of this news, traffic remains constant (i.e., it does not decrease), while for the other half it actually rebounds after an initial drop. This finding suggests that social media, and the sharing those networks facilitate through personal connections, play a crucial role in perpetuating interest in a fraction (small, but still significant) of all news.

Overall, these studies offer a more detailed account of informal talk and engagement with mass media than Tarde (and those who followed in his steps) could ever have dreamed of. "If no one conversed," he wrote, "the newspapers would appear to no avail. … They would be like a string vibrating without a sounding board" (Tarde 1969, 58). To his credit, we can now measure the frequency of the sounds that come out of that board—and understand why some can be heard so much louder. Digital data still offers incomplete slices of reality: it misses much of the relevant action that goes on offline and that is (fortunately for our privacy) still untraceable. But it would be hard to argue that digital data offers a poorer representation of the power of communication than, say, the sample of Ohio housewives that Lazarsfeld used in his study.

The analysis of online talk is refining our understanding of opinion leaders, how they mediate the propagation of news and how that propagation unfolds, in terms of time and distance. Chapter 5 considers the constraints that networks impose on those dynamics (in the end, information can only flow if there is a tie or passage); and the following chapter examines in more detail the social mechanisms that trigger influence, or the decision to pass on news and perpetuate a chain. For now the argument will remain on aggregated dynamics of collective attention, because those dynamics help us understand how tsunamis (to recover the analogy introduced above) get assembled—precisely what Tarde wanted to find out when statistics could only depict, for the most part, a stationary world.

3.4 Unpacking Collective Effervescence

We now know that communication dynamics can be characterized by rapid spikes of activity, and that every so often people converge around those spikes, quickly raising awareness on specific issues with or without the help of mass media. How does this relate to the emergence of what Durkheim called "collective effervescence," the moment when "social interactions become more frequent and more active" (Durkheim 2001 [1912], 158)? Or to what Tarde called "higher aggregations," that is, groups of people "closely associated without ever seeing or knowing one another" (Tarde 1969, 55)? These dynamics are the beating heart of the sort of collective behavior that cannot be reduced to social structures or bureaucracies; they are the hidden engine that keeps much social life in motion. So who starts the process when effervescence bubbles up? Who leads and who follows? And when do collectives reach the point where their actions (their messages) stand out from the uniform sea of attention? Recent research has started to look into these questions using social media data; as a byproduct, this research is also trying to find a solution to the problem of scale, that is, to find the temporal aggregation that best represents the communication dynamics underlying effervescent behavior.

The problem of scale is the type of question that was not even on the radar for much social research before digital data became (overwhelmingly) available. Most communication activity today can be obtained with a temporal resolution that goes down to the second; so the question, again, is how much we should adjust our observation lenses to capture the action as it unfolds. What is the best way of aggregating temporal data so that we can reveal significant patterns—for instance, who is leading a process of collective upheaval and who is following to make it grow? The problem of aggregation, in fact, affects not only the temporal resolution but also the granularity of the observations: social media, for instance, allow us to track communication dynamics from the level of individual accounts to the level of millions of users, so how do we adjust the zoom of our measurement devices to capture dynamics across these different levels of analysis? The answer to this question is partly an empirical matter and partly a computational one. Individual users might not be active enough at certain time scales, which leads to scarcity of data; and analyzing millions of time series (and, in particular, how they affect one another) is still a prohibitively expensive use of computational resources. In recent research, colleagues and I have proposed a new method to solve the time scale problem given a geographical aggregation of the data (Borge-Holthoefer et al. 2016). Crucially, our approach (a collaborative effort that brings together insights from physics, information science, sociology, and communication) helps

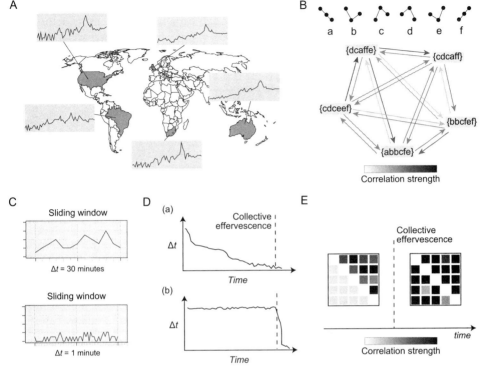

Figure 3.2
The evolving signature of collective behavior

identify the tipping point that makes collective effervescence brew into existence.

Figure 3.2 illustrates our take on the problem. First we use a geographical partition to reconstruct the time series tracking activity patterns (panel A). These time series contain information about the role that each geographic area plays in shaping the rhythms of the overall communication dynamics. In this example, the geographic areas correspond to entire countries, but we could also aggregate the information on a higher resolution level (e.g., cities), or for a conceptually different partition (e.g., sociodemographic groups). Then we apply a technique to determine who leads and who follows in the exchange of information. This technique first transforms the time series into a shorter sequence of symbols that simplifies the complexity of the original signal (panel B). The sequence of symbols acts like a sort of DNA encoding the profile of communication dynamics, and it helps find patterns of directional influence, i.e., whether activity in one region helps predict activity in another region. This symbolic transformation is important in this context because it controls for the amplitude of each time series; that is, it eliminates the impact that more densely populated regions have on volume. More social media users lead trivially to more messages and higher spikes; by transforming spiky series into a sequence of symbols that only map the ups and downs of the trends, not the magnitude, the method eliminates noise and helps identify more clearly the driving dynamics across regions. These driving dynamics can be represented as a network mapping the influence of each region on the others.

When a time series helps predict another time series, it means that there is a transfer of information from the first geographic region to the second, in other words that the second region is following the first. In his writings, Tarde talked about "a trickle-down of imitation and influence from the elites of the capital cities down to the rest of the populace" (Katz, Ali, and Kim 2014, 9). This is similar to what our method aims to capture: Are there some regions that lead the way when it comes to drawing attention to some issues? This question requires, again, finding the right scale to reconstruct the time series. A wider aggregation span (pulling together activity generated over a longer period) will result in fewer data points and smoother trends; narrower spans, on the other hand, will produce more data points but spikier and noisier signals (panel C). Luckily, the computational tools available today help us solve this question of temporal aggregation in a data-driven way. This solution entails the following: for a given sliding window, consider all possible pairs of geographical units (in this example, countries) and compute the total amount of information being transferred between them for different aggregation spans (e.g., a few minutes, an hour, a day). The amount of information transferred is the metric that serves as a proxy for leader-follower dynamics: the higher the total transfer of information among regions (i.e., the stronger the ties in the network depicted in panel B), the more leading-following trends are revealed by the data. This metric changes depending on how we aggregate the time series, so if we use different aggregation rules we can then compare how the metric varies for each of those rules and select the aggregation span that maximizes information flow. This is the temporal scale that best captures the intrinsic rhythm of decentralized communication.

What our method reveals is that this rhythm is not constant: it gets progressively smaller as the onset of massive collective events (i.e., a social mobilization) approaches (panel Da). However, this is only the case when the momentum is built up endogenously, from the bottom up; in cases where collective effervescence results from mass media interventions (e.g., breaking news triggering buzz), the characteristic temporal scale remains stable until the news breaks in, bringing the scale suddenly down by accelerating interest and the pace at which communication flows (panel Db). Overall, the method shows that the temporal scale of communication decreases systematically as the levels of global coordination increase: social influence ends up aligning all the time series to the same tempo, which means that all regions are in ebullition and it is no longer possible to identify leaders or followers. This build-up process is not visible when an external force (e.g., mass media) suddenly drives collective attention to the boiling point. If we represent the network of influence across regions as a matrix encoding the correlation strength for each pair (panel E), what we see is that communication dynamics transition from a hierarchical structure where a few regions dominate the flow to a horizontal structure where all regions are driving one another. The method, in other words, captures the transition from a small tune to a symphonic variation—from a state where a few regions start the "trickle-down of imitation" to a state of collective effervescence where all regions are increasing the momentum and raising public attention. This is when the tsunami has already assembled.

The lens offered by this analytical approach is a long way from the metaphorical conception of effervescence first proposed by Durkheim or Tarde's "higher aggregations," those individuals "closely associated without ever seeing or knowing one another." We can now measure how this type of association relies on communication and the transfer of information across groups of people. What our analyses reveal is not that the speed of information flow decreases as the volume of communication goes up; instead, they show that communication accelerates as coordination among groups (or regions) increases, which means that interdependence is more strongly felt as days pass. To return to the Dreyfus example, historical accounts consistently tell us that mass newspapers played an important role in triggering the chain reaction that escalated to become the affair, and that the unfolding events encouraged many readers to take action— from Sorbonne students disrupting lectures to members of the École Militaire mobilizing in defense of the French army (Arendt 1973, 110; Clark 1973, 173; van Ginneken 1992, 217). Informal conversation—the sounding board amplifying the story, the breeding ground of public opinion— surely played an important role in those events; but historical records are not very useful when it comes to measuring those dynamics. This is what social media and other digital technologies are changing today: by providing more dynamic data, they allow us to devise new metrics that measure the speed of information flow and how, on the aggregate, collectives are formed.

Our analytical approach to the dynamics of collective attention has several parameters that can be adjusted—just as we can adjust the settings of our camera lenses—but the results are robust to alternative tunings (Borge-Holthoefer et al. 2016). The approach shows that recent episodes of mass mobilization and political protest follow comparable patterns: the dynamics of communication accelerate as the day of spontaneous mass mobilizations gets closer, which is a signal that internal coordination is increasing toward a boiling point of generalized excitement. Because of this, these metrics could potentially be used as we use buoys in the sea: to anticipate the waters rising. The goal is not to be able to predict the future (as the previous two chapters have explained, there are several reasons why the future is intrinsically unpredictable) but to be able to identify significant changes in collective attention and, ultimately, opinion formation. Polls and surveys have traditionally offered the main tools to monitor those changes over time so that the information can be fed back into policy debates and decision making—political accountability depends, in the end, on our ability to strengthen the feedback loop between citizens and representatives. Digital technologies might be offering a new way to enforce that loop. However, this possibility requires solving a prior challenge: the problem of decoding the many signals that give the public a voice, and coming up with measurement devices that can help identify sudden shifts in opinion currents. We are just starting to devise methods that allow us to advance in that direction, and there are still many open questions on the table; but digital technologies have allowed us to move faster in one decade than in the previous century of research on collective behavior.

3.5 Collective Behavior Rehashed

Sixty years after the big debate between Durkheim and Tarde, collective dynamics was still considered a minor field of sociological inquiry. Two members of the Chicago school who perpetuated an interest in collective behavior wrote in 1961: "because of their magnitude and complexity, these phenomena [e.g., crowds, public opinion, social movements] are not directly amenable to observation under the kind of rigorously controlled conditions most sociologists would choose. Simple observations of rather strictly delineated phenomena are therefore preferred" (Lang and Lang 1961, 546). The study of social structure, in other words, was still considered superior because it offered a comfort zone of known metrics and reusable tools. Digital technologies have started to change that perception: we are now in a position to analyze the complexity that was once regarded as too difficult to decode. In the process, we can discover where inequalities in the exchange of information arise, or who is driving those dynamics. As those same sociologists also pointed out, "though concerned with unstructured behavior, collective dynamics is not exactly chaotic or random behavior. In fact, the assumption of some kind of pattern is indispensable" (ibid., 552–553). We have just started to uncover those patterns, adding an important layer of evidence to that gained through more interpretive frameworks—the realm to which collective behavior research was confined for generations.

It is pointless to speculate about how the social sciences would look today if Tarde had had access to the data (and the computational tools) that we now have available. But we can at least measure the progress made in making his ideas testable—starting with the nature of social facts, and why communication is the fundamental current that leads to their emergence. Interactions and the exchange of information create the streams of influence that will make a small idea grow big, a new hashtag turn into a trending topic, or a peripheral social movement rise to the media spotlight. As originally formulated, the two-step flow of information highlighted the importance of intermediaries when interacting with the news. Now we can extend our measurement of influence beyond that mediating step and analyze the pathways of social contagion (to use Tarde's expression) in all their diversity. This shift in focus is important because, as the pathways of influence branch out, they grow very different from one another. We are still far from fully understanding what explains those different patterns, and how they grow or merge to generate spikes in collective attention. This chapter has considered one of their manifestations, namely the communication dynamics that we can observe in the aggregate. New data sources have made those dynamics more tangible and more amenable to analysis, and are also encouraging the development of new metrics that help us parse all that information.

The Dreyfus affair, to put things back in a historical perspective, made visible the difference between crowds and publics. Tarde was the first to see it and make this distinction explicit in his writings. As Park and Burgess put it in their *Introduction to the Science of Sociology*, first published in 1921, Tarde understood that "the limits of the crowd are determined by the length to which a voice will carry or the distance that the eye can survey"; the public, on the other hand, "presupposes a higher stage of social development in which suggestions are transmitted in the form of ideas and there is contagion without contact" (Park and Burgess 1921, 868). The public, in other words, was a product of the technological breakthroughs that made the printing press and the telegraph possible. Digital technologies are, in that sense, a mere sequel of those older transformations. Online networks have accelerated the pace of "contagion without contact" because they have made communication even more decentralized than the telegraph did. And yet, as with the telegraph, networks that are decentralized in their architecture might not be decentralized in their use—something that the leader-follower dynamics described above help reveal.

The interdependencies enforced by communication often give rise to asymmetries that, following the logic of unintended effects, arise regardless of the intentions of the actors involved. The flows mapped in figure 3.2 were not triggered intentionally by any given actor or group; they emerged from the aggregation of many individual decisions to contribute to the flow, and from the correlation of the signals they sent over time. But then, even when the flows of information reveal asymmetry, the evidence suggests that the centers of gravity keep on moving: whoever is driving the dynamics one day might be in the back seat the next. Social change, in all its complexity, results from these ever-shifting dynamics, and digital data puts us in a better position to map that constant flow.

We have just started to identify the temporal signatures of collective attention as it is propelled by informal communication. The analyses of digital data help draw a picture of the public that is less focused on the grasp that the media have on opinions and more on how interdependence and influence contend with media coverage. This is helping to illuminate the forces that challenge prevalent views. The process has been referred to as the emergence of "counterpublics" (Fraser 1990), a form of discourse that disputes mainstream opinions that are not necessarily inclusive or representative. Social movements are the traditional instigators of opinion change, and interpersonal ties have, traditionally, been theorized as core to their organizing potential—the reason being that networks allow activists to raise awareness and recruit more people to their cause (McAdam 1986; McAdam and Paulsen 1993). Today, those ties are mediated by digital technologies. Social media have become not only a conduit for information diffusion but also a public domain where opinions and alternative discourses are forged (Gerbaudo 2012; Tufekci 2017). Social media, in other words, have become a space where the public develops—where, to paraphrase Park and Burgess again, there is "contagion without contact." And as the political use of newspapers in the nineteenth century illustrates, a public engaged in open communication often leads to the formation of crowds. Today crowds are powered by the diffusing potential of online networks, as my empirical work analyzing political mobilization shows (González-Bailón et al. 2011; González-Bailón 2013b; González-Bailón, Borge-Holthoefer, and Moreno 2013; Barberá et al. 2015; González-Bailón and Wang 2016). But online networks also help to articulate publics. Chapter 5 returns to the question of why analyzing the structure of those networks is so important to understand diffusion dynamics, and the speed with which publics form.

As the early representatives of collective behavior research emphasized, people's awareness of one another "sets up a lively exchange of influences, and the behavior that ensues is both social and collective" (Park and Burgess 1921, 865). It is social because it creates reactions that link individuals into larger chains; and it is collective because the aggregate will behave in ways no individual could reproduce on their own. We have known for a long time that the media exert power on the public. Now we can also analyze the more subtle, decentralized form of influence that triggers collective behavior. We can only uncover this form of influence by analyzing the complex dynamics of interpersonal communication.

Recent instances of hashtag activism offer contemporary examples of the sort of power that arises from informal communication—i.e., the irregular dripping of information that is channeled through personal connections. These flows sometimes converge to give rise to waves of attention that mainstream media can no longer ignore, as in the case of the #BlackLivesMatter and similar movements in the United States, escalated with the help of online networks (Jackson and Foucault Welles 2015). Once again, the mechanisms that allow politically charged hashtags to become trending topics (and thus gain public visibility) are not deterministic: as with other contagion phenomena, the diffusion pathways that allow hashtags to grow are sometimes long enough to make them noticeable to the overall public; but more often than not, those pathways are cut short by low levels of activity.

Finding the conditions that allow collective behavior to reach the tipping point of effervescence requires more empirical research. The good news is that we are closer to finding answers to those questions because social media (and other digital spaces) have made collective behavior more amenable to observation. And this matters for understanding change. As Tarde realized, "ideas conflict and coalesce as they travel through the networks, strata, and regions that constitute society"; this form of interaction "constitutes public opinion, infuses public policy, and contributes to social stability and change" (Katz, Ali, and Kim 2014, 8). Also, we should add, if we are to rebalance asymmetries in the flow of ideas, we first need to identify where those asymmetries come from.

This newly gained ability to analyze "statistics of conversation" is also shifting the metaphors we use to talk about public opinion. We are moving from the traditional (cybernetic) conception of opinions as thermostats, adjusted "when the actual policy 'temperature' differs from the preferred policy temperature" (Wlezien 1995), to the analogy of early-warning systems that is common in disaster prevention (Sakaki, Okazaki, and Matsuo 2010). This analogy sees social media as a network of distributed sensors that pulsate when users react to local circumstances: if many of these users start sending signals simultaneously (in the sort of decentralized fashion that characterizes Tarde's definition of the public), then collectively they are producing a form of intelligence that individuals would not be able to produce unilaterally—for instance, a strong signal of dissatisfaction with the status quo, stronger than any poll would be able to communicate with its snapshots of the public mood. Of course, there are many measurement issues that also need to be considered and solved when analyzing social media data—for which more research is again necessary. But the current mindset is a long distance from nineteenth-century crowd behavior researchers and their normative attempts to control what were considered irrational masses (Le Bon 1903 [1895]). Now research on collective dynamics is being used as a source of intelligence that can inform policy interventions, as chapter 7 will discuss in more detail. Decoding the logic of collective behavior requires developing new methods, and those methods are agnostic about how the findings are used. Without the analysis, however, it is not even possible to have a discussion of how we want to use digital technologies for the public good. As Tarde would say, the elements would be lacking.

This chapter, to recap, has considered one part of the problem of unintended effects by looking at the aggregate dynamics that result from individual actions, that is, from the decisions to contribute to the flow of information around specific issues at specific times. These actions concatenate to form collective dynamics that we can now observe and analyze with digital data. Communication dynamics, this chapter has argued, have temporal signatures that can help us understand how effervescence and sudden shifts in public attention emerge. More than a century ago, the Dreyfus affair taught statesmen and intellectuals that public opinion is untamable, as malleable as it seems. Today, digital technologies have made it even more difficult to take control of the bridles of an always restless public. But they are also offering new avenues to unpack old accounts of social influence and "magnetic chains," especially as they relate to what makes the public tick. The level of observation considered in this chapter intentionally disregards the mechanisms that social influence activates on the individual level; since the focus of attention has been on aggregated dynamics, interdependence has been presumed but not dissected. This is what the next chapter considers: the social logic of influence as it prompts individuals to coordinate their actions and behave as a collective.

4 The Social Logic of Influence

In July of 1518, a woman started to dance joylessly but frantically in one of the narrow streets of Strasbourg, ignoring her pleading husband, oblivious to her audience and the oddity of such a public display. After a few hours of uninterrupted dancing, she collapsed out of exhaustion, only to get back to her feet and start dancing again early the next morning. In a few days, more than thirty people had followed her example and started dancing in public as well, barely stopping for food or rest. Within a month, as many as four hundred people had joined the "madness," and the whole city was paralyzed in fear as the epidemic started to claim the first victims: some of the unrestrained dancers forced themselves to such fatigue that they fell unconscious and died (Waller 2009, 1–4). This episode of dancing mania was one of several that spread across Europe during the fourteenth and the seventeenth centuries, a social epidemic compared by some historians to the Black Death (Hecker 1888) and that still stands as one of the greatest mysteries of the Middle Ages (Donaldson, Cavanagh, and Rankin 1997). What made the epidemic so dangerous, in the minds of those witnessing it, was that "merely seeing another person dance" could trigger the same condition in the observer: this plague was not spread "by foul breadth, vermin, or dirty water, but through the equally potent forces of sight and suggestion" (Waller 2009, 108). All the authorities could do to prevent the epidemic's spread was to try to hide the dancers from public view.

Fast-forward a few centuries to American college life in the 1970s. Streaking (or running in the nude in front of an audience on a dare or as an act of protest) became so common that the press started to call the fad an epidemic. "The phenomenon," wrote the *New York Times* in 1974, "spread from the nation's collegiate campuses to shopping centers, factories, spring-training baseball diamonds, the hallowed halls of the Michigan State Capitol and on Wall Street" (McFadden 1974). Mass media and preexisting social ties were presumed to help the streaking fad spread: "some division of labor was nearly always present ... most cases involved organizers, actors, spectators, reporters and TV camera crews, and social control personnel" (Aguirre, Quarantelli, and Mendoza 1988, 578). The media, of course, also tried to create firewalls to the diffusion of streaking in an attempt to prevent the audiences from being inspired. "Directors of live television programs," wrote again the *Times*, "have put themselves on an alert for streakers, fearing that television might present a new frontier for nude runners determined to reach a larger audience"; as the vice president of sports operations for NBC put it, "we're on our guard because we don't want to encourage this thing" (Brown 1974). Exposure to bare bodies, they worried, would embolden others to want to strip off their clothes as well.

Back to the eighteenth century: in 1761 two small earthquakes made the streets of London tremble and chimneys fall within a month of each other. A man named William Bell prophesied that a third earthquake would arrive in another month to destroy the city and its inhabitants, and Londoners soon echoed the rumor and spread it widely, taking measures to escape from the calamity: "As the awful day approached, the excitement became intense, and great numbers of credulous people resorted to all the villages within a circuit of twenty miles, awaiting the doom of London. ... The fear became contagious, and hundreds who had laughed at the prediction a week before, packed up their goods, when they saw others doing so, and hastened away" (Mackay 1841, 224). St. Paul's dome, it turned out, did not crumble to the ground and Bell soon lost his credibility—having first enriched landlords in the surrounding towns, who made a fortune renting their accommodations to the escaping crowd. When a devastating earthquake did hit San Francisco in 1906, survivors were as starved for information as Londoners had been eager to consume false rumors: "no bread wagon, no supply of blankets aroused as much interest as the arrival of news" (Shibutani 1966, 31). When the news available proved insufficient, rumors arose fast, this time to help cope with uncertainty. In the absence of accurate forecasting, rumors still abound today about when the next big earthquake will strike the city again.

The last months of 1989 also brought much uncertainty, if for political reasons. The communist regime in East Germany was about to collapse, and the number of public protests demanding change were multiplying in the country. Leipzig became the first scene of massive demonstrations before they spread to other cities, and the turnout there far exceeded the numbers of protesters elsewhere. The layout and geographical location of Leipzig allowed the city to become the focal point of the demonstrations: it helped organize "frustrated people who were willing to participate in mass protest but somehow had to coordinate their individual decisions without knowing or being able to identify one another" (Lohmann 1994, 67). Demonstrators paraded every Monday along the ring road encircling the center of town, making themselves visible and recruiting other people as they advanced in their march. The visibility of the protests allowed "the spontaneous coordination of thousands and later tens and hundreds of thousands of individual participation decisions" (ibid., 68). The first protests were important because they triggered an information cascade that made public what had been hidden until then: the extent to which citizens opposed the regime and how many were ready for change. This awareness helped encourage other people to join the wave.

Epidemics, fads, rumors, and social unrest are all examples of the same type of collective behavior, situations in which individuals act under the influence of what other people do. In fact, these are all examples of the more general case of diffusion in which behavior, information, or ideas travel from person to person. In these dynamics, some actors play the role of leaders (or initiators) and the rest follow, allowing a rumor to spread or a protest to grow. The dancing woman, the first nude runner, the unlikely prophet, or the first demonstrators to go to the streets triggered a reaction that made other people decide to join the chain. Today, many of these dynamics are mediated by digital technologies. Social media allowed the "Ice Bucket Challenge" to go viral, raising millions of dollars and public awareness for a degenerative disease in just a few days (Steel 2014; Surowiecki 2016); but social media also facilitate the spread of rumors and misinformation, as happened during the 2015 Zika virus outbreak (McNeil 2016) or, most significantly, during the 2016 presidential campaign in the United States (Lazer et al., 2017). Online networks encourage the emergence of new forms of activism (Sengupta 2012) and the expression of political discontent (Eligon 2015), but they can also turn political action into a contagious fad with little consequence (Carr 2012). Digital technologies, in brief, have transformed the way in which collective dynamics emerge—but they have not changed their substance or the underlying mechanisms: collective behavior still results from people reacting to people and triggering a contagious chain.

4.1 The Contagion Metaphor

So how do we go from early metaphors of social contagion to the analysis of exposure and its viral effects? How can we identify the conditions that make ideas or behavior spread? Early sociologists, as the previous chapter explained, saw in contagion a source of social change: they realized that social influence could help people break away from the certainty of customs and associated routines. In the absence of biological vehicles for transmission, this sort of contagion could only be channeled by communication—a channel for influence that is strengthened every time new technologies arise (e.g., the telegraph, the Internet). As early as 1921, sociologists were writing about the consequences of expanding communication infrastructures for social life:

World-society of today, which depends upon the almost instantaneous communication of events and opinion around the world, rests upon the invention of telegraphy and the laying of the great ocean cables. ... The traditional cultures, the social inheritances of ages of isolation, are now in a world-process of interaction and modification as a result of the rapidity and the impact of these modern means of the circulation of ideas and sentiments. (Park and Burgess 1921, 343)

As discussed in the previous chapter, Park and Burgess contributed much to importing Tarde's ideas to American sociology. And like Tarde, they often emphasized that communication technologies multiplied the opportunities for information exposure and therefore the avenues for contagion to spread. Social contagion became a shorthand for "the relatively rapid, unwitting, and nonrational dissemination of a mood, impulse, or form of conduct" through interpersonal interaction. In its more extreme form, these early accounts suggested, contagion could adopt "the character of a social epidemic" (Blumer 1946, 176). The dancing manias of the Middle Ages often served to exemplify what these sociologists meant by "collective excitement"; but they also referred to more modern hysterias like those associated with patriotism and war, encouraged to a great degree by the media. As American commentator Walter Lippmann wrote in 1920, "at the present time a nation easily acts like a crowd. Under the influence of headlines and panicky print, the contagion of unreason can easily spread through a settled community" (Lippmann 1920, 56). Sociologists realized that those waves of "patriotic hysteria" (of which, alas, many still reverberate today) have similar formal properties to the dancing manias: they are just different manifestations of collective behavior turning irrationality into a dominant trend.

The same sociologists were also quick to acknowledge the problems implicit in their metaphors. Mania, hysteria, contagion were all terms that seemed to assume some pathological condition: "unrest in the social organism," early theories implied, "is like fever in the individual organism, a highly important diagnostic symptom" (Park and Burgess 1921, 876). But of course social change is not a pathology; it is the normal state of affairs, the healthy beating heart of social life—which is nothing but a stream into which, to paraphrase Heraclitus, you can never step twice.

Those taking the baton from Park and Burgess soon had to recognize the difficulties of doing actual empirical research on collective behavior, given that, by definition, it is spontaneous and unpredictable. "The phenomena," wrote sociologists Lang and Lang, "are generally transitory as well as characterized by an element of unpredictability ... only a lucky accident puts an observer in a position to make significant observations on how a gang forms or to trace the career of a crowd" (Lang and Lang 1961, 546). "Collective behavior," wrote Turner and Killian, "is not yet an area in which generalizations can be presented in precise form and with the backing of experimental or quantitative evidence. There is no dearth of ideas derived from historical analysis and from the impressionistic examination of cases. But few steps have yet been taken toward the verification of these ideas through more rigorous procedures" (Turner and Killian 1957, 13). Yet around this same time, some other researchers were taking the metaphor of contagion literally, paving the way for the "more rigorous procedures" that sociologists were seeking.

In a 1964 paper published in *Nature*, an information scientist and an epidemiologist decided to analyze the spread of ideas within a population as a process analogous to the transmission of an infectious disease (Goffman and Newill 1964). Their goal was not to take the analogy too seriously (unlike sociologists, they did not speculate about the type of "collective fever" that contagious processes can trigger) but instead to determine whether the known mechanisms in epidemic spreading could help understand the diffusion of ideas. The answer to this question was important because, they argued, it could help improve strategies for information retrieval—like those used in online databases, which offer a crucial compass when searching for information in this age of overload. Analogies are only useful if they help uncover essential patterns, the bones in the anatomy of social life to which "historical analysis" and the "impressionistic examination of cases" (to echo Turner and Killian's words) can then add some flesh and garments. Modeling social epidemics in the language of mathematics requires generalizing on the basis of a few basic principles, which by necessity involves disregarding some elements of the process. As the authors put it, "intellectual epidemics are often desirable while biological ones usually are not. This difference, however, does not pertain to the structure of the processes but only to external factors" (Goffman and Newill 1964, 226). Whether we want to encourage or prevent contagion, in other words, we first need to understand how it unfolds.

In general, models of epidemic processes assume that the population can be split into three groups, as illustrated in figure 4.1: those susceptible, those infected, and those removed (because they either die or become immune). The transition from susceptible to infected is caused by exposure to some contagious material, for example an idea—or perhaps a frantic dance. Actors in the infected group are the hosts of the contagious material, so exposure to these actors will increase the number of susceptible people that transition to the infected group as well. There are two factors that are important for understanding the contagious dynamics in a system thus defined: the probability of being infected after exposure (captured by the parameter β), and the rate of recovery (captured by the

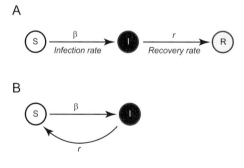

Figure 4.1
Epidemic models of contagion

parameter *r*). Contagion dynamics, in other words, depend on how the three groups of people (susceptible, infected, and removed) interact with one another. Some versions of the model do not allow a transition to the removed group but only back to the susceptible category, where the contagion cycle starts again (panel B in the figure). This or other possible variations of the model aim to ultimately shed light on how different assumptions on group interactions affect the emergence of large epidemics. The length of time during which actors are infected is an important element in the equation because it determines the chances of exposure for susceptible actors. In the end, the analysis of different scenarios, in which actors are distributed across the group categories according to different rules, aims to predict possible outbreaks and bring them under control—or, in the case of the contagion of worthy ideas, to encourage dissemination.

That is what the original model of the contagious transmission of ideas aimed to do: find the moment when a system for information retrieval could help spread content among a community of scientists. The analogy worked this way: instead of infectious material, hosts carry with them ideas that are transmitted through communication, which takes the form of published articles. The authors of those articles are the equivalent of infected people, and the readers are the susceptible group. Contact happens when the articles are read, i.e., when those susceptible get exposed to the ideas. The transition of actors to the removed group happens if they don't become interested in the content or if they lose interest; if they do become interested, they join the infected category and feed the contagion process by publishing articles that contain those same ideas. This might expose other actors and infect them as well. What the analogy reveals is that an epidemic cannot develop within a given population unless there is effective contact between susceptible and infected actors; and this only happens when scientists encounter articles to begin with—hence the importance of information retrieval, a tool that can provide contact when it does not exist.

From this perspective, intellectual epidemics differ in substance but not in form from infectious disease epidemics. One important advantage of this modeling approach, compared to prior metaphorical treatments, is that simple models offer a starting point from which to progressively incorporate more sophisticated assumptions and add extensions that will make the models more attuned to specific empirical scenarios. The mechanisms of rumor spreading offer one such scenario. In the rumor interpretation of the epidemic model, susceptible actors are those who have not yet heard the rumor; those infected are the ones actively spreading the word (Dietz 1967, 523). As with other epidemic models, the final proportion of people who hear the rumor will depend on how the groups interact and how the transition probabilities are defined. However, there are several possible mechanisms that are compatible with this basic framework: rumor spreaders could transition to the removed group through a process of forgetting, which is proportional to time; or they could transition more abruptly after meeting another active spreader: when this encounter happens, they might think that their rumor no longer has any "news value" and decide to drop it (Daley and Kendall 1964). This small difference in the hypothesized mechanism, which translates into different transition probabilities to the removed group, makes a big difference when it comes to determining the population threshold that is conducive to epidemics: in one case, it is possible to identify the initial number of susceptible actors that is necessary to generate an epidemic; in the other case, this population threshold effect disappears.

The theory of contagion has traveled a long distance since these initial models were formulated—and that, again, has a lot to do with the emergence of digital technologies. Mathematical models are theoretical expressions that capture a range of possible scenarios, but only empirical data can help narrow down that space to the settings that are most likely to occur. Online communication allows us to determine those empirical boundaries. Spontaneous, unstructured social action now leaves a trail that can be analyzed with the benefit of hindsight, so "lucky accidents" are no longer required in order to "make significant observations" (as Lang and Lang put it).

Digital marketing, and the design of campaigns aimed to encourage the viral diffusion of content, have done much to revive old metaphors of contagion. The analysis of online communication is helping us identify the mechanisms that drive those diffusion dynamics. In a 2012 study, for instance, researchers looked at the decisions to adopt a new product among a population of more than a million people (Aral and Walker 2012). These researchers used Facebook as their experimental setup; the product to be diffused was an application allowing users to share information on movies. The experiment was designed so that notifications about the application would be sent to randomly selected friends: when a given user interacted with the app, a random subset of her friends received a message with information of that activity and a link to instructions on how to start using the app as well. The question this research aimed to answer was whether exposure to the activity of peers leads to higher adoption rates.

This question falls within the boundaries of the broader problem introduced at the beginning of this chapter, namely whether exposure is enough to trigger social contagion. Exposure was the assumed mechanism in the dancing mania of the Middle Ages and during the streaking wave among college students in the 1970s: being exposed to the behavior of those affected could inspire—or so it was believed—similar behavior in others, which led those in authority to try to prevent exposure by all means. In the context of online marketing, interest in contagion has the opposite goal: to encourage spreading. The issue at hand, however, is essentially identical: Does witnessing what others are doing push us to want to join them?

The Facebook experiment showed that those influencing and those susceptible to influence have demographic characteristics that also mediate the process. Many users would have adopted the application even without any influence because of their propensities and preferences—in the end, it takes a certain type of person to want to share information about movies. Determining the actual role that social influence plays in processes of contagion requires first isolating the impact of other sociological factors on diffusion rates.

Those other factors, like gender, age, or marital status, are important for a number of reasons: they not only affect susceptibility (i.e., the probability of adopting a new product and transitioning to the "infected" group) but confer status in the web of social interactions. People's positions within that network are important because they determine their ability to reach other people. Peers within reach might themselves be more or less susceptible and therefore more or less likely to join the chain of interpersonal influence. These peer effects have been discussed by sociologists since at least the 1950s, when they started paying attention to the role played by mass media in patterns of interpersonal influence (Katz and Lazarsfeld 1955; Merton 1957). The Facebook experiment provided much stronger evidence of peer influence than those early studies; crucially, it showed that exposure to the behavior of others is a driving force in the adoption of behavior even when demographic factors and individual propensities are taken into account.

Similar contagion effects have been identified in the context of political mobilization (Bond et al. 2012), reinforcing the conclusions drawn from cases like the Monday demonstrations in the Leipzig of 1989. This study also used Facebook as the experimental platform, but this time the goal was to boost a get-out-the-vote campaign: users logging in from the United States on the day of congressional elections were reminded to vote, either in generic terms or using the photographs of friends who had already reported voting. What the experiment found is that the users exposed to this information were more likely to vote than those in the control group, who were shown no explicit encouragement to vote; in fact, exposure to information about friends was more influential than exposure to a generic voting message. Contagion, in other words, is more likely among people who know each other than when a message is spread through impersonal channels. In the offline world of the old East Germany, the ring road that enabled the Leipzig demonstrations served a function similar to that of social media today: it turned private information into a public expression—and a set of recognizable faces.

Randomization was crucial in the two experimental studies just described: allocating people to different conditions allows researchers to control for the impact that other factors have on behavior. This is obviously very difficult to do when social interactions take place in settings that cannot be easily controlled or manipulated, as in the Leipzig protests but also during the streaking wave in the 1970s. The directors of live television programs targeted by streaking students were on alert to avoid broadcasting the streakers' actions: this was their attempt to create a firewall against contagion. But then there was no control group of directors willing to give streakers air space, so we will never know whether lack of exposure helped contain contagion in this case. By all accounts, however, attempts to censor those actions did not manage to stop the wave, so surely there were other means than television through which social influence spread—streaking episodes, after all, took place in very public spaces, and university campuses are connected in myriad ways that are not mediated by mass media. Digital technologies make those interpersonal ties more traceable, which means that peer effects (and their consequences for contagion) can be more clearly identified, especially when exposure to different conditions is randomized.

Digital technologies also offer the possibility of analyzing collective behavior in retrospect: once we know which fads become trends, or which messages go viral, we can look back and reconstruct their paths to success. We can then compare those paths with the mathematical space of what is possible, and consider in a more systematic way the always difficult question of why an alternative course of events did not materialize.

4.2   Milling, Herding, and Wildfires

Contagion is just one of the many metaphors used in the study of collective behavior. Once exposure triggers individual reactions, social influence generates cascading effects that grow through reinforcement and feedback. The phenomena that result from these behavioral cascades have been described as "milling," "herding," and "fires that go wild," also referred to as the "elementary mechanisms of collective behavior" (Blumer 1946, 174). The focus of attention here is not on what makes individual actors transition from susceptible to infected but on the bigger picture of group behavior. The diffusion dynamics that underlie these phenomena are similar to those that trigger epidemics, but in this context the population of interest can be defined in more restrictive ways. For instance, it may refer to groups that self-select, like crowds in concerts; or to individuals that share predispositions, like protesters in a public demonstration. Epidemics do not require conscious awareness of the dynamics at play; the forms of collective behavior described as milling or herding do: they result from the actions of individuals who are constantly reading social signals.

The analogy with milling brings to mind the somehow unfortunate image of "cattle and sheep who are in a state of excitement" (Blumer 1946, 147). In reality, however, milling is essentially a communication process: in conditions of uncertainty, actors try to find cues in the behavior of other individuals that will help them react to the ambiguity (Turner and Killian 1957, 58–59). Anyone marooned by a canceled flight knows how the process works: other stranded passengers, otherwise regarded with polite indifference, suddenly become a point of reference; as everyone becomes more responsive to one another, milling results from a common (and frustrated) adjustment to the circumstances. The reaction to the earthquake prophecies in eighteenth-century London also conforms to this definition of milling: it shows that, in the end, "even the most skeptical tend to waver when they see everyone else acting on the basis of a rumor" (Shibutani 1966, 142). In this sense, the behavioral effects of rumor spreading can be considered as a type of milling, only one that manifests with words.

Social media have created a venue in which to test and unpack old ideas on milling, especially as it responds to the spread of rumors. A modern instantiation of *The War of the Worlds* hoax that, allegedly, caused mass panic (and catapulted Orson Welles to fame) can be found in the waves of paranoia that surround privacy concerns on the Web. In recent years, legitimate aspirations to protect data and confidentiality have repeatedly translated into the propagation of misleading information. As one hoax goes, users should post privacy notices on their walls if they don't want Facebook to use their data for evil goals. Though this hoax rests on misleading information (if only because the terms and conditions agreed when joining Facebook cannot be modified by posting a status update), it has repeatedly spread over the years (Victor 2015). The propagation of such hoaxes follows a similar pattern to the propagation of fears in other domains of social life—situations in which, to echo Shibutani's words, even the skeptical waver. The dynamics are such that "once a rumor is under way, it cannot be controlled by any one of the participants, any more than a lynching mob can be stopped when a few members change their minds" (Shibutani 1966, 15). The analysis of social media is at least helping us to identify the diffusion signature of rumors—which is a first step if we are to devise strategies to counteract their effects.

A good way to assess what makes false claims or misinformation special is to compare their diffusion patterns with how truthful information spreads. This is what a team of researchers did using Facebook data (Del Vicario et al. 2016). They analyzed 32 public pages publishing conspiracy theories (i.e., alternative or controversial information with no empirical support) and 35 about science news (published to disseminate scientific information). All the posts that were published for the years 2010 to 2014 were analyzed, which involved reconstructing sharing trees, that is, the way in which people contributed to disseminating the information. Someone sharing a post for the first time created the root of that tree, and subsequent sharing expanded its branches. The analysis of these structures revealed that the patterns of news assimilation differ: conspiracy rumors take more time to assimilate but grow larger with time; science news diffuses faster at first but then stops growing after a while, overall reaching fewer people.

These different patterns, the study concluded, respond to how communities of interest are formed online, "which causes reinforcement and fosters confirmation bias, segregation, and polarization" at the expense of "the quality of the information" (ibid., 558).

These diffusion dynamics, and the way digital technologies encourage them, have become increasingly relevant to the public, especially given the prominence that "fake news" and misinformation have gained in recent electoral campaigns (Cadwalladr 2016; Woolf 2016). The ability to track the contagion dynamics of misinformation has crucial policy implications, especially at a time when the value of truthful statements is often challenged and distrust of expert advice is on the rise (Drezner 2016). The debate on how to regulate the spread of misinformation is still open (Dutton 2017; Lazer et al. 2017), and finding a solution will inevitably require more research. The difficulty of this problem lies in the normative dimension of regulating information and the legitimacy of the task—this, once again, is not a technological problem but a social one, the resolution of which requires drawing the limits of censorship and the right to free expression.

Research on the propagation histories of false rumors, however, has already started to inform the question of how to best solve tradeoffs of information credibility in less politicized contexts, like emergency response situations (Castillo 2016, chapter 8; Mejova, Weber, and Macy 2015, chapter 6). When relevant information is generated organically, from the bottom up (as is common when established communication channels and infrastructures are disrupted in disaster settings; Spiro, Acton, and Butts 2013), automated methods can use the signals identified in the crowd to filter out the messages that are least likely to be true while harnessing valuable information to guide decision making. If one of the problems is how to best allocate limited resources (as happens in most emergency situations), then noisy signals are better than no signals at all. The tradeoff consists in accepting some level of inaccuracy if, in return, the data still offers some useful information.

Overall, the problem of reducing the effects of misinformation offers another example of the ways in which digital technologies (supported by research) can help redirect dynamics that are perverse for everybody. The hoax about privacy notices, for instance, turns the public's attention away from the actual channels that exist to protect personal data, thus making everybody (ironically) more vulnerable to privacy violations. Analyzing how misinformation spreads online can also help identify the segment of the population that is more susceptible to manipulation, either because those individuals don't engage with other verified sources of information, or because they are embedded in groups that overwhelm their attention with conspiracy or untruthful claims. Both cases call for intervention strategies that help counteract perverse information flows.

The analysis of information dynamics can also inform the design of mechanisms to rein in the effects of herding—a perverse effect to the extent that it introduces bias in individual decisions and turns attention away from more optimal courses of action. The problem of herding was introduced in chapter 2 in connection with information cascades—situations in which people disregard their own information in favor of inferences based on the behavior of other people (as in the example of choosing a restaurant because many diners are already sitting inside). Social influence here takes the shape of sequential decision making, and it impacts behavior by shifting the weight we give to private information. Choosing a restaurant is a mundane manifestation of this effect, in which we give more credit to what other people do than to our own initial preferences. But there are also other, more consequential settings where the behavior of others will tip us into acting differently.

Civic participation is one of those settings. Petition signing stands today as one of the most direct channels to try to influence policy making and push for social change. Until recently, however, the fate and histories of all these civic initiatives could not be researched because traditional records would only keep information on the few petitions that succeeded. Digital technologies changed this, making available "the entire transaction history for both successful and unsuccessful mobilizations around petitions" (Margetts et al. 2015, 80). An analysis of this history reveals two things: first, that the vast majority of petitions (more than 90%) never cross the threshold of signatures required to receive an official response; and second, that the proportion of signatures received by a petition on its first day is the most important factor explaining its ultimate success (ibid., 83). An early advantage in popular support is, in other words, a necessary condition for petitions to reach their visibility goals.

This pattern of early, swift growth suggests that social influence leads citizens much in the same way as diners are brought into restaurants: the more signatures collected, the worthier the cause is assumed to be. The good thing about these feedback dynamics is that they encourage partic-ipation. Citizens might not sign petitions on the street if they have no direct information on how many other people have already signed, which weakens their sense of political efficacy; the online counterpart of petition signing exposes participants to immediate information on overall support and momentum, and this helps generate the rapport that triggers the swift, early growth (Margetts et al. 2015). Social influence, in other words, acti-vates a chain reaction because it helps participants reassess the efficacy of their actions. The dark side of herding, however, is that the most visible petitions might not necessarily be the most urgent or the most important from a societal point of view. The actual demands of different petitions depend, of course, on the interests of different constituencies: some peti-tions will be more relevant for some groups than others, and will therefore gather different levels of support. But we also know that social influence often leads to biased outcomes, especially if we assume that the decisions made by others are more informed than ours and we just follow the flow. Examples of this sort of bias, to which chapter 7 returns, can be found in different domains of decision making (Lorenz et al. 2011; Pentland 2014). Here again we find the footprint of unintended consequences: no single actor is responsible for collective outcomes that turn out to be suboptimal; but understanding how those outcomes snowball from individual decisions makes it possible to devise mechanisms to correct the bias.

Yet another popular metaphor has been applied to the diffusion dynam-ics that result from cascading effects: wildfires. The analogy works this way: "Where people already have a common disposition to act in a certain way, such as to seek gain, to flee from danger, or to express hatred, the display of such behavior under conditions of collective excitement easily releases the corresponding impulse on their part. Under such conditions the given kind of behavior will spread like wildfire" (Blumer 1946, 176). This has become a common image in the analysis of protests and social movements, often referred to as "contagious collectivities" (Hedström 1994) that behave like "forest fires" (Biggs 2005). Not only can social movements spread through a geography thanks to the exposure and contact that social interactions facilitate, but the larger a protest grows, the faster it will keep on grow-ing. Mechanisms like interdependence and positive feedback, this research shows, explain the growth of protest waves and the spatial diffusion of collective action efforts much as they explain epidemics. Exposure to other people's behavior is, again, the key to decoding dynamics of contagion. However, one question has remained, so far, unanswered: How do we delimit the reference group that will influence the behavior of an actor? Or, put differently, how do we draw the boundaries within which exposure and contagion happen? The first models of epidemic spreading assumed that anyone could interact with (and be infected by) anyone else. Research conducted since then has moved far from this simplistic assumption.

4.3   Exposure and Reference Groups

Contagion relies on exposure: seeing someone dance in public, run naked across a playing field, relocate in anticipation of an earthquake, or join a protest campaign increases the chances that observers will decide to follow that behavior as well. Information is one aspect of the process: we change our assessment of the situation when we receive social signals that push us to update our private information. But who sends those signals, or whose signals we pay attention to, is another important element of these dynamics. The political mobilization experiment described above showed that personalized information was more influential than generic messages; at the same time, research on online petitions suggests that exposure to generic, global information is also a relevant trigger of behavior. Of course, it could very well be that referrals to the petition site through personalized social media are actually the main reason why the number of signatures goes up so fast—the total number of signatures published on the site would then be less important than the actual number of friends encouraging us to sign through social media channels, which are local and personal. This highlights an important aspect of social contagion: if exposure is the trigger, does it matter whether the sources of information we react to are global or local?

Global information refers to sources that facilitate common exposure: everyone accessing a petition site will see the same number of signatures; audiences watching the same broadcast of a sports event will also see the same spectacle if a streaker decides to strike. Local information, on the other hand, refers to the effects that peers have on peers: if a Facebook user sees many of his friends posting a privacy notice on their wall, he might decide to post it as well; likewise, only those walking the streets of medieval Strasbourg were likely to join the crazy dance because only they would have known it was happening soon enough to join. As intuitive as these examples may be, research on peer effects (i.e., local social influence) has traditionally had difficulty controlling for all possible sources of global information, that is, those unobserved factors that could also be driving the diffusion process (van den Bulte and Lilien 2001). Mass media are usually the main source of common exposure: actors often engage in a given behavior not because they are influencing each other but because they are all responding to the same external driver, like a marketing campaign or mass media coverage. Digital media are, once again, helping researchers disentangle this confluence of forces, not only because they make possible the sort of randomized experiments described above, but also because digital technologies create endogenous systems in which both sources of influence, global and local, coexist.

One of the early studies on Facebook activity considered precisely this question, that is, how social influence arises from the interplay of those two forms of social signaling (Onnela and Reed-Tsochas 2010). This research made use of one of the site's functionalities when the data was collected, between June and August of 2007. Back then, Facebook allowed users to install third-party applications that encouraged them to engage in a range of social activities, like gaming or exchanging information about movies (it was one of these applications that provided the basis for the randomized experiment described above). Every time a user installed one of these apps, friends were automatically notified, creating the local source of social influence: some users were exposed to some applications; other users were exposed to a different set of applications; and still others did not learn anything about any application through their friends. At the same time, everyone could access a list of applications ranked by overall popularity, which, as the authors of the study wrote, acted as a "best-seller" list. The key factor here is that both sources of social influence were endogenous to the system: the apps were not receiving media coverage (although Facebook itself was), and this meant that the dynamics of adoption and the diffusion histories of these applications could be analyzed as driven by the choices users made depending only on what happened on the platform—either as a response to the ranking provided by Facebook or to the activities of friends (global and local information, respectively).

What the study shows is that successful applications were propelled to the higher popularity ranks by social influence; the history of unsuccessful apps, on the other hand, revealed no correlation in adoption rates and, therefore, no evidence of social influence (whether channeled through local or global signals). This finding holds even when the characteristics of the applications are taken into account; in particular, researchers paid attention to network externality features, which make an app's usefulness increase with the size of its user base. The evidence shows that applications that had these features were represented in both the successful and unsuccessful groups, reinforcing the conclusion that mechanisms of social influence were responsible for the fate of applications—not necessarily their design. Although the study could not separate the contribution of global and local signals to the behavior of users, it still offered robust evidence that social influence was responsible for the collective dynamics that emerged in the platform—in particular, for the differentiation of successful and unsuccessful products. Most importantly, it offered empirical support to a theoretical tradition that, since the 1970s, had analyzed the effects of social influence under the rubric of threshold models.

Threshold models are still today among the most widely cited models of interdependent decision making. The motivation for these models came out of the realization that "knowing the norms, preferences, motives, and beliefs of participants in collective behavior can, in most cases, only provide a necessary but not sufficient condition for the explanation of outcomes; in addition, one needs a model of how these individual preferences interact and aggregate" (Granovetter 1978, 1421). Without such a model, the theory suggested, it is "hazardous to infer individual dispositions from aggregate outcomes"—the typical cautionary message that accompanies the analysis of all unintended effects. Granovetter was following here the same intuition that led Schelling to conceive of his segregation model, introduced in chapter 2 as one of the classic examples of unintended consequences. What threshold models suggest is that exposure to a reference group, and the prevalence of a given behavior within that group, will change an individual's assessment of the costs and benefits associated with joining that behavior. Granovetter used the example of a riot. Different actors, he claimed, will require different levels of assurance before joining in: there is safety in numbers, but not for everyone or not to the same extent; in addition, the benefits derived from rioting will vary depending on the number of other rioters. So he came up with a definition of a threshold conceived as an individual attribute that measures the proportion of the group that need to join a collective effort before a given actor decides to join as well. "Radicals," according to his terminology, have low thresholds; the threshold is high for those he calls "conservatives."

As originally formulated, this definition of threshold is equivalent to global social influence: everyone is exposed to the same signal (i.e., the number of people already participating). The assumption is that some will react to that signal sooner and some will react later, depending on their intrinsic dispositions. A range of models have been developed since this original formulation to incorporate local influence—or the effects of personalized information, which changes from actor to actor depending on who is included in their reference group. Today, these reference groups often take the form of friends in social media (as in the Facebook studies discussed above), but more generally they refer to the communication networks in which actors are embedded—regardless of the specific technology, or of whether any technology is actually involved. Exposure is then defined by social networks and what these networks allow actors to see from their local positions (Valente 1996; Watts 2002). There are several aspects that are important in the definition of exposure in this local sense, illustrated in figure 4.2. The first is that the definition of thresholds depends on the size of the network. The focal actor i depicted in panel A, for instance, gets activated (i.e., decides to join, say, a protest) once two of her contacts have activated, which means that she has a threshold of 0.5: half her reference group needs to be in for her to join the cause. The same threshold in a larger network (say, eight contacts instead of four) would require the activation of four people. What this means is that, even if two actors have the same

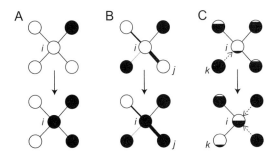

Figure 4.2
Modeling approaches to local influence

threshold or intrinsic predisposition, they might activate at different times if their reference groups differ in size.

The research that I and collaborators have conducted on protest recruitment through online networks uncovers this diversity in the chronological activation of actors that otherwise share the same threshold (González-Bailón et al. 2011). Online activism has come to complement older forms of political participation, and the question here is what makes an issue become a trending topic and spread ("like wildfire") through social media. The analysis I and colleagues conducted on online recruitment dynamics shows evidence of the same feedback effects (or "circular reactions"; Blumer 1946, 170) that make collective behavior so unpredictable and inflammable. Indeed, an increasing amount of research shows that protest mobilizations benefit from exposure to information through social media, especially when mainstream media do not cover the mobilizations until they are already in full swing (Barberá et al. 2015; Borge-Holthoefer et al. 2016; Conover, Ferrara, et al. 2013; González-Bailón et al. 2011; Steinert-Threlkeld et al. 2015). So, as simplistic as online measurements of individual predispositions are (in the end, social media are just one layer of many relevant forms of communication), they still make one important contribution: they offer an empirical window on dynamics that before could only be analyzed with abstract mathematical models (or by way of superficial metaphors).

One reason why the effects of local influence can be so counterintuitive is that local influence introduces variability that cannot be captured in terms of individual attributes alone; for instance, predisposition or number of friends. Social signals travel through networks like a chain reaction: activations cascade depending on the timing of other activations and where in the network they happen (Watts 2002; Watts and Dodds 2010). The following chapter looks in more detail into the reasons why the structure of networks beyond the immediate neighborhood of an actor is so important. For now, it will suffice to say that the activation of an actor depends not only on her threshold and the size of her reference group, but also on what happens beyond her immediate sphere of influence.

Even on the level of local interactions, however, there are other important factors that also mediate the process of contagion. One refers to the number of active sources to which the focal actor is exposed; that is, the extent to which a particular course of action is reinforced by different contacts. This extension has been formulated as the theory of complex contagion (Centola and Macy 2007), originally devised on the basis of simulation results but later supported by experimental and observational data in online environments (Centola 2010; Romero, Meeder, and Kleinberg 2011). This theory extends classic threshold models by suggesting that in many social contexts it is the total number of distinct contacts, not just the proportion of an actor's contacts, that prompts an actor to engage in a particular behavior. Social influence, in other words, often requires reinforcement from multiple sources to effectively encourage someone to act.

The strength of the signal, or the bandwidth of the communication channel that mediates exposure, is another important factor to take into account when analyzing influence (figure 4.2B). The idea here is that the strength of the tie that links the focal actor to members of her reference group is as relevant as her predisposition to act. If some contacts are more important than others because they are held in more esteem or are more trusted, or simply because they communicate more often (which, in the figure's schematic example, is captured by the weight of the tie connecting actors i and j), they will end up being more influential in activating the focal actor. This possibility echoes some elements of the famous strength-of-weak-ties argument, also formulated by Granovetter (1973) and originally devised to determine how often people receive information on job opportunities from acquaintances. Granovetter's argument was that people who belong to different social circles are more instrumental in finding a job because they are a better source of novel information: ties that are weak in terms of frequency of interaction are strong in terms of outcomes.

These theoretical intuitions have recently been refined to incorporate insights gained from the more granular data facilitated by online communication. The core of a recent argument is that there is a tradeoff between the frequency of interaction (e.g., the bandwidth of the tie) and the extent to which novel information circulates through that channel (Aral 2016; Aral and Van Alstyne 2011). This tradeoff changes the way in which we think about thresholds. In the example of figure 4.2B, the focal actor i activates only when the strong contact j has already activated. With no measurement of the bandwidth of each tie, we might infer that the threshold for the focal actor is 0.75; however, given the differences in tie strength (and information bandwidth), it is probably misleading to assume that all three activated contacts are equally influential.

Finally, research on social influence also pays attention to the correlations that local activations generate over time. Classic threshold models assume that actors only make the decision to activate once, and that they remain activated for the rest of the diffusion process. In recent research, colleagues and I relax this assumption in an attempt to offer a more accurate representation of how communication dynamics unfold in social media (Piedrahita et al. 2017). The proposal is not so much an extension of threshold models as a logical next step motivated by this question: What happens once an actor decides to join a collective action effort?

The answer to this question entails thinking about collective action as a two-step process. First, actors decide whether they want to participate; this stage of the process is what threshold models aim to capture. But then, once actors have opted in, there is the problem of coordinating their actions with other participants, which relies on communication events that are recurrent. As discussed in the previous chapter, activity in social media reveals dynamics that lead to large-scale coordination in the form, for instance, of hashtag activism (e.g., the sudden emergence of political hashtags like #Occupy, #UmbrellaRevolution, or #BlackLivesMatter). For these hashtags to become visible, social media activists need to converge in the use of certain keywords and in the timing of their messages. The question is, how do they accomplish that without the support of mainstream media or other global sources of exposure?

Local influence is again the key in thinking about this question. Panel C in figure 4.2 illustrates the way in which we have modeled the process. Every time a member of the reference group activates (e.g., sends a tweet, posts a comment), the focal actor i progresses faster toward an activation threshold that, when reached, will tip her into activation as well. When an actor activates, as represented by node k, she sends a signal to all the members of her reference group that pushes them toward their own thresholds. The difference from traditional threshold models is that the cycle starts anew after every activation takes place: once an actor sends a signal, she will start progressing again toward her threshold as a function of activity happening in her reference group (which in turn depends on activity in the

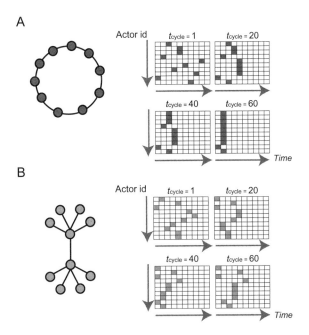

Figure 4.3
The unintended effects of interpersonal influence

rest of the network, etc.) At some point, this local adjustment of timings will result in some actors activating simultaneously; under some conditions, the group of coordinated actors will grow to become globally visible.

This dynamic process depends on how communication networks shape the boundaries of reference groups. Figure 4.3 illustrates how. Panel A depicts the activation dynamics that arise from a network where each actor is connected to two adjacent actors (her reference group). In this example, the initial state places actors in random stages in their progression toward activation, which means that they activate at different times, as illustrated by the matrix in the first cycle (every cycle represents the time it takes for every actor in the network to activate at least once). As time progresses and cycles accumulate, the timing of those activations starts aligning as a result of social influence, up to the point when all actors except one have coordinated their activation. The network in panel B, by contrast, is less conducive to coordination: the presence of hubs, and their greater influence over the peripheral nodes that are only connected through them, hampers the alignment of activations—this is why in the last cycle most actors still activate with different timings.

This simple example is a good illustration of the logic of unintended consequences: the simulated actors behave according to the same mechanism (illustrated in figure 4.2, panel C); the difference lies in the conditions in which they interact, captured by the two different networks. Changes in the structure of interdependence lead to very different collective outcomes, even though these outcomes are not intended or envisioned by the actors involved—who follow, in the end, identical rules. Dynamics like these explain why unknown hashtags suddenly become prominent symbols of a social movement or protest; or why decentralized communication results in the bursts of collective attention explored in the previous chapter, or the spikes in rumor activity discussed above—dynamics that emerge rapidly and unpredictably, seemingly out of nowhere.

Crucially, these dynamics exhibit clear patterns of temporal correlations that cannot be reproduced by classic threshold models, which assume activation to be a one-off event. As with previous models, however, models of repeated activation can also be extended by varying the strength of the signals depending on the nature of the tie, or by distributing thresholds so that connected actors are more similar in their propensity to activate. All these possibilities, and how closely they manage to reproduce observed patterns in empirical data, are still questions that require more research.

There are many other assumptions that could be made about the way in which social influence affects collective dynamics, and there are still many empirical gaps that need to be filled. However, the analysis of digital data is prompting researchers to think in new ways about very old problems, and this is an important step forward because, for decades, the discussion was stuck in the difficulties of collecting appropriate evidence. As those reviewing the history of research on collective behavior have claimed, "a field that consists only of scholars contradicting each other from the armchair can easily degenerate into sterile scholasticism. The most important need in the study of crowds is to get the main questions off the debating rostrum and move them to a level at which measurement, controlled observation, and imaginative experiment can begin to play some part in choosing among competing views" (Milgram and Toch 1969, as cited in Marx and Wood 1975, 372). This is precisely what digital technologies are doing: moving the debate from abstractions and metaphors to concrete mechanisms that can be measured and tested. Of course, the history of social research also offers examples of experiments that, though imaginative, also managed to cross the line of what we now deem ethically permissible (Blass 2009). Research on social influence has already triggered some alarms of this sort, especially as it informs the design of interventions.

4.4   The Double Edge of Contagion

Stopping epidemics that put people at risk is, everyone would agree, a good thing to do. So is designing mechanisms that prevent the spread of misinformation or encourage exposure to new ideas in the hopes that this will boost innovation. However, manipulating the effects of peer influence to increase the sales of a product, restrict consumer options, or more generally curtail the range of free choices an individual can make shifts the discussion closer to the territory of ambiguous ethics—especially since, given the nature of digital data, those interventions often take place without the explicit consent of the subjects involved (boyd and Crawford 2012). Research that unpacks the social logic of influence helps fill an important gap in our understanding of social life: it adds the empirical insights that for long were missing in theoretical discussions. But when experimental setups interfere with the private lives of individuals—which is becoming increasingly the case to the extent that digital technologies blur the line separating private from public life (Nissenbaum 2009)—concerns other than those of designing good research should also be explicitly considered.

The debate on how to use social influence to instill behavioral change is central to the design of many policies and public interventions (e.g., Contractor and DeChurch 2014; Valente 2012). The idea behind this approach is that peers are in a better position to modify behaviors and change community norms than external actors who, as well-intentioned as they may be, are not part of the system they want to change. This debate often tiptoes over different normative conceptions of what counts as a legitimate intervention. Is it always justified to try to engineer peer influence or manipulate the dynamics of contagion? And how compatible is this approach with individual choices and the right to autonomy and self-determination? These questions, which are revisited in chapter 7, cannot be answered by discussing research designs, devising new methodologies, or coming up with new ways of measuring influence effects. They are questions that transcend the internal logic of research and that demand attention to the concerns of the general public.

An example of how sensitive such questions are can be found in the reactions to a recent study analyzing emotional contagion in online networks (Kramer, Guillory, and Hancock 2014). The study manipulated the newsfeeds of Facebook users to test the impact of the emotions expressed by their friends on their own emotions. The experiment involved about 690,000 people, and it consisted of reducing exposure to positive and negative content by omitting relevant posts from the newsfeeds. The findings suggested that when positive posts were reduced, users produced less positive content; conversely, less exposure to negative posts led to more positive activity.

This research aimed to provide unprecedented large-scale evidence of emotional contagion, and cast light on how this form of social influence operates without people's awareness. In the end, however, the study ended up stirring a very public debate about the role of informed consent in social research (Arthur 2014; Goel 2014). As a result of this controversy, an editorial expression of concern was published soon after the original publication acknowledging that "the collection of the data by Facebook may have involved practices that were not fully consistent with the principles of obtaining informed consent and allowing participants to opt out" (Editors 2014). Since then, Facebook has adopted its own internal review board to evaluate the ethics of its research and, more broadly, assess the impact of that work on "our society" (Jackman and Kanerva 2016, 454). As some have already argued, though, important questions remain about how to measure positive impact, what constitutes societal improvement, and whether this sort of change can be left in the hands of corporations (Hoffman 2016).

The more general question underlying the debate is an old and difficult one, namely how to use research to fulfill normative visions of society—a worthy goal that is nonetheless not conducive to easy agreement. Normative statements cannot be assessed by the same means as empirical facts: even if we agree with the statement "ought implies can," determining what is possible (the domain of research) is only one step in the justification of what should be (the moment when normative aspirations are drawn). Normative justifications can rely on research, but ultimately it is up to the public, and to civil society, to define the norms that regulate social life.

The emotional contagion study made clear that researchers' assessment of risk does not necessarily coincide with the public's assessment. And one of the reasons has to do, again, with metaphors—with how the public think about technology, and whether those analogies have positive or negative connotations. As the senior author of the study, Jeff Hancock, writes in an essay reflecting on the public's response to the study, "if users think of a system like Facebook with the metaphor of a platform, or a window, then when that system violates expectations associated with that metaphor (e.g., a platform conducting experiments) this can upset and anger users" (Hancock, forthcoming). It does not matter that Facebook's newsfeeds were already being curated before the experiment (behind the curtains of corporate A/B testing or algorithmic filtering); what matters is that published research made the possibility of those manipulations, and their effects, transparent to the wider public.

The motivations that drive research are, in the end, as important as the novelty or the quality of the work. The tools of data science can be applied to target advertisements or to improve collective decisions: there is nothing in the science that instructs us on how to discriminate between different applications; this is a decision that has nothing to do with the tools but with how we want to use those tools. One of the core arguments in this book is that the unintended effects of human action are one of the problems that digital technologies are helping us solve, making interventions not only legitimate but possible. Social influence is one of the reasons why unintended consequences arise so often, for instance in the form of inequality (as explained in chapter 2) or as waves of misinformation (as explained earlier in this chapter). Unpacking the dynamics that generate those outcomes is necessary if we are to use policy to restrain the perverse effects. Interventions designed without that knowledge are likely to fail or, even worse, to accentuate the perversity of the process.

4.5 The Unpredictable Paths of Influence

The paths that social influence follows, as this chapter has explained, are not fully erratic, but they are also not easy to foretell. This does not mean that all policy interventions are doomed to fail, but that they should take into account the intrinsic unpredictability of the systems they aim to regulate. These policy considerations bring to mind Robert Coates's 1947 short story "The Law" (Coates 1947). In this fictional world, Coates described the adverse effects that mathematical flukes could have in social life. What he called the Law of Averages was one day suddenly broken: "The lady starting downtown for a day of shopping," he wrote, "could never be sure whether she would find Macy's department store a seething mob of other shoppers or a wilderness of empty, echoing aisles and unoccupied salesgirls." Roads would either be jammed with traffic or deserted; theaters and stadiums would be packed or empty; and the shade of that uncertain turnout would grow to cover most facets of social life, corroding the confidence of people, businesses, and government. The chaos that ensued was such that legislators felt forced to step in to control the "unconscious subversiveness of the people." And so they required by law that everyone be average again, imposing some patterns to help make things predictable once more: "a person whose name began with G, N, or U," the solution went, "could attend the theater only on Tuesdays, and he could go to the baseball games only on Thursdays, whereas his visits to a haberdashery were confined to the hours between ten o'clock and noon on Mondays." In such a system, of course, influence peddling soon ensued to obtain favorable exceptions to the rules.

The story offers a vignette of the paralyzing effects of unintended consequences—and the even more crippling effects of cumbersome policies to try to restrain them. Coates did not get the science quite right, however: what his story missed was a credible mechanism explaining the sudden concentrations of people, or their overwhelming absence; without that mechanism, it is no wonder that his policymakers could only come up with a clumsy intervention. Social influence, this chapter has argued, offers one reason why collective behavior can become so unpredictable. The following chapter describes how networks offer the other half of the explanation.

5 Networks and Social Distance

The first cable linking the European and US telegraph networks was laid across the Atlantic seabed in August of 1858. The ships carrying the cable, the American *Niagara* and the British *Agamemnon*, met in the middle of the Atlantic and joined the two halves they were each transporting before sailing off in opposite directions. There had been two failed attempts before. In the first, the cable snapped and fell into the depths of the sea just 350 miles into the journey. In the second attempt, the cable snapped twice and twice the fleet sailed back to their starting positions; when the cable snapped once again, all the ships could do was to return to port to take on new provisions (Briggs and Burke 2009; Briggs and Maverick 1858; Standage 2009 [1998]). So it is no surprise that when the cable was finally landed, jubilation erupted on both continents. Queen Victoria and President Buchanan telegraphed each other to rejoice at the accomplishment. Immediately after, the mayor of New York City sent a message to his London counterpart to celebrate "the triumph of science and energy over time and space" (Briggs and Maverick 1858, 187–189). It did not matter that the cable soon stopped working, and that the enthralled audiences had to wait until 1866, when another cable was laid, to fully rely on the telegraph's promise (Briggs and Burke 2009, 134). The first, if brief, success already settled the world into a new reality: continents that before had been days apart were suddenly "within whispering distance of each other" (Briggs and Maverick 1858, 193). Diplomatic and commercial ties had never reached that level of intimacy.

The trans-Atlantic cable built an unprecedented bridge. As *Scientific American* wrote soon after the achievement, the telegraph offered an "instantaneous highway of thought between the Old and New Worlds" (Standage 2009 [1998], 74). It offered "the connecting link between

America's web-work of forty-five thousand miles, and Europe's system of fifty-five thousand miles of Telegraph wires" (Briggs and Maverick 1858, 12). Other lines would in subsequent years connect to other continents, all the way to India, New Zealand, and Australia, overcoming what some historians have called "the tyranny of distance" (Blainey 1968). And so it is that the telegraph created the fastest global communication infrastructure known to man (and woman). The world was made smaller than it ever had been: the electric network "speeded up the transmission of information, public and private, local, regional, national and imperial"; and this meant that "distance was conquered as information relating to family, business, government affairs, the weather, and natural and manmade disasters was transmitted" (Briggs and Burke 2009, 134). "Time itself," declared London's newspaper the *Daily Telegraph*, "is telegraphed out of existence" (Standage 2009 [1998], 102). The Enlightenment belief that science could bend the rules of nature was vindicated, with fanfare, by the telegraph.

But it was not only time and distance that the telegraph lines helped bridge. A more intangible form of isolation, of social rather than geographic origin, was also altered by the touch of the electric wires. The traditional boundaries separating private and public life, and the lines drawing class distinctions, became increasingly blurred. In a world suddenly electrified, "new forms of communication put communities like the family under stress by making contacts between its members and outsiders difficult to supervise. They permitted the circulation of intimate secrets and fostered irregular association with little chance of community intervention. This meant that essential markers of social distance were in danger, and that critical class distinctions could become unenforceable" (Marvin 1988, 69–70). The more porous circulation of information and the fostering of new associations triggered consequences that would come to characterize the larger social and political transformations of the nineteenth century.

The telegraph was responsible for giving rise to public opinion as we understand it today. The public, as chapter 3 discussed, rose hand in hand with mass newspapers, which in turn evolved to their modern form thanks to the expansion of the telegraph. In fact, the name of the nascent *Daily Telegraph* in London was chosen "to give the impression of rapid, up-to-date delivery of news" (Standage 2009 [1998], 102). Readers connected by nothing other than the printed pages they read began to be aware of each other. Workers in one part of the world became mindful of fellow workers beyond their national borders. The telegraph played a crucial role in the 1848 revolutions that swept across Europe because, even if the electric network was still largely a tool for diplomatic communication, journalists also used it to disseminate the news of escalating social turmoil. Because of this, governments were concerned about opening the use of the telegraph to the public. Nicholas I, the emperor of Russia, banned the circulation of any information about the electric telegraph "on the grounds that it would be subversive" (Briggs and Burke 2009, 137). And history proved him right: technologies have a defiant side when they make it possible to see common grievances and urge those suffering to take action, encouraged by the knowledge that there are also many others willing to push for change.

The telegraph revolution, in brief, already put on the table many of the questions that concern us today: the way the Internet spans social distance, connects isolated groups, brings together people who would otherwise not associate, and facilitates the actions of those who organize for social change (Chadwick 2006; Earl and Kimport 2011; Rainie and Wellman 2012; Rheingold 1994; Shirky 2008; Tufekci 2017). The difference is that digital networks have made it possible to analyze the specific reasons why those communication ties matter. The telegraph cable, everyone agreed, created a geographic shortcut that allowed information to flow faster and reconfigured the bounds of social life: citizens on both sides of the Atlantic could now follow each other like neighbors over the fence of their backyards. The full implications of this reduced distance were, however, not really apparent at first, if only because actual facts (as is often the case) were buried in the noise of bombastic claims. In the years that have passed since, the science of networks has evolved to make sense of the impact that connections, and their architecture, have on dynamics that affect every dimension of social life.

Digital technologies (our current revolution) have allowed us to gain much of that knowledge because they have made the analysis of networks easier and more immediate. We know that networks create an infrastructure that allows information to travel fast around the world; but digital technologies are also helping us decode the more subtle ways in which networks reduce social distance—when they actually do. Networks are the reason why influence and contagion, discussed in the previous chapter, can roll out on a large scale, tipping many individuals to act in a particular way. Yet networks can also create firewalls to those dynamics, enforce social divides, or make ties fragile, compromising patterns of global connectivity—as that first oceanic cable did when it stopped working.

The only way to determine the consequences of living in a connected world is to analyze the myriad ways in which networks emerge and evolve. And while technology broadens opportunities for interaction, in the end it is up to social actors to use those tools to rewire or navigate their ties. Many networks share important properties in the way ties are assembled; but they also differ in small ways that turn out to make a big difference. The good news is that networks offer not only a communication infrastructure but also an analytical language that helps us map distance, and its consequences, in new, powerful ways.

5.1 Network Chains

Networks measure distance as the number of hops that are required to reach one node from another node. The transatlantic cable created the bridge that made London and New York suddenly adjacent to each other: 3,000 miles of ocean reduced to just one link. Traversing that link required the same effort on the part of the operator as connecting with Birmingham from London or with Washington from New York. There were no intermediaries, just a direct connection. Two nodes in a network (two cities, two people) might be geographically very far from each other, but as long as they have a direct link (e.g., a telegraph line, an email connection), there is a direct pathway through which information can flow. As the number of intermediaries grows, so does the network distance between the two nodes. More intermediaries means that the chain of links that need to be crossed to connect two people grows longer; and the longer that chain is, the lower the chances are that those two people will actually manage to get in touch. Creating a tie not only brings closer those directly connected; it also shortens the distance between the nodes that are connected to the heads of the tie. The cascading impact of new links on the average distance in a network is why the world can suddenly get much smaller.

Communication technologies connect parts of the world, but most crucially they connect people. Technologies have an impact on distance precisely because they help form ties that span social divides. A network explanation of this phenomenon and, more generally, of why we live in a small world was first formulated in the 1950s. In a draft paper that took two decades to get published, Ithiel de Sola Pool and Manfred Kochen wrote that "it is almost banal to cite one's favorite unlikely discovery of a shared acquaintance, which usually ends with the exclamation 'My, it's a small world!'" (de Sola Pool and Kochen 1978, 5). The key of their argument was that these chance meetings are, in fact, a clue to social structure, that is, to the factors that make people inhabit the same or different circles and consequently interact with more or less frequency. Two people with the same background or class (defined by things like profession or nationality) will be more likely to meet than two people with different characteristics. Networks help determine the probability of those encounters using the number of intermediaries required to bring two people together. People that are similar, de Sola Pool and Kochen claimed, will need on average fewer intermediaries to connect.

This tendency to interact with similar others translates into networks where ties are not randomly distributed but instead create pockets of dense connections. "The clustering in a society," they wrote, "is one of the things which affects who will meet whom and who can reach whom" (de Sola Pool and Kochen 1978, 13). This clustering means that the contacts a person has are likely to overlap with the contacts his contacts have—in other words, that friends are likely to be friends with each other. This is the main reason why ties that act as bridges are so important: they open up paths that venture away from clusters of mutual acquaintances. And this is where communication technologies make a difference. As de Sola Pool and Kochen put it, "the [1950s] contact pattern for an Indian villager *sans* radio, telephone, or road to his village is of a very different order from that of a Rotarian automobile dealer" (ibid., 7). In one case, it is difficult to escape the constraints of local ties; in the other case, there are many more opportunities to interact with people of different backgrounds and lifestyles. Communication networks offer more or less diversity, and access to more or less opportunities, depending on how they help actors create and rewire their ties.

The question of distance between two random actors depends, then, on how clusters and bridges mix in a network. Measuring this intuition, however, was very difficult to do empirically: researchers did not even have reliable estimates of the number of acquaintances that an average person was expected to have. The lack of empirical data was in fact the main reason why de Sola Pool and Kochen took two decades to publish their manuscript:

they were asking more questions than they could actually answer. By the time they did publish their paper, two approaches to the question of social distance had been developed. The first, led by Stanley Milgram, was an experimental method that tried to make visible the web of acquaintances that connect random people (Korte and Milgram 1970; Milgram 1967; Travers and Milgram 1969). The second, conceived by Mark Granovetter (and briefly discussed in the previous chapter), was a survey-based study that aimed to analyze how ties facilitate access to novel information (Granovetter 1973, 1974). Milgram's experiment aimed to uncover the contact chains that connect an arbitrary pair of people by asking participants to send a message to a random target in a distant city. The task, however, had one condition: participants could only transmit the message to one person they knew on a first-name basis. Granovetter's survey, on the other hand, asked participants to recall how often they saw the contact through whom they found a new job. This measure of frequency of interaction aimed to capture the strength of communication ties.

Milgram's experiments showed that, on average, chains connecting two random actors are short: the length of the chains completed varied from two to ten intermediaries, but a median of five steps was enough to reach the target person (Milgram 1967, 65). This was an empirical confirmation of the small-world phenomenon, that is, the hypothesis that everyone is at a short distance from anyone else. Granovetter's survey, on the other hand, showed that not all ties are equally relevant when it comes to finding a job: as the previous chapter explained, ties connecting people with distant social circles are better at fulfilling that role. If a person rarely interacts with others outside of the cluster of mutual friends, information accessed through those ties will tend to be redundant. In the context of job mobility patterns, this means that novel information about job openings will not abound in tight clusters. It is ties that connect to remote acquaintances (remote because there is no overlapping of friends) that will open up new employment opportunities. And those ties are weaker because interactions with acquaintances are less frequent than interactions with friends: they offer bridges to remote social circles much in the same way as the transatlantic cable built a bridge between the Old and New Worlds.

As imaginative as these attempts to measure social distance were (attested by the fact that these studies are still highly cited today), they were also limited in important ways. First, they had to work with small samples.

Conclusions about the strength of weak ties relied on 54 interviews with a sample of professionals living in a Boston suburb. Different implementations of the small world experiment, on the other hand, started with over a hundred chains, but only a few of these chains were completed (44, 64, 88, or 35 depending on the experiment). This attrition biased the reported results about the number of intermediaries required to connect two strangers; the reason is that "some of the incomplete chains would have been longer than those that were completed" (Milgram 1967, 65). Had those interrupted chains been continued until reaching the target, the reported average number of steps would have been higher.

The survey data on weak ties has additional problems: not only does it rely on a small sample of individuals, but it also likely contains measurement error due to the problem of recall—or the difficulties we have, in general, in retrieving from memory the list of acquaintances we interact with and the frequency of those interactions (Adams and Moody 2007). Even the categories used to measure frequency of contact ("often," "occasionally," and "rarely") seem prone to noisy assessment. In the end, these weaknesses reflect the empirical limitations that existed at the time this research was conducted, of which the protagonists of the research themselves were well aware: "the problems of processing data about social networks and drawing inferences from them," wrote de Sola Pool and Kochen, "still face serious obstacles" (de Sola Pool and Kochen 1978, 32). This is what digital data changed.

Digital technologies lifted important limitations in the analysis of communication networks. Not only did they make possible their computational treatment; they also helped collect the data necessary to qualify in crucial ways the theoretical discussions on social distance. One important development is the differentiation of two problems associated with the small world phenomenon: the first relates to the structural properties of the network; the second to how people navigate those ties. Communication networks may allow any pair of nodes to be within a short distance of each other; but "the mere existence of such a minimum chain does not mean ... that people will become aware of it" (de Sola Pool and Kochen 1978, 6). This means that understanding social distance requires answering two related but ultimately different questions: When does a network create a small world? And how do people find the shortcuts that will help them connect with someone else? The first question implies that not all networks reduce average distance. The second question implies that individuals often cannot find the short chains, so even if shortcuts exist, effectively people in the same network are still far away from each other.

5.2   Structure and Navigation

The first mathematical model examining the possibility space where small world networks emerge was developed in the late 1990s (Watts 1999; Watts and Strogatz 1998). This groundbreaking work gave proper formulation to some of the intuitions advanced by de Sola Pool and Kochen. Instead of assuming that networks are small, the model considered the conditions under which large networks (in the sense of distance) become small without also becoming completely random—a scenario in which networks stop reflecting social structure and therefore offer inappropriate maps of social life. Distance, again, is measured as the number of links required to connect any two nodes, which in network terminology is also called path length. A network where connections are highly clustered (where friends are friends of each other) and ties do not venture beyond those local clusters is a large network because it will require longer chains or paths to connect any two nodes. So the question is, how many ties need to be rewired (i.e., reconnected to distant nodes) to allow everyone to be closer together and thus make the large network become small? The model measured the impact of this rewiring procedure on average distance. The striking finding was that a small number of rewired ties was enough to contract the network: distance was reduced not just between the pair of nodes just connected "but between their immediate neighborhoods, neighborhoods of neighborhoods and so on" (Watts and Strogatz 1998, 440). The impact a few rewired ties had on clustering, on the other hand, was much smaller. The model, in other words, found the conditions under which a network that preserves social structure can still bring everyone closer together—and those conditions involve a small number of long-range ties.

The rewired ties in this model capture a similar idea to the bridges, or weak ties, identified by Granovetter in his job mobility study: these are connections that lead to different social contexts, distant because there is no overlap of contacts for those creating the tie. However, those bridges are just one link in the paths that put every pair of nodes at a short distance of each other. From the global vantage point of the researcher who looks at networks with full information, it is easy to identify where the shortest path is; but when we are navigating our own networks, and thinking about who might be in a position to shorten a transmission chain (i.e., who might be building a bridge), we only have local information. We know who we know, but we do not necessarily know who our friends are in touch with, even less for the friends of those friends. From the position of our own local networks, therefore, we can only envision narrow horizons, not the full branching structure that might lead us toward one target or another. So the question is, how do people actually know who, among their acquaintances or friends, is in a position to shorten a transmission path? Digital technologies have allowed researchers to replicate Milgram's experiments to address this question but this time on a global scale, and overcoming many of the limitations of the original study.

One experiment used the web to recruit participants, who were then asked to perform a similar task to those in the original experiment—only instead of a postal package, they had to send an email to someone they knew who they thought would be closer to the target (Dodds, Muhamad, and Watts 2003). More than 61,000 participants contributed to create chains that were to reach 18 targets in 13 different countries. Of all the chains that were initiated (more than 24,000), only 384 were completed by reaching the final destination. After accounting for this substantive attrition, the results suggested that most chains could be completed in five to seven steps, offering important confirmation to the original study—but also added evidence on how difficult it is to complete chains from a given starting point to the predefined target.

The experiment also illuminated the rationale behind individual choices on whom to contact next in the chain. Participants chose the next step in the transmission mainly based on geographical proximity and similarity of occupation. These dimensions offered the most important heuristics that guided the search for the shortest path. One additional finding was also relevant: in the successful chains, weak ties (i.e., acquaintances rather than close friends) were chosen more frequently as the next relay step than in unsuccessful chains, adding unprecedented evidence in support of the claim that weak ties hold the key for global connectivity. In a later study, however, the effects of attrition were further qualified to show that some chains are, in fact, much longer than the median (Goel, Muhamad, and Watts 2009). This is an important finding because it suggests that even in small worlds, some people find it hard to connect with others.

The main message of this research is that the properties of a network are not enough to understand the dynamics that take place through those ties. Finding short chains is easier in some structures than in others (Kleinberg 2000); and in the specific context of social networks, demographic attributes and identity features are especially important when it comes to devising successful search strategies (Watts, Dodds, and Newman 2002). A network may contain many bridges, and if we have global knowledge we can find the best route to transmit information from one random point to another. This is what recent maps of global networks like those created with Facebook or Twitter data can offer: they contain the full structure of pathways that could connect any pair of people (Edunov et al. 2016; Kwak et al. 2010). However, individuals do not usually have access to the full map of their connections—and even if they did, due to the sheer size of those networks they would not be able to visualize them or assess social distance without some serious computation. For most purposes, in our daily lives we simply do not know how we are embedded in the bigger picture of global communication; so when we are tasked with reaching a particular individual, the best we can do is apply different heuristics to decide to whom to send a message. The important conclusion of recent research is that different search strategies will generate different outcomes even if two actors are at the same distance from a particular target. Networks are as much about infrastructures as about the mental maps we build to represent our ties and the pathways they create.

When there is no intentional targeting, the structure of networks becomes more relevant. The dynamics of social influence discussed in the previous chapter roll out following available links: there is no intentional zeroing in on any specific target, but on as many as the cascading wave can reach. And here structural properties other than local clustering or path length matter greatly. Recent research has been particularly useful in characterizing networks on the intermediate level that spans local features (of which actors are aware) and global statistics like distance (of which they are not). The properties of networks on this intermediate level of analysis are crucial to determining the position different actors occupy (e.g., their reachability and their reach); but also to understanding how their ties are assembled within the bigger picture of everyone's ties and how this, in turn, will affect dynamics like the diffusion of information. The building blocks of networks are like pieces in a dissection puzzle with tiles of different size:

they can be put together to form very different configurations. This is also the reason why networks are so complex, and the dynamics they channel so difficult to anticipate: changing one piece in the configuration can completely change the shape—and how a network behaves.

5.3   Components, Communities, and Cores

One of the features that characterize networks is how cohesive they are. If we were to start removing ties one by one, what would happen with the overall connectivity? This is what a study tracking mobile phone communication patterns did for a network of about 7 million users (Onnela et al. 2007). The study analyzed phone call records for a period of 18 weeks to create links between users if they had at least one reciprocated phone call. The strength of each communication tie was then defined as the aggregated duration of calls between pairs of users, measured in minutes. This is a more accurate measure of actual frequency of communication than responses to survey questions, like those used by Granovetter in his empirical work. Remarkably, however, his theoretical intuitions about social distance were confirmed by these better measurements. One of the findings in the analysis of the mobile phone network is that the strength of a tie between a pair of users increases with the overlap of their friendship circles, "resulting in the importance of weak ties in connecting communities" (Onnela et al. 2007, 7333). In line with Granovetter's idea, the strongest ties are concentrated in clusters, "indicating that users spend most of their on-air time talking to members of their immediate circle of friends" (ibid.). The study also showed that removing the weakest ties has a much stronger effect on the global connectivity of the network than removing strong ties: their absence results in a network that breaks down into separated components; eliminating the strongest ties first, on the other hand, progressively shrinks the network but does not compromise global connectivity.

Components in networks are like unconnected islands: they are unreachable from each other. The more technical definition describes a component as a subnetwork in which any two nodes are connected to each other by paths. If two nodes cannot be connected by a path, they do not belong to the same component. The small world experiment found that most people are part of the same gigantic connected structure (i.e., a single component) and that a few bridging ties are enough to reduce overall distance. In most social networks, those structural bridges have a lower bandwidth because they are sustained by less intense relationships: they link us with acquaintances, with whom we talk less often, not with friends. But these ties are relevant because without them there would be fewer global pathways (if any) linking random nodes: the network would turn into a set of separate circles. And this matters because diffusion processes require connectivity to reach people who would otherwise be secluded in their friendship pockets. The counterintuitive effects of network structure on these dynamics is what digital technologies are helping us decode today.

The impact of weak ties on diffusion dynamics, for instance, is mixed. On the one hand, they create the channels for information to diffuse globally; on the other, because of their lower bandwidth, they impose constraints on the stream, effectively creating bottlenecks that hamper diffusion. A simulated diffusion process run on the mobile communication network showed why this is the case. The simulation worked as follows: at time 0, a randomly selected node (i.e., a mobile user) is seeded with some novel information. At each time step, each infected individual can pass the information to a contact with a given probability; the more time two individuals talk on the phone (encoded as the strength of the ties), the higher is the chance that the information will be passed on. This diffusion mechanism is, in fact, very similar to the susceptible-infected model discussed in the previous chapter; the difference is that here exposure is not random but determined by the structure and tie strengths observed in the real-world mobile network. What researchers found is that, compared to a control scenario where all tie strengths are replaced with their average value, diffusion dynamics are slower in the observed network, "the difference being rooted in a dynamic trapping of information in communities" (Onnela et al. 2007, 7335). Weak ties channel fewer interactions, offering fewer opportunities to pass on information. As a result, information ends up being trapped in local clusters for a longer time.

The way in which weak ties mediate these dynamics is reminiscent of the diversity-bandwidth tradeoff also discussed in the previous chapter (Aral and Van Alstyne 2011). This tradeoff referred to the fact that weak ties are more likely to channel novel information, being the contact points of different social circles. But because strong ties actually involve higher volumes of communication, even if overall they channel less novelty, in the end new information will also circulate through those redundant ties. The broader claim behind the tradeoff argument is that determining whether ties are weak or strong in the structural sense is not enough to understand their role in the diffusion sense—much in the same way as the existence of short paths in a network does not mean those paths are easy to find or navigate. Weak ties might create the bridges that keep the network together and help integrate different social spheres; but they also act like firewalls to diffusion because, being weak, they are only activated occasionally.

Weak ties are, in fact, only part of the story in understanding diffusion dynamics; the number of distinct social contexts to which an actor is connected matters as well. Recent research calls this network feature "structural diversity" (Ugander et al. 2012). This measure helps characterize the number of components in the neighborhood of a node, that is, the number of disconnected islands that would remain if a person's ties with her contacts were removed. Since we build our networks in different contexts and over different periods of time (e.g., we interact with work colleagues, family, or old college friends), our networks tend to have clusters that are only bridged by us. By definition, we are connected to everybody in our personal network; the question is, what is left when we remove those egocentric ties? How will our contacts be connected to each other, if connected at all? In general, the more components result from this exercise (and the larger each of these components is), the higher the levels of structural diversity will be—and the richer the social life of a person, at least as mapped by their network.

The relevant finding that came out of this study is that structural diversity has a positive impact on social contagion. Using Facebook data, the study analyzed two diffusion processes to sustain this claim: the dynamics of recruitment to the site; and the process of engagement with the site once users are recruited. In both instances, people who were connected to more diverse circles (as assessed using the network of friends already using the site) were more likely to enroll and be active in the platform themselves. This held even when structural diversity was measured in alternative ways. Exposure to social signals received from multiple contexts, these results reveal, makes contagion more likely than if all the signals come from several individuals in the same group of friends.

Core-periphery structures offer another way to look at the bigger picture of network connectivity to determine how it affects information diffusion. In general, networks have a core-periphery structure when there is a subset

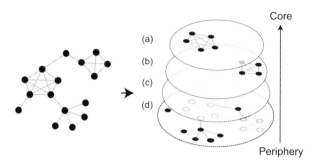

Figure 5.1
Core-periphery structures

of nodes that are densely connected to each other and a subset of peripheral nodes that are connected to the core but not to each other (Borgatti and Everett 1999; Csermely et al. 2013). Various techniques are available that help differentiate core from peripheral nodes, but they all share the same goal: to identify parts of a network where connections are denser and more redundant; this is where information will also tend to travel more easily or faster. Figure 5.1 illustrates one of the ways in which a network can be decomposed into layers of increasing cohesion or "coreness." This specific technique looks at the number of connections of each node and, iteratively, classifies them in groups in which all nodes have the same degree of connectivity (for a technical definition see Alvarez-Hamelin et al. 2005; Seidman 1983). The nodes that are in layer (a) of figure 5.1 are the most cohesively connected, and they form the core of the network because this is where the most intense interactions (as mapped by the ties) take place. Nodes that are closer to the periphery, on the other hand, are the dead ends of the flow, and on average they are farther away from each other than the other nodes. At the same time, some of these peripheral nodes are extremely important for global information diffusion. The node in layer (c), for instance, is a global bridge: without its communication activity, the network would break into two separate components.

This core-periphery structure, by the way, is also the reason why some people are easier to find in search problems like those posed by the small world experiment: it is simply easier to find a path to the core of a network than to find a path to the periphery. And to the extent that social distance reflects lack of opportunities for some groups of people, core-periphery structures are also a measure of social inequality. However, this is not the case in all networks, and in fact some networks self-organize in a core-periphery structure to maximize reach in the spread of a message—a message that would not find an audience otherwise. Rather than creating inequality, in some contexts this organization helps overcome old asymmetries of media reach: for instance, in situations where there is a core of highly engaged actors creating relevant content and a large periphery disseminating that information. This is precisely what colleagues and I found in the context of political mobilization.

In this research we looked at the communication dynamics that emerged in social media (Twitter) during protest events including the Gezi Park mobilizations that erupted in Turkey in the spring of 2013 (Barberá et al. 2015). What our analyses show is that the minority of social media users who reported being on the streets at the time of the protests were also at the core of the communication network, which is where most of the information was being generated and sourced from. Surrounding this core, there was an immense periphery of users who only engaged marginally with information about the events but who, on the aggregate, provided most of the visibility and reach for the protest messages. Since media coverage of these events was censored during the first hours of the mobilizations (Tufekci, 2017), those interested in following the protests had to follow social media activity. The division of labor between core and peripheral users helped relevant information reach an international audience in a matter of hours. These findings are consistent with prior research where we also analyzed communication dynamics during protest mobilizations, this time in the context of the Spanish Indignados, a protest movement that emerged in Spain in 2011, partly inspired by the Arab Spring, partly an instigator of the Occupy movement (González-Bailón et al. 2011). This research found evidence that core users in the protest communication network were more likely to trigger large information cascades (measured as correlated activity) than users who were more peripheral—and the reason lies, again, in the better connectivity of core users and their closer proximity to everybody else.

A more macroscopic way to measure social contexts, and their cohesion, is through a different set of techniques known as community detection. Broadly defined, communities are parts of a network where connections are denser internally than externally. Nodes are classified as belonging to one

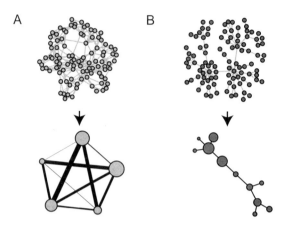

Figure 5.2
Network reduction with community detection

community or another depending on who they connect to and how the rest of the nodes are connected to each other. As with the analysis of cores, there are many different techniques that allow identifying communities in networks, each with strengths and weaknesses; many of these techniques are, in fact, still being developed (Fortunato 2010; Fortunato and Hric 2016; Lancichinetti and Fortunato 2009). All these approaches, however, share the same goal of reducing the complexity of networks by drawing boundaries that help illuminate the logic of their organization. Figure 5.2 illustrates how this reduction technique works, using stylized examples.

The two networks in this figure have the same size (100 nodes), but they differ greatly in how the nodes are connected. Some differences are already visible from a glance at the upper panels: the network in panel A, for instance, has denser local clusters than the network in panel B. These differences are made even more patent when the networks are reduced to their communities (the specific technique applied or the validity of the output is of no importance for the purposes of this example). Every node in the lower panels represents a community (which encapsulates individual nodes that have more ties with each other than with nodes in other communities). In one case, the network is reduced to five communities; in the other case, to eleven. The way these communities are connected to each other also varies. If we are interested in how information diffuses through these ties, then network A seems better placed for facilitating global flows. Even if information flow also depends on where the diffusion process starts, in general network A is more cohesive than network B and therefore offers more channels for information to travel far and fast.

One of the virtues of this reduction technique is that it allows us to think about bridges in a different way: bridges are now the ties that bring entire communities closer together. In large networks (of the sort that social media now make available for analysis) this is particularly useful because it helps highlight the most important channels for information diffusion. These global ties have a strength that depends on how many individual channels exist from node to node. Within each community, some nodes might be better connected to nodes in other communities, and some might be more peripheral. Communities, in fact, can vary drastically from each other in their internal arrangement of ties: some might have, for instance, a clear core-periphery structure while some others might be more densely connected.

We are still far from understanding the many ways in which communities in networks can differ; but the known differences provide the basis for role identification techniques that help us find the actors creating global bridges and assess how their activity impacts information flows in the network. In past research, for instance, colleagues and I show that actors creating global bridges play an important role in collective dynamics like protest campaigns because they help connect different movements (contained, for the most part, within demarcated communities; González-Bailón, Wang, and Borge-Holthoefer 2014). However, since these bridging actors are a minority, they also create bottlenecks in the network that undermine the potential of social media to be an efficient platform for the diffusion of campaign information (González-Bailón and Wang 2016). The analysis of communication networks on this level of analysis, in other words, is helping debunk a few claims about the impact of social media on social distance and collective behavior. Just as with the telegraph two centuries ago, the revolutionary nature of online networks has often been assumed and celebrated. But once we start looking at the more specific mechanisms that make networks the backbone of collective dynamics, their role turns out to be ambiguous and full of paradoxes—though, luckily, also far more interesting.

5.4   Dynamics and Layered Connectivity

The analysis of networks requires us to decide which structural feature we pay attention to. If the goal is to understand diffusion dynamics, social distance is an important feature because it affects the chances that the diffusion process will escalate globally. The footprints of social structure (e.g., clusters, cores, communities) are also important because they allow us to determine where connections are more redundant and, therefore, where information will travel faster—or where it will circulate for longer periods of time before it can cross a bridge to another pocket of dense connections. The social contagion examples explored in the previous chapter all take place in communication networks like the ones discussed here. Assuming we can reconstruct the structure of those ties, we can then locate where the diffusion chain starts and how neighboring ties, and the ties of those ties, determine the course of the chain reaction. Diffusion chains can then be visualized as cascade forests, where trees map the paths that diffusion follows as it flows (Goel et al. 2016). These trees have a root (i.e., the initial seeding node) and branches that grow more or less depending on the behavior of subsequent adopters, starting with the neighbors of the seeding node. The characteristics of these diffusion trees depend on the characteristics of the network in which they grow. Finding out how diffusion trees and networks relate to each other is anything but intuitive—and is the goal of an increasing number of studies.

Recent research, for instance, has tracked interactions in Social Life (an online multiplayer game) to find evidence of the cascading effects of social influence (Bakshy, Karrer, and Adamic 2009). In this game, users can create content and transfer it to other users. The study tracked those transfers among users that had friendship connections—which, in this context, means that they had reciprocated permissions to see one another's online status. The analyses show that the rate of adoption increases as more friends adopt (although users with many friends are less likely to be influenced by any particular one). In addition, the data suggested that some users play a more active role in diffusion chains, and that part of this variability could be attributed to the underlying social network. Another study conducted around the same time using Facebook data showed that although diffusion chains are often extremely long, they are not usually the result of a single chain reaction; instead, small chains are started by many users, and they become large as they merge together (Sun et al. 2009). And a yet more recent study, also using Facebook data, designed an experiment to randomize exposure to information about information-sharing activities of friends (Bakshy et al. 2012). The findings confirmed that users who are exposed to friends' signals are significantly more likely to spread information; results also confirmed the theoretical intuition that while strong ties are individually more influential, weak ties play a more dominant role in the global dissemination of information. The strength of friendship ties was measured using several metrics of interaction frequency on the site (e.g., direct communication, being tagged in the same photos). These metrics capture different dimensions of social distance, and they offer more stringent definitions than a simple friendship tie.

Two recent developments in the analysis of networks are further shifting the way in which we think about contagion. The first is the ability to model temporal changes in the activation of ties (Holme and Saramäki 2012; Moody 2002; Snijders, van de Bunt, and Steglich 2010). Attention to time dynamics has been facilitated by the fact that digital technologies usually add time stamps to communication events. The second development is the ability to place actors in not one but several communication networks, acknowledging the well-known fact that our interactions take place through many communication channels (Haythornthwaite and Wellman 1998) and that networks have multiple layers through which information can flow (Kivelä et al. 2014). Figure 5.3 illustrates the logic behind these two recent developments. Panel A depicts the path dependences that time imposes on diffusion. The fact that communication events have a temporal order means that chronology creates one-way roads in the way information can flow. In this example, if Sam and Jen talk on Tuesday, and Jen and Tim talk on Wednesday, whatever Jen learns from Tim during their conversation will be unknown to Sam—at least, until they talk again (and assuming the

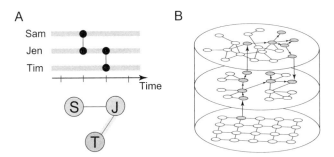

Figure 5.3
Temporal and multilayer networks

news cannot travel any other way). If we aggregate these interactions into a single snapshot, disregarding the temporal ordering of the ties, we have the misleading impression that Jen acts as a mediator—but of course, she can only relay to Sam what she knows at the time of their interaction. This ordering effect is crucial to understanding how information, or rumors, spread.

Panel B illustrates how multilayer structures can also channel information diffusion—and how they challenge us to think in yet another way about social distance. Each of these layers could account for a social media platform, mobile phone communication, or face-to-face interactions. Actors who engage in all these different forms of communication create bridges across interaction domains that will, in turn, facilitate spillover effects across networks. The links that actors form across layers, and the bandwidth of those links, determine the extent to which dynamics in one layer will affect dynamics in the other layers. For this reason, these actors play a special role, similar to those that bridge network communities—only now they are bringing together different contexts for interaction. One of the ways in which these actors can be identified is through a centrality measure called "versatility" (De Domenico et al. 2015). Versatile nodes are those that are not necessarily salient in any specific layer but that contribute to the overall cohesiveness of the different networks. Recent research has shown that using multilayer structures to combine information from different online networks (in this case, Twitter and the location-based Foursquare) can improve models predicting the formation of new links (Hristova et al. 2016). This is the sort of insight that can then be fed back into recommendation systems to rewire a list of contacts —or, perhaps, to even find the one shortcut that connects us to a distant target (thus providing a technological aide that the subjects of the small world experiment did not have to find the shortest transmission chain). Overall, these research directions are still incipient, but the increasing availability of digital data means that they are likely to grow significantly in the next few years.

5.5   Network Interventions

The nineteenth-century telegraph or our modern Internet fiber-optic cables create systems that are engineered from above: they can be designed or rewired to improve resilience or transmission efficiency. Governments and regulators oversee the process to ensure that the changes work for the public good—also to make sure they have control over an important source of power: information (Braman 2009). Whether regulators succeed in defending the public good, or whose interests they really advocate for, is not always clear, as recently manifested by the heated debates around the world over net neutrality, the principle that Internet service providers should not discriminate among data and route it preferentially through fast or slow channels (Editorial Board 2015; also Crowcroft 2007). Social networks, however, are not designed from above: we can build infrastructures to bridge geographic distance, but how do we encourage people to rewire their networks so that they span social divides? Or how do we seed a network in the hopes that worthy ideas will trigger a chain reaction that spreads far and wide? And is it actually legitimate to even try to exert that sort of change?

The answers to these questions depend heavily on the context in which interventions are designed—in line with what the previous chapter discussed about engineering peer effects. The additional difficulty in network interventions is that they not only assume that peers will influence each other; they also require a decision on which ties to activate first in order to maximize influence flow, or which nodes to target as the best entry points to disseminate practices or instill behavioral change. In general, there are four types of network interventions (Valente 2012). The first consists in identifying individuals who stand out on the basis of their network position. Their relevance can be defined in terms of their diffusing potential or in terms of their ability to disrupt the network if removed, properties that relate closely to the theoretical discussion above about how best to measure social distance. The second strategy requires identifying groups that can help segment the network and target relevant people, for instance communities that are unlikely to change their behavior if the rest of the group do not change theirs as well. This intervention strategy is particularly relevant in scenarios characterized by network effects, for instance when new communication technologies are being adopted: the more people embrace those technologies, the faster they diffuse and the more useful they become (Rogers 2003). The algorithms for community detection discussed earlier can help identify these groups.

The third intervention strategy involves activating relevant links with the goal of encouraging diffusion or facilitating the spreading of relevant behavior. Word of mouth campaigns are frequent examples of this form of intervention, which are also at the root of classic theories of communication (Katz and Lazarsfeld 1955). This third type of intervention is related to the first two: finding relevant nodes is usually the first step when thinking about seeding a network with a message in the hopes that it will spread through word-of-mouth dynamics. As much as we have advanced in our understanding of networks, however, it is still unclear whether targeting central nodes is always the most successful strategy to trigger large-scale diffusion (Aral, Muchnik, and Sundararajan 2013; Watts 2002). Research showing that central individuals are more likely to trigger chain reactions usually focuses on chains that are known, with the benefit of hindsight, to have grown large. When research pays attention to a broader universe of cascades, i.e., those that grow large and those that don't, conclusions about who is in the best position to initiate a cascade become less well defined. As the research reviewed above suggests, some of these cascades grow large only when smaller chains initiated locally manage to merge.

Finally, the fourth intervention strategy offers the most aggressive approach: it involves changing the network by removing or adding nodes and removing or adding connections. This is a strategy usually employed in the context of crisis response and by criminologists in their attempts to disrupt covert networks (Carley 2006; Everton 2013; Lin et al. 2006). Most empirical applications of network interventions operate in this context of epidemic control, crisis response, or law enforcement. These same tools and approaches, however, can also be applied (and are, in fact, being applied) to curtail political liberties and hamper legitimate forms of organization.

In September 2013, for instance, China announced new antidefamation laws expanding the scope and severity of criminal offenses covering online speech. Social media users posting libelous messages could face charges if their posts were viewed by more than 5,000 users or reposted more than 500 times. In April 2014, a microblogger was sentenced to three years in prison for disseminating rumors about a former minister (Freedom House 2015). Governments have also engaged in more drastic measures, like cutting off Internet access in the middle of massive political mobilizations, as happened in Egypt in January 2011 (Richtel 2011); or blocking access to social media platforms (YouTube and Twitter), as the Turkish government did in

March 2014 after some users posted recordings and documents showing evidence of government corruption (Rawlinson 2014). The Turkish courts have since ruled the bans unconstitutional, but the government still has leverage to pressure Twitter to close the accounts of critical writers (Freedom House 2015). Also in Turkey, 25 people were arrested in June 2013, at the height of the Gezi Park protests, for using social media to spread antigovernment sentiment and calls for mobilization (Harding and Letsch 2013). These are all strategies that aim to disrupt the operation of communication networks, either by removing nodes that are supposed to be central to global connectivity or by making the ties unavailable as conduits for diffusion.

The good news is that networks are malleable and can quickly adapt to external interventions intended to disrupt their functioning. For instance, during the protests that arose in Hong Kong in September 2014 (the so-called "umbrella revolution"), participants on the streets communicated using mesh networks, that is, direct connections between phones via Bluetooth or Wi-Fi. They did so in anticipation of the Chinese government blocking local phone networks, turning to this alternative mode of communication to ensure that they could still distribute news and information (Knibbs 2014; Rutkin and Aron 2014). These networks look like the structure depicted in the lower layer of figure 5.3B. They are especially resilient to government intervention because they cannot be easily shut down (e.g., Bluetooth would need to be deactivated in every cell phone to break the information chain). However, because they require physical proximity, these networks are only useful in dense crowds, that is, once a critical mass of protesters has already been mobilized. This is why taking a multilayer approach to networks is so important: different communication structures interact with each other at different stages of information diffusion and mobilization. How or with what consequence are questions that require more research.

So the analysis of networks can indeed be used to inform surveillance practices, but it can also be used to circumvent censorship and help groups pushing for social change organize their actions. Again, there is nothing about the analytical techniques or the knowledge we gain through network research that privileges one use over another. Of course, it is true that existing structures of power give some actors a privileged (when not illegitimate) access to the sort of data that informs network interventions. As recent revelations have made clear, it is not only authoritarian states that have unrestricted access to personal data. Intelligence organizations and private corporations with headquarters in Western democracies also play a disturbing role in illegal surveillance practices (Greenwald 2014; Poitras 2016). There is now uncontested evidence that democratic governments authorize bulk data collection (without public scrutiny or appropriate checks) that involves tapping into infrastructures like fiber-optic cables or submitting queries to the databases of social media companies. Metadata like that used in the mobile study described earlier is also routinely used for surveillance practices. The difference is that in research, actual phone numbers are replaced by random keys to protect the anonymity of the subscribers. In the mobile study described above, there was an additional constraint that limited the reach of the data: the operator that provided the call logs had a market share of about 20% in the target country, which is a significantly reduced sample of the underlying (unobserved) phone network. Government agencies engaged in surveillance activities do not operate with those constraints or anonymity guarantees.

Digital technologies create serious challenges to privacy and individual liberties if they are used to engage in indiscriminate data collection. Chapter 7 returns to some of these challenges as they relate to policy design and decision making. And yet the fact is that cynical assessments of the current risks are not very useful if no solution or alternative plan is offered. Many contentious discussions of privacy issues show that it is easy to identify vulnerabilities, but far more difficult to find ways of minimizing or eliminating those risks. The threats to privacy require critical thinking but also constructive solutions; and we can only come up with those solutions through more research. An example of these efforts goes under the name of differential privacy, a line of cryptography that aims to make databases and networks searchable while minimizing the chances of identifying specific individuals through the records (Dwork and Roth 2014; Kearns et al. 2016). This approach starts from the premise that ever-growing databases containing all sorts of information about our daily activities are here to stay—the technologies that generate the data are not appendices to social life but have become its backbone. We cannot obliterate those trails, but the idea of differential privacy is to add enough noise to them that identifying specific individuals becomes more difficult.

5.6 Hidden Architectures

The analysis of networks has uncovered many aspects of social life that before were only apparent in their puzzling, anecdotal manifestation—for instance, the ability of communication to reduce social distance in ways that transcend the specific exchange between pairs of people. Most importantly, the analysis of networks has offered a theoretical bridge connecting individual actions as they respond to local circumstances (discussed in chapter 4) with collective outcomes that do not necessarily reflect individual motivations, even if they respond to them (discussed in chapter 3). Every technological breakthrough brings with it speculations about change, narratives that try to make sense of the transformations triggered by new forms of interacting, by the creation of new channels through which information or behavior spread. But those narratives—as the historical dimension of this book aims to illustrate—often fail to account for actual change because, alas, anecdotes can only go so far in their depiction of the social world and its inner workings. The analysis of networks, which are now more tangible because of their digital form, offers an X-ray to the hidden architecture that articulates social dynamics as they escalate from individual actions to collective outcomes.

Digital technologies are also making more tangible the conditions under which those networks emerge, and easier to determine whether space constrains the formation of ties or encourages, instead, the creation of new connections. This is how the offline world still claims a central role in the configuration of communication patterns: although increasingly mediated by digital technologies, communication still relies heavily on the designs of human geography. The following chapter considers the way in which geography still matters, paying special attention to the flaws and gaps that undermine the representativeness of digital data—and the validity of the pictures of the social world we can draw through that lens.

6 Communication in Space

The expression "the map is not the territory" highlights the gap that separates representations from the things being represented. If we ask locals to draw a map of the city they inhabit, their drawings will quite literally reveal very different realities—imprints of their individual routines and the priorities that define their daily lives in this territory. Research conducted in the 1970s by social psychologist Stanley Milgram asked two hundred Parisians to draw maps of their city "in which they were to mention all of the elements of the city that came to mind" (Milgram 1977, 78). One of the subjects, a 33-year-old butcher, visualized the major stockyards and slaughterhouses of Paris—points of interest that were (understandably) completely disregarded by another subject, a 50-year-old woman who instead made sure to annotate landmarks such as the Louvre and the Palais Royale. The interesting question this study presented is not why there is a lack of correspondence between the maps and the city but what those discrepancies reveal. What can we learn about the biographies of people by looking at how they represent the urban space they live in? And, most importantly, what can we learn about a city by looking at the aggregate of the individual maps and the elements they share?

It is well known that city life offers more communication possibilities than other social arrangements (Milgram 1970; also Simmel 1971 [1903]). Swarming streets are conducive to random encounters and the formation of ties—the threads that have long been known to weave the fabric of urban life (Jacobs 1961; Whyte 1980). But the social dynamics that turn space into meaningful places also impose constraints on communication: some neighborhoods are isolated not so much by geographic distance as by social barriers that tear the urban fabric apart. Mobility patterns, or what people's commuting habits reveal, are a way of assessing the tapestry of urban life.

The maps individuals draw of their cities capture those patterns indirectly: their sketches reveal, in the end, how they navigate space, which paths they are more likely to take, and, more generally, how they imagine their urban environment (Lynch 1960). Now we can assess those dynamics with less impressionistic, more objective data—the digital breadcrumbs that we leave behind as we move around, interact with others, or fail to cross borders that would be invisible if we did not analyze the flows of urban life (Batty 2013). Digital data tracking collective dynamics allows maps to come alive.

Both the hand-drawn maps of the 1970s and today's digital traces reveal that some places act as the centers of gravity where most individual paths converge; many other places emerge as visible only to certain types of people—and some are invisible to all but a few. The borders that cartographers draw for administrative reasons often do not match the patterns people enforce with their feet or commuting habits (Jacobs 1961). For this reason, ordinary people can add valuable experience to the techniques and skills of cartographers. This additional layer of information is important because the life of cities depends on the many choices individuals make. Cities are, after all, a social fact: "a city is as much a collective representation as it is an assemblage of streets, squares, and buildings" (Milgram 1977, 81). The elements that are highlighted by the collective, in other words, are as important as the physical spaces that exist in a city. And so even if the map is not the territory, we are now in a position to add layers of information that allow maps to encode a richer depiction of the social world (González-Bailón 2013a). In the process of adding those layers of information, we can also identify places where there is a scarcity of data (revealing a new form of online discrimination); or where bureaucratic homogeneity overwrites local diversity (thus impoverishing our representations of social life).

Maps, in the end, are tools of legibility: they translate a complex reality into summarized stories that are then used to plan interventions—some of which can go terribly wrong if the maps misrepresent underlying facts (Scott 1999). Maps are useful because they offer a standard grid that can be centrally recorded and monitored. For this reason, they have played a historical role that is inseparable from the emergence of the modern state: "the premodern state was, in many crucial respects, partially blind … it lacked anything like a detailed 'map' of its terrain and its people" (ibid., 2). Lack of context and particularity was not an oversight but a premise in the historical, bureaucratic approach to mapmaking, which simply assumed that "standardized citizens were uniform in their needs and even interchangeable" (ibid., 346). This form of "social straitjacketing" has informed interventions over the last two centuries that failed to take into account the spontaneity of human behavior—and the tendency of crowds to color outside the lines. This rigidity in the representation of space is what digital technologies are changing by allowing diversity to bubble up directly from people's mobility (Eagle and Greene 2014; Ratti and Claudel 2016). Today, we can move beyond old simplistic standards and still measure (and read) the social world, this time incorporating the knowledge that comes from actual experience as manifested through the aggregation of many digital trails.

Maps, of course, are not intended to reproduce the complexity of the world in all its detail—that would defeat their purpose, as Jorge Luis Borges, the Argentinian writer, illustrated in one of his short fictions. Borges imagines an empire where "the Art of Cartography attained such Perfection that the map of a single Province occupied the entirety of a City, and the map of the Empire, the entirety of a Province." This was not enough for the proud cartographers, who ended up drawing "a Map of the Empire whose size was that of the Empire, and which coincided point for point with it." The generations that followed, the story continues, "saw that that vast Map was Useless, and not without some Pitilessness was it, that they delivered it up to the Inclemencies of Sun and Winters" (Borges 1998 [1946], 325). Using the territory as its own map is an illogical aspiration, similar to those that populate the pages of literary nonsense—including the work of Lewis Carroll, who also wrote about a fictional chart "on the scale of a mile to the mile" just after having one of his characters praise pocket maps (Carroll 1893, 169). The reason why maps on a 1:1 scale are useless is that they are as unmanageable as the world they are trying to capture. Even if digital technologies help us reconstruct the spatial flows of communication with unprecedented accuracy, we still need to decide what aspects of the data are more relevant so that we can disregard the rest. The important question in this realm, as in many others, is how we transform all the available information into knowledge that we can act on.

6.1 Collective Maps

Our current communication technologies allow researchers to "effectively borrow the eyes of the population" (Ratti and Claudel 2016, 52). This takes quite a literal form in platforms where users upload and share photos, for instance Flickr and OpenStreetMap. Data from Flickr has been used to reveal mobility patterns in cities and to infer the preferences of different groups of people (Girardin et al. 2008). As the authors put it, "positioning a photo on a map isn't simply adding information about its location, it's an act of communication that embodies locations, times, and experiences that individuals consider to be relevant to themselves and others" (ibid., 42). The aggregation of these experiences uncovers, among other things, what the authors call "desire lines," that is, paths through the city that capture the sequential preferences of visitors. Of course, there is bias in these lines because Flickr users will tend to point out the highlights of their visit and skip the trip's lows (not to mention the fact that many visitors will simply not be inclined to use social media to keep a log of their travels); but even this bias reflects as much about the experience of moving around a city as the mental maps social psychologists asked subjects to draw in the 1970s. One important difference is that digital data allows using that subjective information in a more reactive way to enable a more efficient management of urban infrastructures. The governance of cities, in other words, can now respond to more voices (or footsteps) than it could in the past—or it can identify where those voices are missing and determine what the gap reveals.

Other research used similar data to compare different cities in terms of what the researchers called "magnetism" (Paldino et al. 2015). Magnetism was measured globally (across cities) and locally (within cities) using activity density, that is, the number of photos taken both by locals and visitors at different points in the urban landscape. This measure of attractiveness involved the analysis of 100 million publicly shared geotagged photographs taken during a period of 10 years in more than 3,000 different locations. These researchers analyzed the attractiveness maps that derive from placing photos on locations, but they also looked at the flows of visitors across cities in the form of origin-destination networks—creating a relational map that, following the discussion in the previous chapter, invites us to think about social distance in ways that are not necessarily related to geographical proximity. According to these networks of visitor flows, New York and London are closer to each other than San Francisco and Los Angeles.

The analysis of urban attractiveness as revealed by the choices people make can also be used to improve the governance of cities: "not only do people need efficiency, better transportation and green energy"; they also need "a better experience of living in cities enjoying the things that they have interest in and that they find attractive" (Paldino et al. 2015, 15). This vision is far from the old aspirations of top-down urban design; far from the vision of Le Corbusier, who "embraced the huge, machine-age, hier-archical, centralized city with a vengeance" (Scott 1999, 104), and closer to a more democratic, street-level view of cities (Jacobs 1961). In this view, urban life cannot be designed to behave in an ordered, predictable way; instead, it responds to the shifting choices people make as they interact with each other and with the space they inhabit.

There are two different ways of thinking about space, and traditionally maps could only make one of them operational. The first, which used to monopolize most urban planning efforts, "consists of a representation of the streets and buildings, tracing the routes that the planners have pro-vided for the movements between workplaces and residences, the delivery of goods, access to shopping, and so on." Superimposed on this map there is a second layer which "consists of tracings, as in a time-lapse photograph, of all the unplanned movements—pushing a baby carriage, window shop-ping, strolling, going to see a friend, playing hopscotch on the sidewalk, walking the dog, watching the passing scene, taking shortcuts between work and home, and so on" (Scott 1999, 348). Digital technologies are making more visible this second layer and, in so doing, are prompting a shift from a mindset focused on designing efficiency to another way of understanding urban planning. Instead of building or recommending efficient paths as determined from the top down, digital data can be used to find distinctive or interesting routes, as defined by pedestrians, from the bottom up.

This bottom-up approach to navigation problems is being followed by researchers who have the ultimate goal of adding a more human touch to the routes that Web and mobile mapping services recommend to users (Quercia, Schifanella, and Aiello 2014). This approach entails taking three steps: transforming a city into a network where nodes are locations and links connect geographic neighbors; adding information on people's perceptions of those locations (as being beautiful, quiet, or happy); and selecting a path between any two locations that is as short but also as pleasant as possible. This methodology can also ultimately benefit from personalization—to allow for the fact that streets vibrant with action might be appealing for some people but a nuisance to avoid for others.

Another way in which researchers have borrowed the eyes of the popu-lation is by asking them to recognize places—and thus elicit measures of visibility across neighborhoods or boroughs. Back in the 1970s, researchers did this with a random sample of New Yorkers, who were asked how well they could recognize various parts of the city (Milgram 1977, 63–76). Set in front of a screen on which color slides of different locations were projected, these subjects were asked to indicate which of the five boroughs they believed each scene belonged to. The findings suggested that relative recognizability varied significantly (and somehow unsurprisingly) across the five boroughs, with Manhattan clearly being the most recognizable. One of the conclusions of the study was that "even a highly distinctive architectural display will not be widely recognized if it is too far off the beaten path; centrality in relation to major population flow is crucial" (ibid., 73). Another conclusion was that the approach could be applied to the analysis of other major cities "to determine how successfully each city, in all its parts, communicates to the resident a specific sense of place" (ibid., 75). Forty years later, researchers are using digital technologies to engage in precisely that sort of comparison.

This question of urban recognition, for instance, has been revisited recently using the streets of London (Quercia et al. 2013). In this instance, researchers designed a game that picked random locations from Google Street View and showed the images to users through the screens of their own devices, asking them to guess the subway location—or borough, or city region—of those places. The sample collected through this game was an order of magnitude greater than in the New York study (more than two thousand users) but it found similar dynamics: central London emerged as the most recognizable part of the city; the less recognizable parts were those suffering from housing deprivation, poor living conditions, and crime.

Lack of pedestrian traffic and street life has often been associated with the decay of neighborhoods (Jacobs 1961). Of course, there are many structural conditions that explain deprivation and the persistence of poverty in urban life; but the analysis of recognizable places, and how they are distributed in a city, can help orient interventions by allowing us to map the invisible borders that arise from local knowledge and subjective risk assessment. These implicit borders can be inferred from self-reported route paths, which often reveal important deviations from administratively defined areas (Basta, Richmond, and Wiebe 2010). Digital data is making the approach scalable and easier to generalize because user-generated content allows reconstructing the paths, hotspots, and forgotten places that emerge out of individual itineraries.

Crowdsourcing has also been used to create maps themselves, i.e., the representation of roads, streets, buildings, and infrastructures. This form of decentralized collaboration has made possible what is essentially a layperson's version of cartography, of which OpenStreetMap (OSP) is probably the most successful example. OSP is a platform that channels the voluntary contributions of large groups of people, coordinated online, into the completion of tasks that traditionally were in the hands of established national mapping agencies, like keeping maps accurate and current (Haklay and Weber 2008). At the end of 2006, Yahoo granted the platform the right to use its satellite imagery Web service; this aerial imagery allowed the platform's contributors to remotely map relatively unknown places, resulting in some of the most detailed online maps available only four years after the platform started to operate (ibid., 14). The quality of the results that came out of this collective effort have been tested against the benchmark of official mapping sources (Haklay 2010) and, most importantly, in the context of emergency situations requiring a swift humanitarian response (Meier 2015).

Initiatives like OSP align with the idea that people can act as "voluntary sensors," that is, as a network of intelligent processors "equipped with abilities to interpret and integrate" information: "the six billion humans moving about the planet collectively possess an incredibly rich store of knowledge about the surface of the Earth and its properties" (Goodchild 2007). Ten years later, many more humans are moving about the planet, with ever more powerful communication tools. The knowledge generated in this decentralized fashion is very valuable, because much of that knowledge, like the names we attach to geographic features, is difficult to automate or is not visible from above, i.e., through satellite imagery. And so this is why the ability to use this form of distributed intelligence is a game changer: historically, only a very small proportion of the information people have of their local environments could be applied to mapmaking—and to our representations of the world.

6.2 Redefining Boundaries

Digital trails encode more geographic information than it was possible to collect using traditional methods. And the analysis of this data is, as a byproduct, casting doubts on the significance of administrative partitions of space. A more granular study of human mobility patterns is revealing effective borders that do not always overlap with those created for bureaucratic purposes—and this matters because those administrative borders are the basis on which many statistics and interventions rely. In one study, researchers obtained mobility data through a website designed to track banknotes (Thiemann et al. 2010). The website allows users to track bills by letting them submit their postal code and the serial number of the bill. The bit of information that is relevant to tracking patterns of human mobility is generated when a registered bill is reentered into the database, something the website refers to as a "hit": when a banknote reappears in a different location, a new segment is added to the trajectory of that note. Researchers using this data assume that the flux of banknotes between locations is proportional to the flux of individuals traveling between those places. In total, the study analyzed the trajectories of close to 12 million bills to draw connections among more than 3,000 counties in the United States. This network was then used as a proxy for human mobility across a wide range of spatial scales, from the short distances of local trajectories (i.e., within the same county) to the longer distances traversing the two coasts of the continent. One of the questions the researchers asked of this data was: Do existing administrative subdivisions capture the most informative partition of space, as revealed by the way in which people (carrying banknotes with them) actually move?

The approach researchers took to this question required analyzing the network connecting the different counties using similar tools to those described in chapter 5. In particular, they looked at the community structure revealed by the network of banknote trajectories. The analyses differentiate ties connecting geographically close locations from ties connecting locations that are farther apart (but that are still close through, say, the air transportation network). These calculations result in a map of effective borders that, although partially correlated with administrative borders or topographical features (like the Appalachian Mountain range), still depart significantly from the information contained in traditional maps. For example, some of these effective borders split states into independent patches: in Pennsylvania, the strongest border separates the state into two regions centered on Pittsburgh and Philadelphia. Being able to identify these geographical partitions from actual mobility patterns is important because it

improves our understanding of dynamic processes like epidemics or information spreading. When exposure is determined by physical interaction,
identifying the places where people actually converge or fail to converge
can inform our theories of why diffusion unfolds with a given speed and
reach—and of how best to encourage or restrain that process.

At the same time, linking online communication activity to the offline
locations where that communication originated sheds light on the spatial
range of information diffusion, and on where the process originates or
intensifies. My collaborators and I, for instance, have reconstructed networks of influence in space using social media activity aggregated as time
series. The nodes in these networks are geographic areas, and the ties map
the flow of influence across those areas using the same methods introduced in chapter 3 (Borge-Holthoefer and González-Bailón 2017; Borge-
Holthoefer et al. 2016). In line with the logic of social distance, proximity
in these networks is not necessarily related to geographical proximity—
often it is not: two regions can be tightly connected in terms of information
flow but geographically far from each other. Figure 6.1 shows the matrices
encoding the network information for two samples of Twitter data: one
tracking communication activity in the United States around the Occupy
Wall Street protests of 2011; the other tracking communication around the
Spanish 15-M (Indignados) movement, which also arose in 2011. The rows
in these matrices correspond to the geographic units of analysis (states and
metropolitan areas, respectively); the columns track time, with the color of
each cell corresponding to the centrality of a particular area in the flow of
information at a given time. On the lower end of the color scale, we have

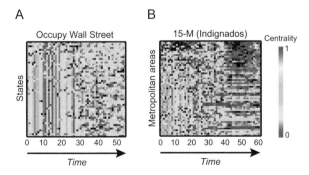

Figure 6.1
Networks of influence in space

regions that have no influence over any other regions (they are followers); on the higher end, we have regions that are strong leaders—and therefore influence activity in a high number of other geographic units.

What the figure reveals is that communication dynamics around these two instances of political mobilization followed very different spatial diffusion patterns. In the Occupy Wall Street case, some states were clearly more central than others in the exchange of information, but there is no clustering or mutual reinforcement. This spatial clustering, on the other hand, is obvious in the 15-M case: toward the end of the observation period, a number of metropolitan areas form a dense network of mutual influence in the creation of protest-related content (the cluster of darker cells in the upper right corner of the matrix). During this time interval, activity is spatially spread and many regions have a positive influence over many other regions; in fact, they are all driving each other and increasing the overall volume of message exchange. Compared to the 15-M case, the Occupy Wall Street social media campaign failed to generate activity that spread in space and triggered similar feedback effects. Of course, these patterns also respond to the granularity of the spatial aggregation, and this is a choice that is guided in turn by the availability of data—and by the characteristics of human geography in different territories. But the patterns nonetheless reveal dynamics of information diffusion that would be very difficult to identify in the absence of social media data.

These different diffusion dynamics, which only become apparent when the analysis of social media activity is anchored in space, offer important insights into the evolution of campaigns and political movements. They also highlight that social media do not always guarantee the ability to bridge spatial distance. Online activity is associated with different degrees of offline presence (as measured by the location of those creating the messages), and this translates into varying degrees of success in the spread and consolidation of collective action. Although social media activity is by no means the only thing that matters in understanding the evolution and impact of social movements, this simple example suggests that social media can still be used to screen important differences in the evolution of collective action. The Occupy Wall Street movement, in the end, failed to attain continuity and consolidate institutionally, whereas the 15-M movement led to the emergence of new political parties that today have representation in national and regional parliaments.

Another way of characterizing the spatial dimension of human interactions—and how they relate to maps—is through the analysis of communication dynamics over telephone networks. A study analyzing 12 billion calls over a one-month period reconstructed the map of Great Britain using the traffic of calls (Ratti et al. 2010). Callers were located in geographic locations that aggregated individual-level activity, and links were then reconstructed between those locations mapping traffic flow, which was measured as total call time. As with the banknotes study, the network was analyzed with community detection methods: the goal was to explore regional cohesiveness not as defined by geographical constraints but as derived from individual communication patterns. This approach shows that communication is affected not only by population distribution in space but also by boundaries that define the level of cultural integration of different regions. One of the metrics devised in the study to assess these boundaries is the call time ratio, "defined as the percentage of time a region talks to itself." According to this measure, Scotland was the region least connected to the rest of Great Britain, followed (with some significant distance) by North Wales, South Wales, and Greater London. In the words of the authors of the study, "if Scotland and Wales were to become independent from the UK, and if the detrimental effect of the secession were considered proportional to the number of external connections, the effect on people would be approximately twice more disruptive on Wales than Scotland" (ibid., 5). The importance of this indicator is that it can complement more traditional measures used to characterize regions, like economic activity or territorial statistics.

A similar study did precisely this: integrate the UK mobile and landline communication network with socioeconomic indicators (Eagle, Macy, and Claxton 2010). The goal of this research was to find evidence of correlation between network diversity and economic prosperity, echoing longstanding theories according to which more diverse networks are associated with more and better economic opportunities (e.g., Granovetter 1974). The directionality of the association cannot be easily determined with observational data: it is difficult to assess "whether network diversity promotes opportunity or economic development leads to more diversified contacts" (Eagle, Macy, and Claxton 2010, 1031). However, the novelty of the study is that it shows how communication diversity, measured on a national scale, can be used as a key indicator of economically healthy communities.

Communication diversity was measured in two ways: as number of active contacts, to determine whether individuals spread their talk time evenly among their social ties rather than focus on a few of them; and as spatial dispersion, to determine whether those ties are spread across different regions or are concentrated within the same geographical area. These two measures of diversity characterize interpersonal ties through which information flows—an important dimension of communication because, as previous chapters explain, it determines how ideas or news spread. Today, these ties can be analyzed on the level of entire nations using actual calling patterns, which offer a good proxy to interaction and information diffusion channels. Although this line of inquiry is still incipient, we can already derive some policy implications. As the authors put it, "the strong correspondence between the structure of social contacts and the economic well-being of populations highlights the potential benefit of socially targeted policies for economic development" (Eagle, Macy, and Claxton 2010, 1031). In other words, while geography still matters, networks allow a different interpretation of space and of how to improve access to opportunities.

Back in 1995 Nicholas Negroponte wrote that communication technologies would override the constraints of geography: "Digital living will include less and less dependence upon being in a specific place at a specific time" (Negroponte 1995, 165). Twenty years later, however, research is still qualifying that statement. Being in the same place at the same time, for instance, still matters for forming ties or interacting with others in the pursuit of collective action, even when communication takes place online. Another study analyzing the Occupy movement shows that the social media network that emerged around the mobilizations had very high levels of geographic concentration, "with users in New York, California, and Washington D.C. producing more than half of all retweeted content" (Conover, Davis, et al. 2013). Unlike the study mentioned above, which focused on aggregated time series on the state level, this study analyzed individual-level data in the form of retweet networks. The authors found that, compared to other streams of political communication, the flow of messages related to the Occupy campaign were highly localized in a few cities. What this means is that, even if the technology makes it possible for anyone to contribute to a movement's stream, "proximity to events on the ground plays a major role in determining which content receives the most attention" (ibid., 6).

More generally, physical proximity often determines the formation of social ties. A different study used data from three location-based social networks, i.e., online platforms that allow users to share their positioning with friends, to show that close to half of all ties are formed locally, within a range of 100 km or 60 miles (Scellato et al. 2011). A prior study also shows evidence that the probability of two people having an online connection decreases with their geographic distance (Liben-Nowell et al. 2005). Communication technologies, in other words, still respond to the constraints of geography—only those constraints do not necessarily coincide with the ones imposed by administrative boundaries.

To sum up, digital technologies offer two ways of collecting spatial data: active footprints in the form of photos, status updates, messages, or voluntary contributions to crowdsourced maps; and passive imprints left through interaction with infrastructures like a mobile phone network (Girardin et al. 2008). There are many privacy concerns associated with the use of this data, especially for the passive trails that are collected for operational reasons (i.e., to improve the delivery of services) but with a lack of transparency on how much information about individual behavior is actually being processed. This data usually has the four-column format of "userid," "longitude," "latitude," and "time." Research often aggregates the data on the level of geographical units to avoid identifying specific individuals, but other research reveals that individual trajectories can be reconstructed with much detail, to the point of revealing for each individual where they live or work (Gonzalez, Hidalgo, and Barabási 2008). The information revealed by these trails is more accurate than for the trails reconstructed from mental maps, but it is also more personal and potentially compromising, especially if the data is linked with other publicly available datasets (de Montjoye et al. 2013). This creates one of the most important tensions in the analysis of digital traces: What counts as a legitimate use of the data we generate as we move around?

The ability to access individual mobility data is good for research: compared to less revealing proxies, like the movement of banknotes, logs on individual trajectories yield more insightful information on how we navigate space; the choices we make cannot be assessed using the traffic of dollars because currency diffuses in the pockets of different people—and this means that they can only be used to reconstruct paths on the aggregate level (Gonzalez, Hidalgo, and Barabási 2008). Individual-level trajectory data is also good for governance because important policymaking decisions, like where to plan a new metro line or how to manage traffic during big events, depend on having better models of travel demand (Jiang et al. 2016). However, the fact remains that call detail records, which mobile phone service providers need to manage for billing purposes, also contain information that is increasingly personal; and subscribers might not want that information shared for research that is only remotely connected (if at all) with the service they paid for. This is an example of the normative tradeoff that digital technologies create between individual value and social value, or between private choices and public control. The following chapter returns to this tradeoff and to why it is so difficult to solve.

6.3   Selection Bias and Digital Gaps

As abundant as digital data might seem, online representations of the world still suffer from important gaps in their coverage. Crowdsourcing might improve our depictions of space by allowing more people to have a say in how space is annotated and constructed; but this form of knowledge generation is still subject to the bias of self-selection—or to the fact that not everyone contributes equally to the task of generating data. And this begs the question: How does the online division of labor affect the representativeness of the information made public? Attempts to answer this question have uncovered inequalities in content production that reproduce linguistic, cultural, political, and economic barriers (Graham 2014). Most of the information about the world is being generated in the Global North, even if Internet penetration rates keep on rising. In that sense, the world has not changed much since thirteenth-century maps that offered an accurate representation of the Mediterranean, a less accurate representation of peripheral Europe, and no information at all about the rest of the world (ibid., 101). Today, some places still receive more attention in the creation of data than other places, and this impacts on the accuracy of our representations, generating asymmetries in how those places are perceived. Some parts of the world are, simply, more legible than others—even with the data abundance that characterizes the digital age.

One study, for instance, analyzed user-generated placemarks uploaded to Google Maps to reveal some of those information asymmetries (Graham and Zook 2011). Placemarks are used to annotate specific points of the earth, and they offer one of the ways through which people can contribute to the peer production of geographical data (in a similar way to the OSM initiative described above, only under licensing terms and conditions defined by Google). A cartographic visualization of the density of these annotations reveals big disparities across the globe but also at different national scales. One example: Louisville, Kentucky, was found to have almost 50% more user-created content than the entire country of Iraq. Another example: Beijing and Shanghai were heavily annotated, but the rest of China was represented by only a small amount of information (partly because there is a limited ability for Chinese users to contribute geographic information within the country, so most of those annotations were likely submitted from abroad; ibid., 130, n. 7). Being able to identify these asymmetries is important because "visibility and invisibility in physical space are increasingly being defined by prominence, ranking, and presence in online information" (ibid., 120–121). In other words, in this digital age the information that is not displayed online is essentially invisible for most intents and purposes. This new form of inequality affects not only our mental representations of places, but also the research we can conduct using peer-produced data.

The asymmetries created by communication technologies are not new. Today there is more indexed content layered over, say, the Tokyo metropolitan region than in the entire continent of Africa; but in the 1990s there were also more landline telephones in Tokyo than in all of sub-Saharan Africa combined (Graham 2014, 108). The reasons for these asymmetries are complex, and they have less to do with communication technologies per se than with complex socioeconomic and geopolitical factors. Recent research, for instance, shows evidence of politically motivated discrimination against ethnically marginalized groups in the provision of digital communication, "with governments extending these services primarily to politically favored groups" (Weidmann et al. 2016, 1154). The evidence for these conclusions was based on a spatial estimation of Internet penetration using the number of active Internet subnetworks during the period 2004–2012. This way of measuring Internet penetration uses observed traffic and is more granular than the statistics provided by agencies like the International Telecommunication Union, which are offered only at the level of countries and do not allow the analysis of differential access across ethnic groups at the subnational level (ibid., 1152). By geolocating the observed active subnetworks, the researchers could aggregate the data to the level of subnational geographic units that they then combined with known ethnic group settlement regions. Using this information, they found evidence that governments play a discriminatory role in the allocation and control of digital communication.

At a time when the Internet's role in foreign affairs is often praised and politicized (to the exasperation of some; Morozov 2011), these findings come as a reminder that development policies should take into account the uneven provision of digital services: "Only if this digital inequality is alleviated can we expect these modern channels to empower people and societies in order to foster lasting political and economic development" (Weidmann et al. 2016, 1154). Even then, access to infrastructures is only part of the problem; the other part is who produces the content that will be published through those infrastructures. Digital technologies have leveled access to content production, but, as the previous paragraphs suggest, the production of that content still leads to discrimination—even if this is often an unintended consequence of how crowds self-organize in the contribution of voluntary information. More often than not, there is no intentional discrimination strategy behind online asymmetries, as there is in the provision of some services and infrastructures. Because of these asymmetries, however, Internet technologies are shifting discussions from the causes that lead to the digital divide, which considers inequality in access (e.g., Norris 2001), to the consequences of the data divide, which refers to the uneven presence of data points across the world (Castillo 2016, 126). This asymmetry in data exists on different scales: there is less high-quality data in low- and middle-income countries, but also in less affluent regions within the rich countries.

At the same time, digital technologies are alleviating many of the old difficulties in compiling relevant data on a global scale. One form of annotation that is particularly useful for social research is event data tracking conflicts or other politically meaningful events around the world. This data relied, traditionally, on the analysis of newspaper articles, and their collection was limited by technological constraints; many of these constraints are being shifted by the automated coding from news media that digital technologies make possible (Wang et al. 2016). Event data can be used to analyze a wide range of phenomena, from political debates and foreign policy to conflict escalation or the irruption of protests. Extracting those events from news coverage used to require expensive manual coding, which imposed limits on scalability and also on the quality of the coding. Text-processing techniques offer tools that can help lower the costs of those analyses while increasing the coverage. The validity of these automated modes of data collection is still being tested and assessed; but the hope is that they may lead to global monitoring systems of societal events that can, in turn, help "provide insights into a range of global problems, from national security to the spread of diseases" (ibid., 1503). In other words, digital technologies can now be used to build maps of world affairs—adding yet another layer in the annotation of space.

6.4   Cities as Laboratories

Urban research has traveled far since the sociologists of the Chicago school first turned cities into laboratories for social research. Cities offered the perfect setting for the analysis of collective behavior because, sociologists realized, cities are "rooted in the habits and customs of the people." The city plan, Robert Park would write in 1925, "establishes metes and bounds, fixes in a general way the location and character of the city's constructions, and imposes an orderly arrangement, within the city area, upon the buildings which are erected by private initiative as well as by public authority"; however, he continued, "the inevitable processes of human nature proceed to give these regions and these buildings a character which it is less easy to control" (Park and Burgess 1984 [1925], 4). The research of early sociologists aimed to characterize the uncontrollable and unplanned nature of city life, and analyze how collective behavior shaped urban dynamics—something to be experienced, not designed.

These goals, however, were difficult to attain without deploying "an army of participant observers" on the streets, what anthropologist Bronisław Malinowski called a "nation-wide intelligence service" (Lang and Lang 1961, 551). The approach was taken seriously in Britain. A project called Mass Observation was launched in 1937 under the leadership of a poet, a communist journalist, a filmmaker, and an anthropologist. Their goal was to record the life of ordinary people: what they did, what they felt, and what they thought. For that, the project collected material from a volunteer panel that included personal diaries, but also from a team of paid investigators who went to the streets to record people's behavior and conversation in as much detail as possible. Part of this data collection involved overhearing, "a study of chance conversations unobtrusively collected" (ibid.). Another form of data collection involved asking amateur observers to send in reports about their experience during certain events. One of those events was the spread in 1938 of a dance craze called Lambeth Walk, a dance inspired by a musical and that took the name of one of the working-class residential areas in London. An entire chapter was devoted to this dance in the 1939 Mass Observation book (Madge and Harrisson 1939).

The Mass Observation project can be considered an antecedent of the crowdsourced method for data collection that seems so innovative today. It had, however, many more biases and limitations than digitally crowdsourced data. For starters, observers were far from being a representative sample of the population—people suffering from illiteracy, for instance, could not write a report of their experiences. Other techniques, like overhearing public conversation, demanded an exceptional memory on the part of the observer, who probably filled many more gaps than he was willing to acknowledge with figments of his own imagination. Today, ordinary life in cities can be analyzed without recourse to an army of participant observers. Instead of paid investigators, researchers today have at their disposal sensors, algorithms, and monitoring devices to get a picture of what makes a city, and its people, tick. This data-driven approach to everyday life capitalizes on both active and passive footprints: from the ratings and comments left in recommender systems or social media to pedestrian traffic or call patterns during peak hours and mega-events, like concerts or sports finals.

The analysis of these traces is helping uncover some interesting paradoxes, including the so-called "slower is faster" effect (Gershenson and Helbing 2015). In many settings, the slowing down of individuals can increase everybody's overall speed, and vice versa: individuals trying to be fast can slow down the collective, as when people are trying to evacuate a room too quickly, or when pedestrians are trying to cross a road by being pushy and forcing cars to stop. In these situations, what is good for the individual is not good for the group—echoing many of the paradoxes explored in previous chapters that put individual behavior and collective outcomes at odds. Managing this paradox is what motivates much of the research conducted today on congestion in urban travel, where cities are turned literally into laboratories for the analysis of collective behavior.

Recent research, for instance, analyzed travel demand and travel time estimates in five major cities around the world (Çolak, Lima, and González 2016). The relationship between travel distance and travel time was then used to calculate time lost due to congestion—which depends on the density and the spatial distribution of the population but also on the traveling decisions of the many individuals that clog the roads. The researchers used the crowdsourced data from OSM to obtain the road networks for the five cities, and they then used call detail records to reconstruct mobility patterns and estimate travel demands. With this information, they came up with a model that helped them determine not only shortest routes but also which routes decreased overall congestion. Their goal was to come up with policies that contribute to improving the life of the city as a whole, even if they do not benefit individuals. This, of course, begs the classic question of how individuals can be incentivized to behave in a way that benefits the collective.

Studies like this illustrate that when it comes to understanding collective behavior and unintended effects, individual beliefs and motivations do not usually offer enough information. Communication and space end up shaping the dynamics that come out of individual decisions in ways that no individual can control on their own—not even if they have been elected to do so. The constant reactions to the behavior of others, who in turn change their behavior as they react to ours, and the constraints of space (in the end, and beat poetry aside, there are only so many roads to travel) are all factors that make collective behavior difficult to predict and control. The most we can say is that it is a constantly shifting target.

Back in the 1970s, sociologists interested in the dynamics of collective behavior already pointed out that "space-time proximity" is more important for understanding the emergence of crowds than individual attitude variables (McPhail and Miller 1973). Space shapes that proximity, but it is ultimately communication and interactions that make people converge or collide. What digital technologies have changed is not the nature of the problem: governing a system like this is as challenging today as it ever was. The change comes from how we can represent the problem. Today, after all, "every citizen has a tool with which to perceive and process the city" (Ratti and Claudel 2016, 63)—and, more generally, how they relate to space. Digital technologies have accelerated the feedback loop between representations and the way we react to them. And we have just started to determine the implications of that two-way exchange.

6.5   Measurement and Representation

When it comes to imagining worlds where the inconceivable becomes real, Italo Calvino joins ranks with the likes of Lewis Carroll and Jorge Luis Borges. In one of his stories, written in 1964 under the title "World Memory," he imagines a society where "everything that has ever been since time began" is archived (Calvino 1995, 129). The duty of those in charge of the catalog is, the first-person narrator claims, to make sure that nothing important is omitted "because what is left out is as if it had never been." Of course, in this world "the moment comes when a yawn, a buzzing fly, an itch seem the only treasure there is, precisely because completely unusable, occurring only once and for all and then promptly forgotten, spared the monotonous destiny of being stored in the world memory." The quirk of the profession, the narrator continues, is that as soon as attention focuses on those trivial things, they are immediately included in the files—so compiling the catalog grants "the right to put one's personal imprint on the world memory." The story, in the end, unfolds to uncover the narrator's real motives (not revealed here) and a declaration of intent: "If there is nothing that needs correcting in the world memory, the only thing left to do is to correct reality where it doesn't agree with that memory." This is, again, a world where representations are intended to supplant reality.

The history of scientific research is full of examples where measurement problems lead to misleading representations of the world. These problems sometimes derive from the use of imperfect instruments, which give us distorted or noisy measures. Other times they result from convenient choices, as the streetlight effect illustrates: just as the drunk man searches for his missing keys under a streetlight because that is where the light is, researchers often look for answers where they think it is easiest to find them. And sometimes, measurement problems derive from plain old ideological bias, that is, from wanting to conform reality to an interested view of the world (as, it turns out, Calvino's character wanted to do). The problem of mapping the world accurately, with cartographies or with models, motivates a lot of the good research that digital data makes possible today. How else can we determine the gaps that separate our representations of the world from the world itself than by following the maps we build to see if they lead us where we want to go? The task of research is, among other things, to determine why we might want to build maps to begin with—but also to illuminate whether there are inescapable limits to our ability to anticipate what reality can bring.

One of those limits can be defined by building an analogy with the so-called "uncertainty principle" (Barabási 2011, 197). The principle states that it is impossible to determine the location and momentum of a particle at the same time: the more you know where an object is, the less you know where the object is going. This inequality does not arise from insufficiency in our measurements but from how the world is intrinsically built. Does the same limit apply to human dynamics? Are mobility patterns or communication dynamics defined by the same intrinsic uncertainty? The answer is important because it determines the boundaries within which our interventions in the world in the form of policies can materialize, and the ability of those policies to succeed at regulation. But it is also important from a more philosophical point of view: Does this intrinsic uncertainty rescue free will in a world that is, it seems, increasingly determined by the data we collect?

Research looking at the role of randomness in human behavior, or the extent to which our actions are predictable, does not seem very encouraging: on average, there is a 93% predictability in our daily mobility patterns; that is, only 7% of the time does our location remain a mystery—at least according to mobile phone records (Song et al. 2010). Of course studies like this consider a relatively short period of time, in this case three months of data—hardly a good approximation to the scale of our lives. And yet, would we be more or less predictable over a longer period of time? Is the reconstruction of our past actions as flawed as many of our maps are? Even Calvino's world leaves space for this speculation: "Who could rule out the possibility that the universe consists of the discontinuous network of moments that cannot be recorded?" (Calvino 1995, 132). The way in which we represent the world is, it turns out, always imperfect—if only because, as stated, it is futile to try to build maps at the same scale as reality. On the other hand, speculations only take us so far—and at least maps take us to where we want to go (most of the time). The only way to transform all the data we have into knowledge we can act on is by building models that can inform our actions with the best available information. In the end, the representation of the road we want to travel can only be as accurate as our measurement tools make possible. This is as true for research as for policy-making, as the following chapter aims to discuss.

7   Designing Policy and Action

Stafford Beer landed in Santiago in the fall of 1971 to embark on an ambitious mission: to assist the Chilean government in the design of a system that would help manage the economy by monitoring its behavior in real time. The day of Beer's arrival, November 4, marked exactly a year since Salvador Allende had won the presidential election to become the first self-proclaimed Marxist to lead the country and pave, in his own words, a "Chilean way to Socialism" (Allende 1973). Allende's political career spanned four decades before it ended violently with the military coup of 1973. He was known for his "concern and empathy for the fate of the poor and the most vulnerable in society," but also for "his passion to find pragmatic and logical solutions to social problems" (Clark 2013, 28–29). A reformist for some, a revolutionary for others, Allende's policies aimed to expand the reach of the state while respecting existing liberties and democratic institutions. His policies involved the nationalization of large-scale industries, but also a commitment to decentralized governance and individual freedoms. Implementing these competing goals, however, was a complex task. This is why one of Allende's men decided to write a letter to Beer asking for his advice and inviting him to work with the government in the management of the nationalized sector of the economy (Medina 2011, 15). Beer was not only an internationally renowned operational research consultant; he was also one of the leading advocates of management cybernetics, a branch of the science of feedback and self-regulation that gained prominence following Norbert Wiener's work at MIT in the 1940s (Wiener 1948). Beer had already tested successfully his cybernetic ideas in the steel and publishing industries, but the Chilean request was his first chance to test those ideas on a national scale. His response to the invitation was an excited yes.

Beer's conception of an effective government was driven by the same analogy of the nervous system that had inspired so many before him—and would inspire so many after. The ability of the nervous system to adapt quickly to changing environments, he thought, is what governments should mimic to survive and prosper (Beer 1974, 43). For this, two things were necessary: a network of data collection and information flow (i.e., the nerves) and a control center or operations room (i.e., the brain). The synergies between constantly updated information and human decision making would create, he claimed, the feedback loop that would allow organizations to adapt effectively to ever-changing circumstances. The process was intended to work like the steering engines of ships, "one of the earliest and best-developed forms of feedback mechanisms" (Wiener 1948, 12). Cybernetics had inspired engineers to introduce feedback into industrial regulation processes. Beer went one step further to turn cybernetics into an agent of social change. A few months before he was invited to Chile, Beer had given a keynote address in which he discussed a new technological system for government administration that he called, with characteristic bombast, the Liberty Machine (Beer 1974, 35–69; Medina 2011, 33). This machine was, in fact, a communication infrastructure envisioned as connecting operations rooms with channels that would allow real-time information sharing. The system was conceived to function "as a disseminated network, not a hierarchy" and to treat information, not authority, as the basis for action (Medina 2011, 34). This is the vision that Beer carried with him to Santiago in the fall of 1971. During the next two years, he worked with Chilean engineers and government officials to implement this vision under the name of Project Cybersyn—a blend of the words "cybernetics" and "synergy."

The project materialized in the form of a telex network connecting different industries with one mainframe computer that processed the data received. Statistical software was developed to model that data, monitor metrics of factory productivity, and simulate future scenarios on the basis of those indicators. An operations room (the brain of the network) was designed as the center where all that information could be transformed into decision making. Conceived as a "futuristic dream," the room "broke new ground in interface design, not because of its technical newness but because of the priority its designers gave to the human operator" (Medina 2011, 88). The room was a hexagonal space that contained seven swivel chairs arranged in a circle; there was no table, to discourage operators from looking at papers and promote conversation, and the wood-paneled walls had several screens that could be activated with remote controls to display economic indicators and graphs (these graphs, however, still had to be drawn by hand). What motivated Beer and his team was the belief that this technology could help the government win economic battles by allowing them to make fast, informed decisions as events took place. This was particularly important in a context where political conflict and an economy in decline (destabilized, to a large extent, by foreign intervention) added much unpredictability to the country's governability. One of the walls in the operations room displayed red lights designed to flash whenever economic emergencies required immediate attention. The designers knew that those lights would flash often and fast.

The Cybersyn project was never completed, as the 1973 military coup ended the aspirations of Beer and his team. However, the experience of designing that system put on the table many of the issues that we confront today as digital technologies grow more entrenched in policy, governance, and political action. Detractors of the project were quick to denounce its totalitarian nature, its potential for Orwellian control. It did not matter that the project was, in fact, conceived as a tool for liberation, for peaceful revolutionary change, as a mechanism to strengthen Chilean's right to self-determination. As Beer actually knew, "designing freedom" is an oxymoron difficult to swallow for those who hold a less engineering view of governance and political life (Beer 1974, 88).

The project was also criticized because it encouraged policymakers to place too much trust in numbers that oversimplified complex dynamics. These concerns echoed the sociological maxim that "not everything that can be counted counts, and not everything that counts can be counted" (Lohr 2015, 10). The critics emphasized that counting is often a political process, reflecting the values and the biases of those drawing the numbers. This lack of neutrality was, in fact, also present in the design of the Project Cybersyn operations room. The remote controls that gave this room such a futuristic touch did not include keyboards because this eliminated "the girl between themselves [the decision makers] and the machinery." By "the girl" they meant the female secretaries who, back then, had to do all the typing because their bosses lacked the skills (Medina 2011, 127). The

Liberty Machine, it turns out, was not free of the prejudices that dominated the age.

Many digital applications today respond to aspirations similar to those motivating the Cybersyn project, but they also present many of the same challenges. The notion of "algorithmic regulation" as it relates to the future of governance, for instance, is not so different from what Allende's government tried to do in the early 1970s. The idea behind algorithmic regulation is that constant measurement and monitoring are necessary to determine the success of policies and make adjustments, if needed, based on the data (O'Reilly 2013). This idea captures the same spirit behind Beer's implementation of his Liberty Machine, and the same policy goals that Chileans wanted to accomplish: to increase the efficiency and adaptability of the decision-making process.

Digital technologies have also renewed the tension between the potential of new data sources to improve governance and the dangers to privacy, autonomy, and discrimination. On the one hand, digital traces help pull together the data that is necessary to make informed decisions on policy scenarios. On the other hand, those traces often turn individuals into unwilling sensors. The information compiled from online sources can be fed into applications that discriminate or exacerbate inequalities, either through algorithms that magnify undetected bias or through prejudiced technology design. The tension between individual rights to autonomy and privacy and the demands of the common good is as present in the use of digital technologies as it was in the cybernetic approach to socialism. National Security Agency abuses in the name of security (Greenwald 2014); Wikileaks's disclosures in the name of openness (Leigh and Harding 2011); or the actions of the collective Anonymous for the sake of lulz (i.e., their characteristic "deviant style of humor"; Coleman 2014) are all examples of digital technologies shaping policy and action beyond ideological divides.

There is one big difference between our world and the world of the early 1970s, however; and that difference is the Internet. Our communication channels are richer and more varied than the telex lines Chilean engineers had to work with. Likewise, the ability to store and process information has also grown considerably since IBM mainframes were the state of the art. Current notions of crowdsourced governance rely on a similar architecture of decentralized networks for information processing, but today we have many more sensors capturing metrics than we had four decades ago. So the question is: Do we also have better answers to the old problems of governance? Do our numbers still oversimplify complex dynamics, or do they actually allow us to map that complexity more accurately? And are we still vulnerable to the grasp of Orwellian Big Brothers, or do we have more channels to circumvent that form of control and invest in the common good? The Internet has changed many things; prominent among them (and core to this book's argument) is the research we can conduct. As the previous chapters showed, we now know more about collective dynamics, the effects of social influence, how networks articulate social life, and the way in which geography and space shape those dynamics—all of which, as many of the examples already discussed show, often result in unintended consequences. Research that illuminates those dynamics is important because it addresses the context in which policy and governance operate, and in which our intuitions of privacy and autonomy are forged.

7.1 Crowdsourced Problem Solving

Networks have become a tool for thinking about governance today. One reason is that networks help tap into knowledge that is widely dispersed, and aggregate it in the form of better solutions or more accurate measurements. As chapter 5 explained, networks can create ties that span social distance; this means that they help integrate information that arises from different local contexts. Digital technologies have multiplied the avenues for collecting that localized information: they facilitate what would be very difficult to do using a top-down, centralized approach to data collection. Several applications have been developed in recent years to harness this form of collective intelligence. Examples range from platforms that encourage the reporting of nonemergency issues in city neighborhoods, like potholes or faulty streetlights, to software that facilitates information collection, visualization, and interactive mapping during crisis events. Services like the US seeclickfix.com or the UK fixmystreet.com create "adaptive, flexible urban reporting points" that can be used to improve local governance (Johnson 2012, 63). Platforms for interactive mapping like Ushahidi.com mean to generate and archive data when there is none, increasing transparency and accountability and, in fact, facilitating governance when institutions cannot operate normally (Meier 2015). In failed states that do not have governance structures in place, or when standard communication channels break down in emergency situations, decentralized networks of information exchange can fill an important gap in available knowledge.

The problem of selection bias discussed in the previous chapter sometimes renders the crowdsourced information incomplete or misleading. People living in more affluent neighborhoods, for instance, are more likely to report problems with streetlights than those living in poorer parts of a city—where the problems faced, to begin with, are much more severe than the malfunctioning of lights. A lack of data points in some neighborhoods, therefore, does not necessarily mean that they have no problems to report; it just means that the governance channels that new technologies make available are not equally accessed by everybody. The digital divide is still making portions of the population (and the places where they live) invisible online and underrepresented in the databases that increasingly guide policies and interventions (Crawford 2013). But crowdsourced data also makes visible what was not easy to visualize and analyze before, for instance episodes of violence during disputed elections, as happened in Kenya in 2007; or the location of victims during crisis events, as in the Haiti earthquake of 2010 (Giridharadas 2010; Meier 2015). Resources can be allocated to prevent violence and protect citizens in the exercise of their democratic rights; or to organize rescue operations more effectively under time constraints. This planning, however, requires data to guide the decision making. Crowdsourcing is making that data available, helping override censorship or a simple lack of accurate records. In the process, crowdsourcing is also encouraging social activism and public accountability in ways that strengthen democratic life.

That is, at least, the message that scholars and policymakers have been echoing for some years now (Benkler 2006). The main assumption is that public officials can also benefit from having access to the dispersed knowledge that communication networks pull together, and that this collaboration can create stronger ties between citizens and their elected governments (Noveck 2009, 2015). The claim is not just that new technologies accelerate access to information, "which would only drown decision makers"; but that crowdsourcing offers "the collective knowledge and creativity needed to curate and filter innovative solutions" (Noveck 2015, xvi). One example of how these synergies between the government and citizens can materialize is the Peer to Patent initiative in the United States, first piloted in 2009 to help the administration examine patent applications (Noveck 2009). The idea behind this initiative was that volunteers could share their expertise with the US Patent and Trademark Office, which is in charge of issuing patents to inventors—and is overwhelmed with hundreds of thousands of applications. The Peer to Patent platform provided channels through which scientists and experts could share their knowledge and assess the claims of a patent application. The goal, again, was to harness the intelligence contained in distributed networks. The problem, however, is that it proved very hard to attract enough volunteers, so the network did not grow very large—and the initiative failed to take off.

Drawing from this experience, a more recent instantiation of crowd-sourced decision making has been proposed under the label of "brain trust." The term was first used to refer to the experts who counseled Franklin Roosevelt during his presidency. This group "helped Roosevelt flesh out his rough ideas for everything from national agricultural planning and securities regulation to the Council of Economic Advisers and public works projects" (Noveck 2015, 210). The proposal to create a brain trust in the context of crowdsourced technologies follows the same argument that outside expertise can greatly benefit policymakers; but it also contends that valuable knowledge does not need to come from an elite of experts: it can arise as well from the contributions of average citizens who have access to relevant information (ibid., 209–240). Communication technologies have made it possible, in principle, to tap into diverse viewpoints and aggregate all that advice in a way that can inform decisions. In practice, however, the logistics are not that straightforward. We now have enough research evidence to qualify early optimistic claims about the technical possibilities of crowdsourcing, and acknowledge the limitations of this form of collaborative decision making—limitations that result mostly from the human element in the equation.

Wikipedia still stands as the main example of how a decentralized form of knowledge generation can work to produce actual value. An early study showed that the difference in accuracy between the site and the *Encyclopaedia Britannica* was minimal, which offered support to the claim that a network of unpaid editors could match the more hierarchical work structures of paid professionals (Giles 2005). Clearly a change of model in the production of knowledge had taken place. But the problems of this form of collaboration have also been repeatedly discussed since the early days, especially as they relate to gender discrimination and glass ceilings (Hargittai and Shaw 2015; Wagner et al. 2015; Wagner et al. 2016); the lack of diversity among contributors and consequent biases in knowledge representation (Graham, Straumann, and Hogan 2015); and the nature and effects of editorial disputes (Yasseri et al. 2012). The majority of the so-called "edit wars" between contributors take place around politically sensitive topics—precisely the domain where a brain trust would need to operate most of the time.

There are serious doubts about how realistically one can hope to overcome the logistical problems (or the legal barriers) that would make a crowdsourced brain trust possible. But there is one aspect that makes the project very powerful, and that is that it "diffuses the tension between expertise and citizenship by taking seriously the view that all citizens possess expertise" (Noveck 2015, 250). The distrust of experts is one of the main challenges that democracies face today, a cause for cynicism exacerbated by the 2008 economic crisis and the policy reactions that followed. What a project like the brain trust suggests is that the differentiation between citizens and experts is misleading, and that what counts as expertise pretty much depends on the nature of the problem. Professionals on the ground are likely to have more relevant insights into specific questions than experts discussing those problems in general terms behind office doors.

This notion of crowdsourced information gathering has also been applied as an alternative to surveys, which rely mostly on expert input and offer inflexible modes of data collection because questions are "prewritten" (Salganik and Levy 2015). Proposals to crowdsource governance also highlight that problems change constantly and that having channels for continuous engagement is the only way to be responsive: "The broken, staccato rhythm of citizen engagement today does not, and cannot, support meaningful action on the complex problems we face—problems that cannot be solved, only tackled, and then retackled as they evolve" (Noveck 2015, 268). Just like a nervous system, we may add, constantly reacting and adjusting to external conditions—precisely what motivated the Cybersyn project more than four decades ago in a very different political context. The problem of recruitment, however, still looms large in the foreground of these grand visions. Nerves do not volunteer to do their job, they just do it; but the brain trust needs to convince people that they should contribute their wisdom to the public good.

Improving something as gargantuan as government is a big endeavor. On a smaller scale, digital technologies are helping us understand better what motivates people to take part in specific problem-solving activities—for instance, the unlikely task of locating 10 balloons floating randomly across the United States (Pickard et al. 2011). This is a problem of decentralized search similar to that of finding a target person through the shortest chain of acquaintances discussed in chapter 5. The difference is that instead of finding a random person located in some city, participants had to find the coordinates of 10 weather balloons in unknown spots in the fastest way possible. This problem of "blind search" was considered impossible to solve using "conventional intelligence-gathering methods" (ibid., 509). The challenge, which was announced by the Defense Advanced Research Projects Agency (DARPA), came with a $40,000 prize for the successful team. Different research teams had to compete to obtain the balloon coordinates before the other teams, so in the end the challenge boiled down to triggering enough recruitment and mobilization through online networks—that is, to having as many people as possible acting as distributed sensors and reporting back from their respective locations.

The recruitment strategies employed by different teams included attracting participants for altruistic reasons (one team promised to donate the prize money, if they won, to a humanitarian organization); or using the mobilization power of social media celebrities. The winning team, which managed to locate the 10 balloons in under 9 hours, followed a different recruitment approach. Their strategy was to provide financial incentives that propagated through the recruitment chains: the person who found a balloon would receive part of the prize, but also whoever recruited that person, the recruiter of the recruiter, and so on.

This recursive incentive scheme worked well because it motivated participants not only to find the balloons but also to recruit other participants. Such an approach to social mobilization is different from dynamics of recruitment to, say, a political cause, because it does not rely on the intrinsic motivations that usually prompt political action; it encourages working in teams for efficiency and profit, not out of solidarity or respect for a shared political identity. But the study still offered interesting insights into how communication ties are activated, and how online networks are used to spread recruitment calls. Most importantly, the strategy worked and the problem was solved: all balloons were found in less than half a day.

Subsequent challenges explored other aspects of this decentralized form of problem solving. One of them, for instance, scaled up the geographical scope of the search. The challenge, which was proposed by the US State Department, required locating and photographing five target actors in five different cities in the United States and Europe using only a mug shot—and, once more, the mobilizing potential of online networks (Rutherford et al. 2013a; Rutherford et al. 2013b). The targets were visible for only 12 hours, and they were instructed to walk the city streets (in Stockholm, London, Bratislava, New York, and Washington) using average routes. Unlike the balloon challenge, here the search was not blind. Participants could use geographical cues when thinking about who to recruit next to the cause, following similar heuristics to those applied by the participants of the small world experiment described in chapter 5. What this challenge had in common with the balloon search is that there was a fixed time allowed to complete the task (12 hours). At the end of that time, the winning team had managed to locate three of the five target actors.

These studies show that when it comes to recruiting people to a decentralized search task, there are three important elements that ultimately determine success: the incentives offered; the structure of preexisting communication ties; and the geographical coverage of those networks. This means that the potential of crowdsourcing to solve search problems depends on three types of human decisions: the incentives offered to drive recruitment; the heuristics applied to mobilize some ties and not others; and the longer-range decisions (unrelated to the task) to actually form ties with certain types of people—decisions that, as chapters 5 and 6 explained, are determined to a large extent by social structure and spatial constraints. One question that digital technologies make it possible to ask is: Can algorithms improve human judgment in each of those domains (i.e., the design of incentives, the navigation of ties, and the formation of networks)? An increasing number of applications show that algorithms can complement human cognition when it comes to making decisions in a range of uncertain scenarios (Christian and Griffiths 2016). But we also have an increasing number of examples in which human cognition improves the way in which algorithms mediate decision making (Michelucci and Dickinson 2016). This synergy between biological brain and digital machine is far from the horizons that Beer and his Chilean colleagues could envision—but it closely follows their steps.

7.2 Algorithms and Decision Making

One limitation of algorithmic decision making is that it is often partial in its assessment. Prejudices can drive the operation of algorithms in two ways: through statistical inference, if the data used for algorithmic manipulation is incomplete or biased; and through the code itself if it's written with implicit values—much in the same way as Beer's operations room was designed to minimize female input. That code is not neutral, and that it regulates social dynamics similarly to the way law does—only more opaquely—has been a cause for concern for some years now (Lessig 2006). The rising prominence of algorithms in most aspects of our daily lives is making the implicit regulatory power of technology ever more visible. This has prompted some observers to actually claim that "the future belongs to the algorithms and their creators" (Steiner 2012, 212). Others, like computer scientist Latanya Sweeney (who conducted the research discussed in chapter 2 uncovering Google's discriminatory search results), summarize more soberly the significance of algorithmic thinking: "Technologists may now have to think about societal consequences like structural racism in the technology they design" (Lohr 2015, 194). Technologies, in the end, cannot escape the social context in which they originate. When technologies fail our standards of fairness, it is a human failure aggravated by a lack of social and institutional controls.

Recent research, for instance, suggests that Airbnb (the online marketplace to rent accommodations) is built in a way that facilitates racial discrimination. Using a field experiment, researchers have shown that requests from guests that have African-American-sounding names are about 16% less likely to be accepted by potential hosts than identical applicants with white-sounding names (Edelman, Luca, and Svirsky 2016). The platform's design choice is to discourage the anonymity of guests and hosts, with the goal of facilitating trust; but, as in many other domains of social life, this choice triggers unintended consequences—in this case, enabling racial discrimination. The solution to this structural bias is, once again, not technological but social.

An antidiscrimination policy that would audit hosts suspected of discrimination, bar those who are shown to discriminate, and withhold identity information until a reservation is confirmed has been proposed as the sort of institutional measure that could limit the effects of discrimination

(Clarke 2016). This policy, however, suggests that we need to design platforms that restrain human, not algorithmic, prejudice. At the time of writing these pages, Airbnb had just published a report outlining their strategy to fight discrimination, including the formation of a "full-time team of engineers, data scientists, researchers and designers whose sole purpose is to advance belonging and inclusion and to root out bias" (Murphy 2016, 24). Other measures include allowing instant booking listings, i.e., rentals that do not require prior host approval of a guest. However, some have already argued that this policy might actually backfire and trigger more unintended consequences, for instance a two-tiered reservation system that will make the differential treatment of minorities even more conspicuous (Benner 2016).

Cases like that of Airbnb show that algorithms are not the only source of discrimination or in need of regulation. In fact, algorithms can help us identify perverse social dynamics, determine the source of the bias, and overcome cognitive limitations, the existence of which has been extensively documented through psychological research (Kahneman, Slovic, and Tversky 1982; Tversky and Kahneman 1974). Determining when we should stop searching for a good apartment, how we should solve the tradeoff of exploring new options versus exploiting the known ones, or even when to make use of random chance when trying to solve hard problems are all situations where an algorithmic approach can improve human decisions (Christian and Griffiths 2016). The exploration/exploitation tradeoff, for instance, is a problem that digital technologies are helping us address with better resources: they offer data to determine where the optimal balance lies, but also venues for intervention to get us closer to the point where new and old information can be integrated—hopefully in the form of better solutions or ideas. Another way to think about this tradeoff is in terms of social learning versus individual experience: How much value do we give to what other people do (the exploration part) versus what we have done so far (the exploitation part) when making a decision? Is social learning, or exploration, always beneficial for the individual and the group?

This same question was addressed a few years ago in the context of an online trading platform (Pentland 2014, 28–41). What made this platform interesting for research purposes was that it incorporated a social network through which users could look up other users' trades and past performance, and thus be influenced by that group of reference. Users could either place a normal trade by themselves, or place a trade that exactly copied someone else's strategy. Employing the data generated by 1.6 million of these users, the researchers measured the impact of social learning on financial outcomes. One of the findings was that there was a lot of variation in social learning, from isolated individuals who never copied anybody, to highly clustered users who were all copying each other. A second finding was that return on investment was, on average, higher for those users between the two extremes of isolation and clustered redundancy. The reason is that too much social learning triggered herd behavior, and too little reduced diversity and novelty. These findings are interesting on their own since they illuminate the empirical workings of social influence and diffusion; but they are also interesting because they offer the sort of knowledge that can be used to nudge traders into behaving differently for the benefit of all. These same researchers also proposed using this sort of data to design interfaces that recommend "tuning" social networks so that users can escape feedback loops of redundant connections or avoid being too isolated to learn from others.

In general, finding the right balance between the exploration of new options and the exploitation of known solutions depends on the underlying structure of communication bringing people together into groups or teams (Lazer and Friedman 2007; Mason and Watts 2012). The performance of those groups depends on how conducive the exchange of information is to finding better solutions to common problems. The notion of collective intelligence relies precisely on finding the right equilibrium between diversity and social influence: on the one hand, too much influence leads to convergence, which ends up atrophying diversity; on the other hand, too much diversity without influence precludes the diffusion of good information or ideas.

Research has shown that less diverse teams produce worse outcomes in the completion of problem-solving tasks (Woolley et al. 2010). Those tasks included things like solving visual puzzles, making moral judgments, or negotiating over limited resources. The findings showed that teams with more equal distribution of conversational turn-taking performed better; in other words, "groups where a few people dominated the conversation were less collectively intelligent" (ibid., 688). One way to interpret this finding is that the more voices are heard in discussions about how to solve a problem, the wider the exploration range can grow.

At the same time, research also shows that social influence increases the bias of collective estimates because it decreases diversity (Lorenz et al. 2011). A statistical phenomenon known for a long time to operate in crowds is that the average of many individual estimates (on, say, the population of a given country) can be very close to the true value even if, individually, each of those estimates is off-target (Galton 1907; Surowiecki 2004). This form of crowd estimation offers a useful tool for decision makers because they can request and aggregate independent opinions to inform their actions. However, "it is hardly feasible to receive independent opinions in society, because people are embedded in social networks and typically influence each other"; in fact, "in democratic societies, it is difficult to accomplish such a collection of independent estimates because the loss of diversity in estimates appears to be a necessary byproduct of transparent decision-making processes" (Lorenz et al. 2011, 9024). So, given that influence seems inescapable in most social scenarios, can we at least use algorithms to monitor its effects and, if possible, correct the unintended consequences?

One partial answer to this question comes out of organizational research in which digital displays were used to provide real-time feedback on team interactions (Pentland 2014, 107–112). The tool, called Meeting Mediator, had two main components: a sociometric badge that captured turn-taking behavior, and a mobile phone used to visualize the flow of interactions. The tool helped manage participation with the goal of allowing a balanced conversation by visualizing levels of engagement as a network: at the center of the network, represented in the mobile screen, group members could see a colored node that became darker as overall engagement improved or lighter when engagement went down; this central node would also get closer to one of the other nodes, each representing a person in the group, if that person started to dominate the conversation. The device, in other words, allowed real-time feedback on social interactions and encouraged self-regulation so that teams could steer their way toward more horizontal discussions as those discussions were taking place. Tools like this follow a longer research trail in organizational sociology in which interactions and informal communication networks are mapped and analyzed to assess performance (Burt 1992, 2005). The difference is that digital technologies allow measuring those interactions as they evolve (as opposed to through snapshots) and provide instantaneous feedback.

Another area where people and algorithms are working together is through microtasking, a process that breaks down a task into smaller components that are then distributed to workers over online networks. This is one of the ways in which the power of crowds can be harnessed for specific problem-solving purposes. It is particularly well suited to tackle problems that require applying over and over the same simple steps—for instance, categorizing galaxy shapes through the inspection of images that are difficult to analyze by machines, as in the now canonical Galaxy Zoo, a classic example of citizen science (Lintott et al. 2008). The use of microtasking has opened the way for more complex synergies between crowds and machines: "In creating problem-solving ecosystems," states a recent review, "researchers are beginning to explore how to combine the cognitive processing of many human contributors with machine-based computing" (Michelucci and Dickinson 2016, 32). This includes building online workspaces where contributors can engage in open-ended discussions and prescribe actions to be taken offline. Compared to microtasking, the design of these online workspaces is more attuned to the complex nature of the political world, which is more ambiguous than science in the problems it poses—and not as amenable to agreement as when members of the crowd are asked to assess the shapes exhibited by faraway galaxies.

Developing those workspaces beyond their current prototype stage requires more research to understand "the human-machine feedback loop." After all, "machines tend to give predictable outputs, such that errors can always be traced to faulty code or design, but humans are less predictable in terms of their availability and the quality of their work" (Michelucci and Dickinson 2016, 33). This is the inescapable human condition—and the most challenging element in the puzzle for those who advocate an engineering approach to the social world. Putting the brain trust idea or, more generally, crowdsourced governance into practice depends on finding mechanisms that will make the human-machine loop not only operational but also legitimate and robust. This is not so different from finding the right design for what behavioral scientists call "choice architectures," that is, background conditions that encourage certain choices and nudge people to behave in a particular way (Sunstein 2016; Thaler and Sunstein 2009). Nudge interventions may be designed to encourage recycling, more efficient energy consumption, or greener commuting habits; they may also aim to accomplish other societal goals like reducing poverty, improving health, or encouraging people to vote. And yet nudges still generate resistance among some observers because they are perceived as threats to personal autonomy or as a form of manipulation. Many of these objections dissolve when the interventions are analyzed through the lens of specific examples and an evaluation of the costs and benefits involved (Sunstein 2016). Algorithmic decision making raises similar concerns, which also require a concrete analysis of the costs and benefits that arise across domains. But there is one difference, which is that privacy becomes a much more prominent element in this debate.

7.3   The Two Sides of Privacy

The most important (and contentious) point of discussion involving the role that algorithms play in decision making is privacy. Underlying this debate lies the tension between individual rights and the common good, as tense as a tightrope under the performer's feet—and as difficult to tread in balance. Algorithms constantly judge us on the basis of our data, but it is often difficult to assess their fairness and therefore their actual role in protecting what is collectively deemed good or necessary. Think of the algorithms used by the US Transportation Security Administration to select certain passengers for "special screening" at airports. The procedure is supposed to be for the benefit of all travelers, but without transparency there is no accountability and no way of telling whether this is just another setting where discrimination is unfairly perpetuated (Schneier 2015, 159). Even if we have transparency, we still need to determine how to solve the tradeoff between individual value and social value; or between private choices and public control. This is a hard tradeoff to solve because it is plagued with paradoxes.

One such paradox is the seeming contradiction that "people appear to want and value privacy, yet simultaneously appear not to value or want it" (Nissenbaum 2009, 84). On the one hand, survey respondents consistently report being concerned about how their personal information is used by government and corporations; on the other hand, their behavior reveals an entirely different set of priorities: "In almost all situations in which people must choose between privacy and just about any other good, they choose the other good" (ibid., 85). One answer to this paradox is that expectations on privacy are, in fact, relational: they depend on the context in which data transactions take place. We might be willing to give information away in one setting, but reject having that information used for an entirely different purpose. This approach, which has been dubbed "contextual integrity," sustains that the right to privacy is "a right to live in a world in which our expectations about the flow of personal information are, for the most part, met" (ibid., 211). These expectations change across social contexts, and are encoded in the form of social norms: we might be willing to share personal information for research but not for marketing purposes. It is when those norms are violated that algorithmic technologies are denounced as a threat to privacy. The implication is that technologies should be used in line with our normative expectations. And yet who determines what those expectations are or whether they should, in fact, be changed is anything but clear. As chapter 1 discussed, history tells us that expectations change with every wave of technological development. We just get used to new technologies and redefine the boundaries of privacy accordingly.

Another paradox in discussions on privacy relates to who should restrain abuses of access to personal information. The contradiction here derives from the fact that even if those advocating for privacy "fear Big Brother most, they need to lean on him to protect privacy better from Big Bucks" (Etzioni 1999, 10). The intervention of the state, in other words, is necessary to regulate potential threats coming out of the private sector and corporate surveillance—those "ill effects of the new unfettering of market forces" (ibid.). The perverse twist to this paradox is that the state is, of course, also able to abuse its power and force private corporations to hand over information on their users (Greenwald 2014). The tension between individual rights and the common good (usually dressed in the uniform of national security) manifests itself here most forcefully. This tension offers a reality check to normative orthodoxies that seemingly want to govern the world according to an immutable hierarchy of values. The fact is that "although ideologies can be structured around a single organizing principle—like liberty, or a particular social virtue—societies must balance values that are not fully compatible" (Etzioni 1999, 200). Discussions of how to protect privacy are no exception to this rule.

So how do we translate these normative discussions—for which the two paradoxes just mentioned are only the tip of the iceberg—into principles than can guide policy and action? How do we use digital data for the benefit of society while minimizing the damage to individuals or groups? One analogy that has been used to frame this dilemma compares data to exhaust, "something we all produce as we go about our information-age business," or—taking the analogy one step further—"the pollution problem of the information age" where "privacy is the environmental challenge" (Schneier 2015, 238). This metaphor implies that corporations, the state, and individuals all have responsibilities to preserve privacy limits—much as we are all responsible for the environment. Protective measures range from developing and using software that will only store the data allowed by the user to more institutional and far-reaching attempts at regulation. Relying on individual responsibility seems an ineffective way of protecting privacy, given that it requires some level of technical sophistication and that it stands at odds with the paradox mentioned above: for most purposes, most of us simply do not give too much thought to how our data exhaust is generated or used. In the policy domain, on the other hand, there is a difference between regulating data collection and regulating data use, a difference that marks a divide between Europe (where the former is favored) and the United States (where the latter prevails).

A "new deal on data" has been recently proposed as an example of regulating data use (Pentland 2014, 180–182). The deal draws an analogy with the English common law ownership rights of possession, use, and disposal; in other words, it makes three basic claims: you have the right to possess your data, to control how your data is used, and to destroy or distribute it as you deem appropriate. Again, the approach presupposes that "individual rights to personal data must be balanced with the needs of corporations and governments to use certain data—account activity, billing information, and so on—to run their day-to-day operations," although no specific guidelines are offered on how precisely to find that balance—especially when day-to-day operations force us to consider values that are, as stated above, not fully compatible. The idea, however, has informed the 2012 Consumer Data Bill of Rights in the United States. The Obama administration's big data report published in 2014 followed similar lines in its call to give consumers more control over their information (Lohr 2015, 192). Considering how much data we generate, however, the issue of regulating not just its use but also its collection is on the table.

Proposals on how to regulate data collection have two important precedents: the 1980 OECD Privacy Framework and the 1995 EU Data Protection

Directive (Schneier 2015, 190). Both initiatives enshrined informed consent as one of the principles that should drive the collection of personal information. This notion is based "on legal, philosophical, and moral individualistic assumptions" according to which using information without explicit consent is a violation of personal autonomy; the principle "reflects the classical liberal view of a person as a free agent who knows his or her preferences and is able to act on them rationally" (Etzioni 1999, 155). And yet this principle also presupposes that consent forms are "contracts" that are voluntary and informed, when the fact is that, in most instances, people have no real choice (ibid., 156). In April 2016 the European parliament approved the General Data Protection Regulation, adopted to supersede the 1995 Directive (Gibbs 2016). These new rules were implemented as a response to the challenges created by new online technologies like social media, cloud computing, or location-based services (European Commission 2015). One of the principles addressed by the 2016 Regulation is the "right to be forgotten." This right grants individuals the possibility of having their data deleted, even if consent to its collection was once given. This is an important change, since the regulation assigns data ownership not to the companies that collect it through "informed consent" forms but to the individuals who generated the information in the first place (freedom of expression and historical and scientific research are protected from this right, though).

When the debate on privacy touches the topic of surveillance, the underlying tension is one of trust versus indifference. In some domains, individuals are trusted to use their privacy in ways that do not cause harm, but society "does not forgo its right to act—for example, in cases where a person uses his or her privacy to molest a child or make bombs." In most other domains, individual private choices are met with indifference: "it concerns all those numerous matters about which the society rules that these are matters in which the individual is free to act as he or she deems fit" (Etzioni 1999, 210). Governments have the right and the responsibility to determine the conditions under which certain acts and choices need to be controlled; they also have the responsibility of regulating unwarranted scrutiny on matters that should be met with indifference, especially when the scrutiny comes from private companies—or from the growing breed of data brokers (Lohr 2015, 188). Recent regulatory efforts on the highest policy levels aim to rebuild this other type of trust: trust between citizens and corporations. The question of who watches the watchers, however, still burns in many discussions on privacy.

What makes those discussions so interesting these days is that even if digital technologies have multiplied opportunities for surveillance, they have also encouraged the emergence of new political actors. The role of these actors is to push for transparency when it is the states (under governmental supervision and with the aid of private corporations) that break trust without cause.

7.4   New Forms of Activism

Besides Big Brother and Big Bucks (to reuse Etzioni's terminology), today there is a third type of actor, of a more elusive identity in its networked, crowdsourced architecture—but as influential nonetheless in how we think about data and privacy in the digital age. Doxing, or the practice of broadcasting private information about individuals or organizations (derived from "dox," or "documents"), has become a common form of political action that relies, precisely, on smashing privacy boundaries. It has been the tactic of groups like Anonymous (Coleman 2014) and WikiLeaks (Leigh and Harding 2011), actors that in spite of their recent emergence have already been able to shift the political agenda on a global scale.

The publication in 2010 of the US State Department diplomatic cables, which was a collaboration between WikiLeaks and several global media organizations, is considered one of the greatest journalistic scoops of the last thirty years (Leigh and Harding 2011, 8). Though the documents published were redacted by a team of journalists, soon the unredacted version of the archive started to circulate online through Torrent distribution systems (Ungerleider 2011). The stated motivation for doxing campaigns is to push for transparency, even if the modus operandi of the groups behind those campaigns is, paradoxically, rather opaque. The problem with these campaigns is that innocent people often fall victim to that unfiltered (and unchecked) transparency—whether this is always an unintended consequence is certainly not clear. In these cases, matters that would usually be met with indifference are turned into targets of surveillance.

One of the latest episodes of this unjustified breach of privacy happened in July 2016, when WikiLeaks published hundreds of thousands of emails that were supposed to contain damaging information about Turkish

President Erdogan and his government (days after an attempted coup) but that, in fact, released private and sensitive information of ordinary citizens. The leak contained data "of what appears to be every female voter in 79 out of 81 provinces in Turkey, including their home addresses and other private information, sometimes including their cellphone numbers. ... Their addresses are out there for every stalker, ex-partner, disapproving relative or random crazy to peruse as they wish. ... The files also include whether or not these women were AKP members [Erdogan's Justice and Development Party]—right after a brutal and bloody coup attempt to overthrow the AKP" (Tufekci 2016). Commentators soon pointed out that this and similar episodes have inevitably damaged WikiLeaks's "moral high ground," which was based on its ability to act as "an honest conduit" rather than a "damaged filter" (Ellis 2016). Anonymous has built a similarly "ambivalent" relationship "with the court of public opinion"; the reason is that their methods "are at times subversive, often rancorous, usually unpredictable, and frequently disdainful of etiquette or the law" (Coleman 2014, loc. 126). Their doxing often relies on information that can be found on publicly accessible websites; but, as happens with the use that data brokers make of that public information, the problem is that the data is decontextualized or compiled in ways that were never envisioned by those making the information available.

What lies at the heart of negative reactions to these disclosures is, again, the violation of expectations of privacy: data is used for purposes other than those intended when the data was first made public. In other words, the notion of contextual integrity ("the right to live in a world that meets our expectations about the flow of personal information") is also challenged by actors that operate to confront the abuses of the state and private corporations. The debate has created two different fronts: those advocating for unfiltered transparency and those supporting a curated version. Edward Snowden, the leading actor in the 2013 leak of thousands of National Security Agency classified documents, has openly criticized the unfiltered approach that WikiLeaks takes to the dissemination of government secrets (Chokshi 2016). His own approach to the disclosure was to get the editorial assistance of professional journalists who would help parse, contextualize, and tell the story hidden in the documents leaked. As he told Glenn Greenwald and Laura Poitras, the journalists who would make the story public, "I'm relying on you to use your journalistic judgement to only publish those documents that the public should see and that can be revealed without any harm to any innocent people" (Greenwald 2014, 53). A similar form of curation also took place during the 2010 diplomatic cables leak: "the final piece of the journalistic heavy lifting was to introduce a redaction process so that nothing we published could imperil any vulnerable sources or compromise active special operations" (Leigh and Harding 2011, 5). Up to that point, the ethical framework of WikiLeaks relied, mostly, on just one person. Even so, and in spite of journalistic curation efforts, the unfiltered archive soon found its way to the public.

In addition to human curation, however, the journalistic editorial approach relied heavily on search tools that helped organize and parse all the data. These information retrieval engines have been compared, metaphorically, to the oracle of Delphi: "Like the divinations of the Oracle, the problem with the Snowden archive is that you never find an easy answer … it all begins with typing questions into little boxes. Then doing it again. Above all, what you find are more questions … you ask something and receive cryptic information that may offer you some answers, but only by raising more questions" (Crawford 2016, 140–141). The truth is that information retrieval tools are not so much an oracle as a compass that helps navigate a seemingly boundless sea of information; and this compass will become ever more important if we, as individuals, are to start taking care of our own "data exhaust" as well.

The curation of information will rely, more and more, on algorithms that determine how we search and display data. This means that demands of transparency in the operation of both human and automated curation (as applied by political actors, journalists, the state, or private corporations) will become increasingly difficult to meet without actual research illuminating how algorithms and humans interact. This is because "the interplay of social algorithms and behaviors yields patterns that are fundamentally emergent. These patterns cannot be gleaned from reading code" (Lazer 2015). They cannot be gleaned, either, by asking the actors involved.

These synergies between automated and human decisions are manifested in other recent strategies used to channel protest and civil disobedience. Two of these strategies are distributed denial of service (DDoS) attacks, which bring online services down by overwhelming websites with traffic (Sauter 2014); and obfuscation, "the deliberate addition of ambiguous, confusing, or misleading information to interfere with surveillance and data collection" (Brunton and Nissenbaum 2015, 1). These examples, which have been compared to "virtual sit-ins" or to "weapons of the weak" and stand as transgressive forms of activism, illuminate how the same technologies that are used to implement an Orwellian reality can also be used to create resistance. The so called "big data" that feeds into so much policy and decision making is an unintended byproduct of the Internet; but so are new political actors like Anonymous, WikiLeaks, or Snowden. If anything, their actions show that the algorithmic approach to information processing is most powerful when it is informed by human decisions on who to target and which information to reveal.

7.5   Networked Governance

The above discussion suggests that digital technologies play (unsurprisingly) a complex role in governance: the data they generate is good for informed decision making but also for surveillance; they allow eavesdropping but also the decentralized coordination of political action; they create biases in data collection but they also facilitate solutions to problems that were impossible to solve using conventional data-gathering methods. Above all, digital technologies force us to confront the old irreconcilable tension between private interests and the common good. Our current technologies make a historical statement by casting new light on the old principles of autonomy and privacy. And, as with older technologies, the discussions will soon steer away toward newer technological developments and renewed concerns. Trust and transparency are still the guiding principles of how we think about good governance today; but now they apply not only to human decisions and curation practices but also to the decisions carried out by algorithms. If transparency is not given, new forms of activism are willing to take it—implementing their own algorithmic approach to democratic practice.

In spite of all the controversies, one thing is certain: decision makers have less of an excuse today to design flawed interventions or choice architectures. Chapter 4 ended with Coates's story of a world where policymakers had to intervene to control the "unconscious subversiveness" of the people, who either flooded public spaces or turned them into deserted landscape, always without intent. Their solution was as inefficient as it was intrusive—an attempt to micromanage freedom that aimed to solve one problem but created a heavier burden on the people it tried to help. The use of digital traces to inform that sort of decision making is, for some, also an attempt to design freedom. This attempt is criticized for reasons that are very similar to those used against the Chilean Cybersyn project with which this chapter started: freedom cannot be designed without losing its essence; or, in today's parlance, data science cannot inform actions without reducing politics to technocratic rule. Many of these reactions reveal a confusion about what algorithms can actually do. For the most part, they are less deterministic than many institutionalized forms of decision making operating within bureaucratic machines. Current technologies have cut the verbosity of old cybernetic visions, offering working examples of how we can harnesses the power of collectives and counteract the unintended effects. The next step in this progress is to make algorithms and human intelligence converge more naturally in the solution of problems that change constantly—often in unexpected ways.

8 Conclusions: Questions for Now and the Future

Technologies encode social change. The printing press, the telegraph, the telex network, the Internet: these are all artifacts that reflect the ideas, beliefs, and interests of an era as much as the progress of the science that made them possible in the first place. They are also a reminder that human reactions to the new offer a thin repertoire: audiences acclaim and denounce emerging technologies with similar arguments and fervor across the ages. Our current technologies, it turns out, are not different in that respect. What makes them unique compared to older technologies is that they allow us to analyze the same dynamics of change that gave them prominence. This book has given an account of how we can conduct those analyses, paying special attention to the creative (often perverse) impact of unintended consequences on the paths to change. Digital technologies, and the data science that evolved with them, have given us the tools to uncover the complexity at the heart of those dynamics—the fuel, to offer one more metaphor, that activates social life and all its paradoxes.

The book has offered many examples of how we can extract meaningful patterns from the data we generate in our mediated interactions. We can now study aggregated shifts of collective attention and its temporal dynamics as we can analyze the beating of a heart. We can map networks of information flow and reconstruct the paths that news and ideas follow to reach their audiences. And we can study the individual-level mechanisms that make those higher-order dynamics emerge. Social change unfolds on these three levels, bubbling up from individual actions, reconfiguring the behavior of collectives, and generating aggregated and often unintended effects that can be tracked at the level of populations. Decentralized communication is the moving architecture that connects these three levels of constant action and reaction. This is why digital technologies are offering more and better data to analyze how the shifting parts operate. And yet there are still many unresolved questions around most of the topics discussed here. The progression of knowledge is, by definition, always provisional and open-ended: for every answer we obtain, there are many more questions that follow. Beyond that, new challenges emerge in this discussion about how we define the conditions in which we generate that knowledge.

At a time when the very notion of truth is being contested (Drezner 2016) and the models of the world we build with data seem to be sinking to new credibility lows (Davies 2017), determining the value of evidence-based research (as opposed to mere opinion) seems ever more pressing. This includes some level of critical thinking with regard to who collects, owns, and has the ability to access data; the purpose of research, and the motivations guiding that work; the reasons for storing and retrieving information that will build imperfect (but hopefully still useful) maps of social life; and how to allocate responsibilities in networks that are decentralized in their operation and full of unintended consequences. The following sections consider these questions in more detail, both as a recap of this book's journey and as an invitation to think about the road that lies ahead of us.

8.1   Which Form of Critical?

Back in the 1960s, Karl Popper and Theodor Adorno led a public debate that has come to be known as the "positivist dispute"—even if this label was itself disputed because the participants would not agree on what positivism was and who belonged to that category of thought (Adorno et al. 1976 [1969]). The elements of the discussion boiled down to two fronts: critical rationalism and critical theory. The first was represented by Popper, and it encapsulated an approach to social theory that favored "gradual and piecemeal reform, reform controlled by a critical comparison between expected and achieved results" (ibid., 291). The critical theory represented by Adorno, on the other hand, took a more radical approach: it claimed that the social sciences aimed either to reproduce the existing status quo or to transform that reality. The path to transformation required breaking with science and logic because they, too, were part of the system to be changed, "not only a social force of production but also a social relation of production" (ibid., 4). For Popper, the ideology of those proposing solutions did not matter—as long as that ideology did not destroy "intelligence and critical thought" (ibid., 293); for Adorno, social and ideological forces constrained and biased every single form of knowledge (including, we are led to conclude, his own).

Arguments like these are still very much alive in current discussions of the forces that drive technological developments and their impact on social life. This book unambiguously sides with the approach evoked by critical rationalism. One reason is that, otherwise, we are forced to find a theoretical position from which, in the words of Adorno, "one can respond to the other person without, however, accepting a set of rules which are themselves a theme of the controversy—an intellectual no man's land" (ibid., 4). Such a land, it turns out, offers little more than a logical maze with no possible exit (and the fallible guidance of a rather pretentious rhetoric). Dismissing Adorno's epistemology, however, does not diminish the importance of values, which, as the previous chapters have repeatedly claimed, always play an important role in our approximation to the world. In Popper's words, research is fueled by values that include "truth; the search for truth; the approximation to truth through the critical elimination of error; and clarity" (ibid., 294). If we are to understand the role that technologies play in social life, and how the now-pervasive networks of communication tie us together or set us apart, we need to be able to make statements of truth with the best available data and the best analytical tools. And these do not come packaged in the colorful cellophane of ideologies but as bare empirical claims that can be tested and retested. This is why clarity is such an important value. In this digital era, the promotion of clarity includes the promotion of algorithmic transparency.

Questioning the way in which algorithms operate is crucial if we are to tell truth from falsity. The exercise, however, entails looking at algorithms for what they are, i.e., instructions on how to process data, sometimes on the basis of flawed assumptions or unopened black boxes (O'Neil 2016). Analogies, in this case, won't help much: claims like "the algorithm is the psychoanalyst of the twenty-first century" (Simanowski 2016, 10) do not give much guidance as to how to make algorithms perform better or solve the tradeoff between finding a solution to a problem and making the factors that contributed to the solution easy to explain and understand. If we claim that algorithms maximize the wrong function or fail to produce the intended result, we assume we can correct them and make them better—provided we apply some serious critical and analytical thinking to the task. If we think of algorithms as psychoanalysts, on the other hand, there is no clear starting point to improve how they operate or the role they should be playing.

One of the themes in this book has been the opposition of the scientific and the humane that is implied by many accounts of technologies. This opposition presumes that the scientific and humanistic approaches to social life are incompatible with each other. In reality, they are stronger when their values join forces—and when critical theories do not fall into the trap of self-defeating epistemologies. The use of analytical models to simplify the complexity of the world does not preclude other forms of knowledge from adding additional layers of information and perspectives that are difficult to capture in the language of models. History offers many valuable lessons that are based on the narratives with which we retell the past—hardly a setup for experimentation. History highlights the importance of the social context for understanding how we think about technologies and the priorities that take precedence in their design. These priorities are often aligned with political or economic interests that can only be fully scrutinized when we look at them from different angles. Data science helps us find patterns in a sea of observations. Whether the boundaries of that sea need to be expanded or restricted is not part of the problems data science aims to solve—but it is an important problem, of course.

8.2   Unintended Effects or Collateral Damage?

This book has revolved around a guiding metaphor: the analogy that sees in the social world a cryptogram that we can decode. The starting point of the metaphor is the idea that social life has a structure that is often hidden, buried in noise; and that, much as probability can help reverse-engineer a cryptic code, so data science can uncover the patterns that give structure but also propel change in the social world. This analogy emphasizes the stochastic nature of social life, the fact that its course is never fully random or fully deterministic; it is instead a dynamic process that exhibits path dependence, where the present constrains the future but never fully shapes it; a process that often triggers unintended consequences, neither envisioned nor designed by any one actor involved—which renders meaning less useful for explanatory purposes than when we try to account for other dimensions of social life.

The good news is that unintended consequences often trigger innovation and change; the bad news is that they can also generate mishaps and errors in judgment. Many unintended effects look, in fact, more like collateral damage, the cracks in the system through which specific individuals fall—and of course, those individuals are more than just data points failing to fit a prediction. The question then is how to assign responsibilities—lest the law of unintended consequences become a blank check that justifies everything that goes wrong. This book has considered several scenarios in which policies could try to prevent or mitigate perverse outcomes, as when inequality arises in systems by way of cumulative effects that are not necessarily related to merit but to some random initial advantage; or as when rumors or misinformation spread through networks like wildfire. Algorithmic decision making can also generate unintended consequences across a range of policy domains, including outcomes like discrimination in targeted advertisement; but then algorithms can help identify those effects as well, especially when they result from human prejudice, which, as several examples given in the previous chapters show, is a social (not a technological) condition.

Web technologies, and the political economy that surrounds them, are themselves big unintended consequences—never envisioned by Berners-Lee when he proposed building a "universal linked information system" to help organize knowledge (Berners-Lee and Fischetti 2000). Political actors like Anonymous or WikiLeaks emerge also as the unintended outcomes of technological development—as driven in their actions as they are today, and as intentional as they are in defining their targets. It is here that social change finds much of the fuel that turns its wheels: localized events that induce an interminable chain reaction that generates things other than those originally pursued. This book offered a few examples in which the idea of unpacking unintended effects can be made operational, that is, amenable to actual research with data and findings. The examples have come mostly from the analysis of collective behavior in systems that are linked by communication networks. There are still many open questions about how those networks activate chain reactions, but there is no question about the progress made in our ability to unpack what was once considered an intriguing but unsolvable puzzle.

8.3   What to Archive and Retrieve?

Another recurrent theme in this book has been that better measurements help us devise better theories; our understanding of the world, in other words, improves as we sharpen our measurement instruments. As several historical examples illustrated, our current obsession with measurement is the most recent manifestation of an old impulse—a change of mindset that started, in fact, way before the telegraph revolution, back in the sixteenth century, when a quantitative view of the world forcefully grabbed people's imagination never to let go again (Crosby 1997). It is clear that this obsession with measurement has yielded many benefits: I will ask you, reader, to survey a normal day in your life to determine how important metrics and numbers are in guiding most of the decisions you make. And yet this does not eliminate the always difficult question of deciding what data to collect and which data to analyze. This problem, which has always troubled philosophers of science more than scientists themselves, has come to the fore of public discussions after a succession of events that highlight the limitations of our metrics and analysis. Algorithms and statistical models could not prevent the 2008 economic crisis; in fact, they helped precipitate it by the blind trust put on analytical instruments that were, it turns out, grossly imperfect. Likewise, the failure to predict the outcomes of recent elections (the Brexit referendum in the United Kingdom or the 2016 presidential election in the United States) has also stirred a very public discussion about the accuracy of models and expert predictions. One of the issues here is that, of course, our models can only work with what we feed them. If our measures and data are not good enough, models cannot compensate for that (or not most of the time).

Today, with all the distributed sensors and passive ways of amassing social information, it seems that data collection has lost many bounds. But it is still bounded—if only because data is not a natural resource but the product of historical and cultural contingencies (Gitelman 2013). We pay attention to the things we deem important, and this is not an unguided decision. There are, in fact, important qualitative distinctions between data, information, and knowledge. In the words of a humanist, "data (as givens or facts; *datum* in Latin) embody the lowest level in the chain of perception, preceding both information (as processed data; *informare* in Latin) and knowledge (as interconnected information)" (Simanowski

2016, 129). It has actually been proposed to replace the term "data" with "capta" ("things captured"), to stress the fact that it is we who *take* those measurements, i.e., they are not given to us by nature (ibid.). Again this brings back the discussion of previous pages of how good our representations are of the territory we want to map. As imperfect as they are, having maps is better than having no maps at all—especially since cartographies that reproduce the world in its full complexity are a logical impossibility. The important question then is: Do our maps help us reach the destination, i.e., do they help us solve the questions we ask? If not, then we need to revisit the maps. This is precisely what critical rationalism is for.

An added difficulty to how we think about data today comes from the larger social structures that lie beyond the scope of data science. When a great portion of the data we generate derives from the use of proprietary technologies in the hands of a few corporations, the question of access (i.e., who can analyze the data) becomes very relevant. Historically, the systematic collection of data started as a tool that allowed states to have control over their populations, as chapter 6 explained (Scott 1999). Today, data collection is increasingly the realm of private interests whose goal is to maximize financial gains. The clarity and transparency we need to be able to apply critical thinking, that is, to compare the expected and achieved results that come out of the analysis of that data, depend on having access to that information and to how it is being exploited. Some of the measures that have been proposed to encourage that kind of transparency include auditing and algorithmic accountability (Lohr 2015; O'Neil 2016). This is one of the regulatory issues that will need serious attention in the years to come. At the same time, technologies also risk increasing the knowledge gap between experts and the general public "whose data are analyzed but who do not themselves have the knowledge or means to participate in such analyses" (Simanowski 2016, 75). Disregarding expert knowledge is, of course, not a solution to this problem, but this fact doesn't make the growing asymmetry less urgent.

8.4 How to Control Networks?

Networks are the manifestation of many unintended effects. For instance, their architecture is such that information can travel far and fast through the local activation of ties. Neither the formation of those ties nor the decision to activate them responds to a grand plan: actors connected in a decentralized network make decisions without much awareness of how those decisions will concatenate to give structure and rhythm to the networks of which they are part. Likewise, oftentimes networks derail intentional interventions, as when viral marketing campaigns fail to actually go viral. The way in which cumulative effects roll out in social networks is another example of unintended consequence. On the positive side, when used in the context of recommender systems or collaborative filtering, these cumulative effects might direct attention to content that would otherwise be obscured. These dynamics, in turn, have the potential to flatten access to public attention and democratize culture. The negative side is that these same dynamics can also reinforce inequality and rich-get-richer effects, consolidating asymmetries that are then difficult to overcome.

Many social facts rely on these dynamics, i.e., the definition of a situation as real is not real until it gains the right collective resonance and triggers a large-enough chain reaction. This is one of the limits that restrict constructivist approaches to social life: not everything depends on our mental representations of the world. Yet dynamics like the diffusion of misinformation illustrate the power of networks to build realities that do not correspond with the facts. Can we devise strategies to prevent that flow, that is, to build firewalls that will contain the progress of conspiracies or lies? The previous chapters considered from different angles the challenges that this sort of intervention might pose. Trying to control networks might clash with individual choices and with the right to autonomy and self-determination. This, the previous chapters argued, is a question that transcends the internal logic of research; it demands listening to the concerns of the general public, and engaging in open-ended conversations to try to solve hard tradeoffs. The role that researchers can have in these discussions is to determine the facts—and how much of the problem derives from the tension between what we know and what we still ignore.

Online networks are so pervasive and essential to the current social order that they have, inevitably, become a contested political territory—of which this book has also given a few examples. Online networks have played a very visible role in political protests around the globe; they have also allowed (as a byproduct) the emergence of new political actors whose main weapon is to challenge old gatekeepers of information. At the same time, digital technologies have become a new beacon of power, the golden-eggs goose that triggered the whirlwind of what some call "data capitalism," which is the ideological version of the already aging term "big data." This is yet another way in which technologies encode social change—and the reason why so many actors are trying to control network dynamics.

Technologies have always been instrumental in the organization of social movements and political action. The printing press helped the Lutheran revolution spread; the telegraph allowed news to travel fast as protests contorted the face of Europe in 1848; and mass newspapers became, a few decades later, the most influential agitators during one of the greatest political scandals in modern history, the Dreyfus affair. Social movements have always made use of communication technologies to organize in new ways and to push for social transformations. This is what gives communication so much power: if used instrumentally, it can reach and shape the hearts and minds of the people. Digital technologies, however, have uncovered a different, subtler reason why communication is so powerful. The reason is that it makes actions interdependent, triggering chain reactions that are beyond the control of any one individual.

This book has given many examples of why this type of interdependence can be so consequential—and at the same time so difficult to govern. The network effects that characterize digital technologies are just the skin-deep version of the deeper logic that articulates social life: actions trigger reactions that feed back in the process to build up dynamics that are difficult to anticipate. This form of power cannot be analyzed in the terminology of conflicting interests and media bias. It arises from the way in which communication enforces social influence, and from the feedback effects that amplify random initial advantages to create inequality but also to allow minority voices to suddenly reach the public spotlight. The previous chapters opened a window on how these dynamics unfold, and suggested strategies to think about how to best intervene in those networks, knowing that those interventions will surely trigger further reactions.

8.5   When Is the Code Cracked?

This question is probably the easiest to answer of all the questions asked: as long as communication keeps on adding stochastic dynamics to social life, the code will never be fully cracked. The stochastic nature of social life is the reason why our depiction of the world will never be complete. Much in the same way as cryptographers (to follow up with the metaphor) reallocate probabilities as new encrypted messages are intercepted, we have to keep on updating our judgments of the world as new information comes in. This is why data science can make a difference: it offers the modeling techniques that allow us to adapt our knowledge to that constant flow of information. The key issue here is that, even if we understand the mechanisms that activate social dynamics, we can still be uncertain about the outcomes. We need to constantly revisit algorithms and data analyses—to stay reactive to an ever-changing reality.

And yet there is little doubt (or so it should seem at the end of this book) that we have made great progress since the first social thinkers approximated the social world with the aid of analogies. Analogies offer the first mental bridge to turn the unknown into known territory; they help transform the new and puzzling into familiar concepts that help us grasp the complexity. But progress in actual understanding depends on our ability to unpack those analogies and test the assumed operating mechanisms with specific data. Digital technologies have resolved many of the measurement issues that in the past prevented our taking that step. They have also created other measurement and modeling issues that often require going back to analogies to try to find an entry point that can help crack the problem. Our current communication revolution is, in any case, pushing us to think outside the box—or, rather, outside the spinning circle of usual arguments that are made, over and over, to praise or condemn technological developments.

The cumulative approach to research, on which technological but also policy innovations rely, is a never-ending journey. Along the way, critical voices always arise—which can encourage progress but also distract from the actual challenges. In the end, finding fault is easy; identifying actionable ways to improve the state of the art is much more complicated. This book has advocated for the creative impulse that can help push the current frontiers, encouraged by the distance traveled since the first systematic efforts to explain the social world. The hope is that these pages have made this sense of possibility seem encouraging and real. What is most important is to realize that the technological and the social are no longer separate realms. We reinforce social structure when we build technologies.

We regulate social interactions when we implement algorithms. We change individual decisions with the design of interfaces. Technologies, in other words, are becoming the invisible scaffolding that supports every dimension of social life. The previous chapters have given examples of how to confront the challenges created by digital technologies when it comes to thinking about the world we live in and the world we would like to build. These challenges can only be solved by bringing together the insights of data science and the long-held wisdom of social thought, with its sobering approach to the human condition—but also its undeterred will to understand the social world in its mind-blowing complexity.

References

Adamic, L. A., and Huberman, B. A. (2000). Power-Law Distribution of the World Wide Web. *Science*, *287*, A2115.

Adams, J., and Moody, J. (2007). To Tell the Truth: Measuring Concordance in Multiply Reported Network Data. *Social Networks*, *29*(1), 44–58.

Adorno, T. W., Albert, H., Dahrendorf, R., Habermas, J., Pilot, H., and Popper, K. R. (1976 [1969]). *The Positivist Dispute in German Sociology* (G. Adey and D. Frisby, Trans.). London: Heinemann.

Aguirre, B. E., Quarantelli, E. L., and Mendoza, J. L. (1988). The Collective Behavior of Fads: The Characteristics, Effects, and Career of Streaking. *American Sociological Review*, *53*(4), 569–584.

Albert, R., Jeong, H., and Barabási, A. L. (1999). Diameter of the World-Wide Web. *Nature*, *401*, 130–131.

Allende, S. (1973). *Chile's Road to Socialism*. Harmondsworth: Penguin Books.

Allport, G. W. (1979). *The Nature of Prejudice*. New York: Perseus.

Alvarez-Hamelin, J. I., Dall'Asta, L., Barrat, A., and Vespignani, A. (2005). Large Scale Networks Fingerprinting and Visualization Using the k-Core Decomposition. Paper presented at the Advances in Neural Information Processing Systems.

Anderson, C. (2007). *The Long Tail: How Endless Choice Is Creating Unlimited Demand*. London: Random House.

Aral, S. (2016). The Future of Weak Ties. *American Journal of Sociology*, *121*(6), 1931–1939. doi:10.1086/686293.

Aral, S., and Van Alstyne, M. (2011). The Diversity-Bandwidth Trade-off. *American Journal of Sociology*, *117*(1), 90–171. doi:10.1086/661238.

Aral, S., and Walker, D. (2012). Identifying Influential and Susceptible Members of Social Networks. *Science*, *337*, 337–341.

Aral, S., Muchnik, L., and Sundararajan, A. (2013). Engineering Social Contagions: Optimal Network Seeding in the Presence of Homophily. *Network Science, 1*(02), 125–153. doi:10.1017/nws.2013.6.

Arendt, H. (1958). *The Human Condition.* Chicago: University of Chicago Press.

Arendt, H. (1973). *The Origins of Totalitarianism.* Orlando, FL: Houghton Mifflin Harcourt.

Arthur, C. (2014). Facebook Emotion Study Breached Ethical Guidelines, Researchers Say. *The Guardian* (June 30). Retrieved from https://www.theguardian.com/technology/2014/jun/30/facebook-emotion-study-breached-ethical-guidelines-researchers-say.

Bagehot, W. (2007 [1872]). *Physics and Politics.* New York: Cosimo Classics.

Bakshy, E., Karrer, B., and Adamic, L. (2009). Social Influence and the Diffusion of User-Generated Content. Paper presented at the Second ACM International Conference on Web Search and Data Mining.

Bakshy, E., Rosenn, I., Marlow, C. A., and Adamic, L. (2012). The Role of Social Networks in Information Diffusion. Paper presented at the International Conference on Web and Social Media, Dublin.

Barabási, A. L. (2005). The Origin of Bursts and Heavy Tails in Human Dynamics. *Nature, 435*, 207–211.

Barabási, A. L. (2011). *Bursts: The Hidden Patterns behind Everything We Do, from Your E-mail to Bloody Crusades.* New York: Dutton.

Barabási, A. L., and Albert, R. (1999). Emergence of Scaling in Random Networks. *Science, 286*, 509–512. doi:10.1126/science.286.5439.509.

Barabási, A. L., Albert, R., and Jeong, H. (2000). Scale-Free Characteristics of Random Networks: The Topology of the World Wide Web. *Physica A, 281*, 69–77.

Barberá, P., Wang, N., Bonneau, R., Jost, J., Nagler, J., Tucker, J., et al. (2015). The Critical Periphery in the Growth of Social Protests. *PLoS One, 10*(11).

Basta, L. A., Richmond, T. S., and Wiebe, D. J. (2010). Neighborhoods, Daily Activities, and Measuring Health Risks Experienced in Urban Environments. *Social Science and Medicine, 71*(11), 1943–1950.

Batty, M. (2013). *The New Science of Cities.* Cambridge, MA: MIT Press.

Becker, H. S. (1963). *Outsiders: Studies in the Sociology of Deviance.* New York: Free Press.

Beer, S. (1974). *Designing Freedom.* Toronto: CBC Publications.

Benkler, Y. (2006). *The Wealth of Networks: How Social Production Transforms Markets and Freedom.* New Haven: Yale University Press.

Benner, K. (2016). Airbnb Adopts Rules to Fight Discrimination by Its Hosts. *New York Times* (September 8). Retrieved from http://www.nytimes.com/2016/09/09/technology/airbnb-anti-discrimination-rules.html.

Berger, J. (2013). *Contagious: Why Things Catch On*. London: Simon and Schuster.

Bernays, E. (1928). *Propaganda*. Brooklyn, NY: Ig Publishing.

Berners-Lee, T., and Fischetti, M. (2000). *Weaving the Web: The Past, Present and Future of the World Wide Web by Its Inventor*. London: Texere.

Bicchieri, C. (2005). *The Grammar of Society: The Nature and Dynamics of Social Norms*. Cambridge: Cambridge University Press.

Biggs, M. (2005). Strikes as Forest Fires: Chicago and Paris in the Late Nineteenth Century. *American Journal of Sociology, 110*(6), 1684–1714.

Biggs, M. (2010). Self-Fulfilling Prophecies. In P. Bearman and P. Hedström (Eds.), *Handbook of Analytical Sociology*. Oxford: Oxford University Press.

Blainey, G. (1968). *The Tyranny of Distance: How Distance Shaped Australia's History*. London: Macmillan.

Blass, T. (2009). *The Man Who Shocked the World: The Life and Legacy of Stanley Milgram*. New York: Basic Books.

Blumer, H. (1946). Collective Behavior. In A. M. Lee (Ed.), *New Outline of the Principles of Sociology*. New York: Barnes and Noble.

Bond, R. M., Fariss, C. J., Jones, J. J., Kramer, A. D. I., Marlow, C. A., Settle, J. E., et al. (2012). A 61-Million-Person Experiment in Social Influence and Political Mobilization. *Nature, 489*, 295–298. doi:10.1038/nature11421.

Borgatti, S. P., and Everett, M. G. (1999). Models of Core/Periphery Structures. *Social Networks, 21*(4), 375–395.

Borge-Holthoefer, J., and González-Bailón, S. (2017). Geographies of Change: Networks of Influence in the Spatial Diffusion of Twitter Activity. Working paper.

Borge-Holthoefer, J., Perra, N., Gonçalves, B., González-Bailón, S., Arenas, A., Moreno, Y., et al. (2016). The Dynamics of Information-Driven Coordination Phenomena: A Transfer Entropy Analysis. *Science Advances, 2*(4).

Borges, J. L. (1998 [1946]). *Collected Fictions* (A. Hurley, Trans.). London: Penguin.

Boudon, R. (1982). *The Unintended Consequences of Social Action*. London: Macmillan.

boyd, d., and Crawford, K. (2012). Critical Questions for Big Data: Provocations for a Cultural, Technological, and Scholarly Phenomenon. *Information, Communication and Society , 15*(5), 662–679.

Braman, S. (2009). *Change of State: Information, Policy, and Power*. Cambridge, MA: MIT Press.

Briggs, A., and Burke, P. (2009). *A Social History of the Media: From Gutenberg to the Internet.* Cambridge: Polity Press.

Briggs, C. F., and Maverick, A. (1858). *The Story of the Telegraph.* New York: Rudd and Carleton.

Brin, S., and Page, L. (1998). The Anatomy of a Large-Scale Hypertextual Web Search Engine. *Computer Networks and ISDN Systems, 30,* 107–117.

Broder, A., Kumar, R., Maghoul, F., Raghavan, P., and Rajagopalan, S. (2000). Graph Structure in the Web. *Computer Networks, 33,* 309–320.

Bronowski, J. (1978). *The Origins of Knowledge and Imagination.* New Haven: Yale University Press.

Brown, L. (1974). TV Networks Seek to Avoid Streaking Incidents. *New York Times* (March 29), 71.

Brunton, F., and Nissenbaum, H. (2015). *Obfuscation: A User's Guide for Privacy and Protest.* Cambridge, MA: MIT Press.

Burt, R. S. (1992). *Structural Holes: The Social Structure of Competition.* Cambridge, MA: Harvard University Press.

Burt, R. S. (2005). *Brokerage and Closure: An Introduction to Social Capital.* Oxford: Oxford University Press.

Cadwalladr, C. (2016). Google, Democracy and the Truth about Internet Search. *The Guardian* (December 4). Retrieved from https://www.theguardian.com/technology/2016/dec/04/google-democracy-truth-internet-search-facebook

Calvino, I. (1995). *Numbers in the Dark and Other Stories* (T. Parks, Trans.). New York: Vintage Books.

Candia, J., González, M. C., Wang, P., Schoenharl, T., Madey, G., and Barabási, A.-L. (2008). Uncovering Individual and Collective Human Dynamics from Mobile Phone Records. *Journal of Physics A: Mathematical and Theoretical, 41*(22), 224015.

Carley, K. M. (2006). Destabilization of Covert Networks. *Computational and Mathematical Organization Theory, 12*(1), 51–66. doi:10.1007/s10588-006-7083-y.

Carr, D. (2012). Hashtag Activism, and Its Limits. *New York Times* (March 25). Retrieved from http://nyti.ms/1B9DwAd.

Carr, N. G. (2010). *The Shallows: How the Internet Is Changing the Way We Think, Read and Remember.* London: Atlantic Books.

Carroll, L. (1893). *Sylvie and Bruno Concluded.* London: Macmillan.

Castillo, C. (2016). *Big Crisis Data: Social Media in Disaster and Time-Critical Situations.* Cambridge: Cambridge University Press.

Castillo, C., El-Haddad, M., Pfeffer, J., and Stempeck, M. (2014). Characterizing the Life Cycle of Online News Stories Using Social Media Reactions. Paper presented at the Proceedings of the 17th ACM conference on Computer Supported Cooperative Work and Social Computing, Baltimore, Maryland.

Centola, D. (2010). The Spread of Behavior in an Online Social Network Experiment. *Science*, *329*, 1194–1197.

Centola, D., and Macy, M. W. (2007). Complex Contagions and the Weakness of Long Ties. *American Journal of Sociology*, *113*(3), 702–734.

Chadwick, A. (2006). *Internet Politics: States, Citizens, and New Communication Technologies*. New York: Oxford University Press.

Chokshi, N. (2016). Snowden and WikiLeaks Clash over How to Disclose Secrets. *New York Times* (July 29). Retrieved from http://www.nytimes.com/2016/07/30/us/snowden-wikileaks.html.

Christakis, N. A., and Fowler, J. H. (2009). *Connected: The Surprising Power of Our Social Networks and How They Shape Our Lives*. New York: Little, Brown.

Christian, B., and Griffiths, T. (2016). *Algorithms to Live By: The Computer Science of Human Decisions*. New York: Henry Holt.

Clark, T. N. (1969). Introduction to Gabriel Tarde, *On Communication and Social Influence*. Chicago: University of Chicago Press.

Clark, T. N. (1973). *Prophets and Patrons: The French University and the Emergence of the Social Sciences*. Cambridge, MA: Harvard University Press.

Clark, V. F. (2013). *Salvador Allende: Revolutionary Democrat*. New York: Pluto Press.

Clarke, K. (2016). Does Airbnb Enable Racism? *New York Times* (August 23). Retrieved from http://www.nytimes.com/2016/08/23/opinion/how-airbnb-can-fight-racial-discrimination.html.

Coates, R. M. (1947). The Law. *New Yorker* (November 29), 41–43.

Çolak, S., Lima, A., and González, M. C. (2016). Understanding Congested Travel in Urban Areas. *Nature Communications*, *7*, 10793. doi:10.1038/ncomms10793.

Coleman, G. (2014). *Hacker, Hoaxer, Whistleblower, Spy: The Many Faces of Anonymous*. London: Verso.

Comte, A. (1830–1842). *Cours de philosophie positive*. Paris: Bachelier.

Conover, M. D., Davis, C., Ferrara, E., McKelvey, K., Menczer, F., and Flammini, A. (2013). The Geospatial Characteristics of a Social Movement Communication Network. *PLoS One*, *8*(3), e55957. doi:10.1371/journal.pone.0055957.

Conover, M. D., Ferrara, E., Menczer, F., and Flammini, A. (2013). The Digital Evolution of Occupy Wall Street. *PLoS One*, *8*(5), e64679. doi:10.1371/journal. pone.0064679.

Contractor, N. S., and DeChurch, L. A. (2014). Integrating Social Networks and Human Social Motives to Achieve Social Influence at Scale. *Proceedings of the National Academy of Sciences of the United States of America*, *111*(Supplement 4), 13650–13657. doi:10.1073/pnas.1401211111.

Crawford, K. (2013). The Hidden Biases in Big Data. HBR Blog Network, 1.

Crawford, K. (2016). Asking the Oracle. In L. Poitras (Ed.), *Astro Noise: A Survival Guide for Living under Total Surveillance*. New Haven: Yale University Press.

Crosby, A. W. (1997). *The Measure of Reality: Quantification in Western Europe, 1250–1600*. Cambridge: Cambridge University Press.

Crowcroft, J. (2007). Net Neutrality: The Technical Side of the Debate: A White Paper. *Computer Communication Review*, *37*(1), 49–56. doi:10.1145/1198255.1198263.

Csermely, P., London, A., Wu, L. Y., & Uzzi, B. (2013). Structure and Dynamics of Core/Periphery Networks. *Journal of Complex Networks*. doi:10.1093/comnet/cnt016.

Daley, D. J., and Kendall, D. G. (1964). Epidemics and Rumours. *Nature*, *204*(4963), 1118.

Davies, W. (2017). How Statistics Lost Their Power—and Why We Should Fear What Comes Next. *The Guardian* (January 19). Retrieved from https://www.theguardian .com/politics/2017/jan/19/crisis-of-statistics-big-data-democracy.

De Domenico, M., Sole-Ribalta, A., Omodei, E., Gomez, S., and Arenas, A. (2015). Ranking in Interconnected Multilayer Networks Reveals Versatile Nodes. *Nature Communications*, *6*. doi:10.1038/ncomms7868.

de Montjoye, Y.-A., Hidalgo, C. A., Verleysen, M., and Blondel, V. D. (2013). Unique in the Crowd: The Privacy Bounds of Human Mobility. *Scientific Reports*, *3*, 1376. doi:10.1038/srep01376.

de Sola Pool, I., and Kochen, M. (1978). Contacts and Influence. *Social Networks*, *1*(1), 5–51.

Del Vicario, M., Bessi, A., Zollo, F., Petroni, F., Scala, A., and Caldarelli, G., Stanley, H. E., and Quattrociocchi, W. (2016). The Spreading of Misinformation Online. *Proceedings of the National Academy of Sciences*, *113*(3), 554–559. doi:10.1073/ pnas.1517441113

Dietz, K. (1967). Epidemics and Rumours: A Survey. *Journal of the Royal Statistical Society. Series A (General)*, *130*(4), 505–528. doi:10.2307/2982521.

DiPrete, T. A., and Eirich, G. M. (2006). Cumulative Advantage as a Mechanism for Inequality: A Review of Theoretical and Empirical Developments. *Annual Review of Sociology, 32*(1), 271–297. doi:10.1146/annurev.soc.32.061604.123127.

Dodds, P. S., Muhamad, R., and Watts, D. J. (2003). An Experimental Study of Search in Global Social Networks. *Science, 301*(5634), 827–829.

Donaldson, L. J., Cavanagh, J., and Rankin, J. (1997). The Dancing Plague. *Public Health, 111*(4), 201–204. doi:10.1038/sj.ph.1900371.

Drezner, D. W. (2016). Why the Post-Truth Political Era Might Be Around for a While. *Washington Post* (July 11). Retrieved from https://www.washingtonpost.com/posteverything/wp/2016/06/16/why-the-post-truth-political-era-might-be-around-for-a-while.

Durkheim, É. (1982 [1895]). *The Rules of Sociological Method* (S. Lukes, Ed.). New York: Free Press.

Durkheim, É. (2001 [1912]). *The Elementary Forms of Religious Life.* Oxford: Oxford University Press.

Dutton, W. H. (2017). Fake News, Echo Chambers and Filter Bubbles: Under-researched and Overhyped. *The Conversation,* May 5. http://theconversation.com/fake-news-echo-chambers-and-filter-bubbles-underresearched-and-overhyped-76688?utm_source=twitter&utm_medium=twitterbutton.

Dwork, C., and Roth, A. (2014). The Algorithmic Foundations of Differential Privacy. *Foundations and Trends in Theoretical Computer Science , 9*(3–4), 211–407. doi:10.1561/0400000042.

Eagle, N., and Greene, K. (2014). *Reality Mining: Using Big Data to Engineer a Better World.* Cambridge, MA: MIT Press.

Eagle, N., Macy, M. W., and Claxton, R. (2010). Network Diversity and Economic Development. *Science, 328,* 1029–1031.

Earl, J., and Kimport, K. (2011). *Digitally Enabled Social Change: Activism in the Internet Age.* Cambridge, MA: MIT Press.

Easley, D., and Kleinberg, J. (2010). *Networks, Crowds, and Markets: Reasoning about a Highly Connected World.* New York: Cambridge University Press.

Edelman, B. G., Luca, M., and Svirsky, D. (2016). Racial Discrimination in the Sharing Economy: Evidence from a Field Experiment. Harvard Business School Working Paper, 16(069).

Editorial Board. (2015). Global Threats to Net Neutrality. *New York Times* (April 10). Retrieved from http://www.nytimes.com/2015/04/10/opinion/global-threats-to-net-neutrality.html.

Editors. (2014). Editorial Expression of Concern: Experimental Evidence of Massive Scale Emotional Contagion through Social Networks. *Proceedings of the National Academy of Sciences of the United States of America*, *111*(29), 10779. doi:10.1073/pnas.1412469111.

Edunov, S., Diuk, C. G., Filiz, O. I., Bhagat, S., and Burke, M. (2016). Three and a Half Degrees of Separation. Retrieved from https://research.fb.com/blog/three-and-a-half -degrees-of-separation/.

Eisenstein, E. L. (2012). *The Printing Revolution in Early Modern Europe*. Cambridge: Cambridge University Press.

Eligon, J. (2015). One Slogan, Many Methods: Black Lives Matter Enters Politics. *New York Times* (November 18). Retrieved from http://nyti.ms/1S5uryn.

Ellis, E. G. (2016). WikiLeaks Has Officially Lost the Moral High Ground. *Wired* (July 27). Retrieved from https://www.wired.com/2016/07/wikileaks-officially-lost -moral-high-ground/

Engels, F. (1987 [1892]). *The Condition of the Working Class in England*. London: Penguin.

Etzioni, A. (1999). *The Limits of Privacy*. New York: Basic Books.

European Commission. (2015). Data Protection Reform. European Commission—Fact Sheet (December 21). Retrieved from http://europa.eu/rapid/press-release _MEMO-15-6385_en.htm

Everton, S. (2013). *Disrupting Dark Networks*. Cambridge: Cambridge University Press.

Ferguson, A. (1767). *An Essay on the History of Civil Society*. London: T. Caddel.

Fischer, C. S. (1994). *America Calling: A Social History of the Telephone to 1940*. Berkeley: University of California Press.

Fortunato, S. (2010). Community Detection in Graphs. *Physics Reports*, *486*(3–5), 75–174.

Fortunato, S., and Hric, D. (2016). Community Detection in Networks: A User Guide. arXiv:1608.00163.

Franke, R. H., and Kaul, J. D. (1978). The Hawthorne Experiments: First Statistical Interpretation. *American Sociological Review*, *43*(5), 623–643. doi:10.2307/2094540.

Fraser, N. (1990). Rethinking the Public Sphere: A Contribution to the Critique of Actually Existing Democracy. *Social Text* (25/26): 56–80. doi:10.2307/466240.

Freedom House. (2015). Freedom in the World 2015: The Annual Survey of Political Rights and Civil Liberties. http://www.freedomhouse.org/report/freedom-world/ freedom-world-2015.

Galton, F. (1907). Vox Populi. *Nature, 75*(7), 450–451. doi:10.1038/075450a0.

Gerbaudo, P. (2012). *Tweets and the Streets: Social Media and Contemporary Activism.* London: Pluto Books.

Gershenson, C., and Helbing, D. (2015). When Slower Is Faster. *Complexity, 21*(2), 9–15.

Gibbs, S. (2016). European Parliament Approves Tougher Data Privacy Rules. *The Guardian* (April 14). Retrieved from https://www.theguardian.com/technology/2016/apr/14/european-parliament-approve-tougher-data-privacy-rules.

Giles, J. (2005). Internet Encyclopaedias Go Head to Head. *Nature, 438*(7070), 900–901.

Ginsberg, J., Mohebbi, M. H., Patel, R. S., Brammer, L., Smolinski, M. S., and Brilliant, L. (2009). Detecting Influenza Epidemics Using Search Engine Query Data. *Nature, 457*, 1012–1014.

Girardin, F., Blat, J., Calabrese, F., Dal Fiore, F., and Ratti, C. (2008). Digital Footprinting: Uncovering Tourists with User-Generated Content. *IEEE Pervasive Computing, 7*(4), 36–43. doi:10.1109/mprv.2008.71.

Giridharadas, A. (2010). Africa's Gift to Silicon Valley: How to Track a Crisis. *New York Times* (March 13). Retrieved from http://www.nytimes.com/2010/03/14/weekinreview/14giridharadas.html.

Gitelman, L. (Ed.). (2013). *Raw Data Is an Oxymoron.* Cambridge, MA: MIT Press.

Gleick, J. (1988). *Chaos: Making a New Science.* London: Penguin.

Gleick, J. (2011). *The Information: A History, a Theory, a Flood.* New York: Knopf Doubleday.

Goel, S., Anderson, A., Hofman, J., and Watts, D. J. (2016). The Structural Virality of Online Diffusion. *Management Science, 62*(1), 180–196. doi:10.1287/mnsc.2015.2158.

Goel, S., Muhamad, R., and Watts, D. (2009). Social Search in "Small-World" Experiments. Paper presented at the Proceedings of the 18th International Conference on World Wide Web, Madrid, Spain.

Goel, S., Watts, D. J., and Goldstein, D. G. (2012). The Structure of Online Diffusion Networks. Proceedings of the 13th ACM Conference on Electronic Commerce (EC'12). doi:10.1145/2229012.2229058

Goel, V. (2014). Facebook Tinkers with Users' Emotions in News Feed Experiment, Stirring Outcry. *New York Times* (June 29). Retrieved from http://www.nytimes.com/2014/06/30/technology/facebook-tinkers-with-users-emotions-in-news-feed-experiment-stirring-outcry.html.

Goffman, E. (1963). *Stigma: Notes on the Management of Spoiled Identity*. Upper Saddle River, NJ: Prentice-Hall.

Goffman, W., and Newill, V. A. (1964). Generalization of Epidemic Theory: An Application to the Transmission of Ideas. *Nature, 204*(4955), 225–228.

Gonzalez, M. C., Hidalgo, C. A., and Barabási, A. L. (2008). Understanding Individual Human Mobility Patterns. *Nature, 453,* 779–782.

González-Bailón, S. (2013a). Big Data and the Fabric of Human Geography. *Dialogues in Human Geography, 3*(3), 292–296. doi:10.1177/2043820613515379.

González-Bailón, S. (2013b). From Chiapas to Tahrir: Networks and the Diffusion of Protest. *World Politics Review*, April 16. http://www.worldpoliticsreview.com/articles/12872/from-chiapas-to-tahrir-networks-and-the-diffusion-of-protest.

González-Bailón, S., Borge-Holthoefer, J., Rivero, A., and Moreno, Y. (2011). The Dynamics of Protest Recruitment through an Online Network. *Scientific Reports, 1,* 197.

González-Bailón, S., Borge-Holthoefer, J., Rivero, A., & Moreno, Y. (2013). Broadcasters and Hidden Influentials in Online Protest Diffusion. *American Behavioral Scientist, 57*(7), 943–965. doi:10.1177/0002764213479371.

González-Bailón, S., and Wang, N. (2016). Networked Discontent: The Anatomy of Protest Campaigns in Social Media. *Social Networks, 44,* 95–104.

González-Bailón, S., Wang, N., and Borge-Holthoefer, J. (2014). The Emergence of Roles in Large-Scale Networks of Communication. *EPJ Data Science, 3*(1), 1–16. doi:10.1140/epjds/s13688-014-0032-y.

Goodchild, M. F. (2007). Citizens as Voluntary Sensors: Spatial Data Infrastructure in the World of Web 2.0. *International Journal of Spatial Data Infrastructures Research, 2,* 24–32.

Graham, M. (2014). Internet Geographies: Data Shadows and Digital Divisions of Labor. In M. Graham and W. H. Dutton (Eds.), *Society and the Internet: How Networks of Information and Communication Are Changing Our Lives*. Oxford: Oxford University Press.

Graham, M., and Zook, M. (2011). Visualizing Global Cyberscapes: Mapping User-Generated Placemarks. *Journal of Urban Technology, 18*(1), 115–132.

Graham, M., Straumann, R. K., and Hogan, B. (2015). Digital Divisions of Labor and Informational Magnetism: Mapping Participation in Wikipedia. *Annals of the Association of American Geographers, 105*(6), 1158–1178. doi:10.1080/00045608.2015.1072791.

Granovetter, M. (1973). The Strength of Weak Ties. *American Journal of Sociology, 78,* 1360–1380.

Granovetter, M. (1974). *Getting a Job: A Study of Contacts and Careers*. Cambridge, MA: Harvard University Press.

Granovetter, M. (1978). Threshold Models of Collective Behavior. *American Journal of Sociology*, *83*(6), 1420–1443.

Greenwald, G. (2014). *No Place to Hide: Edward Snowden, the NSA, and the U.S. Surveillance State*. New York: Metropolitan Books.

Grewal, D. S. (2008). *Network Power: The Social Dynamics of Globalization*. New Haven: Yale University Press.

Haklay, M. (2010). How Good Is Volunteered Geographical Information? A Comparative Study of OpenStreetMap and Ordnance Survey Datasets. *Environment and Planning. B, Planning and Design*, *37*(4), 682–703. doi:10.1068/b35097.

Haklay, M., and Weber, P. (2008). OpenStreetMap: User-Generated Street Maps. *IEEE Pervasive Computing*, *7*(4), 12–18. doi:10.1109/MPRV.2008.80.

Hancock, J. T. (forthcoming). Introduction to the Ethics of Digital Research. In B. Foucault Welles & S. González-Bailón (Eds.), *The Oxford Handbook of Networked Communication*. New York: Oxford University Press.

Handy, C. (2015). The Seductions of the Infosphere. *Harvard Business Review* (July 15). Retrieved from https://hbr.org/2015/07/the-seductions-of-the-infosphere.

Harding, L., and Letsch, C. (2013). Turkish Police Arrest 25 People for Using Social Media to Call for Protest. *The Guardian* (June 5). Retrieved from http://www.theguardian.com/world/2013/jun/05/turkish-police-arrests-social-media-protest.

Hargittai, E., and Shaw, A. (2015). Mind the Skills Gap: The Role of Internet Know-How and Gender in Differentiated Contributions to Wikipedia. *Information Communication and Society*, *18*(4), 424–442. doi:10.1080/1369118X.2014.957711.

Hayek, F. A. (1966). Dr. Bernard Mandeville (Lecture on a Master Mind). *Proceedings of the British Academy*, *52*, 125–141.

Haythornthwaite, C., and Wellman, B. (1998). Work, Friendship, and Media Use for Information Exchange in a Networked Organization. *Journal of the American Society for Information Science*, *49*(12), 1101–1114.

Hecker, J. F. C. (1888). *The Black Death and the Dancing Mania*. London: Cassell.

Hedström, P. (1994). Contagious Collectivities: On the Spatial Diffusion of Swedish Trade Unions, 1890–1940. *American Journal of Sociology*, *99*(5), 1157–1179.

Herman, E. S., and Chomsky, N. (1988). *Manufacturing Consent: The Political Economy of the Mass Media*. New York: Pantheon.

Hirschman, A. O. (1982). *Shifting Involvements: Private Interest and Public Action*. Princeton, NJ: Princeton University Press.

Hirschman, A. O. (1991). *The Rhetoric of Reaction.* Cambridge, MA: Harvard University Press.

Hobsbawm, E. (2010 [1962]). *The Age of Revolution: 1789–1848.* London: Abacus.

Hoffman, A. L. (2016). Facebook Has a New Process for Discussing Ethics. But Is It Ethical? *The Guardian* (June 17).

Holme, P., and Saramäki, J. (2012). Temporal Networks. *Physics Reports*, *519*(3), 97–125.

Horowitz, D. (2000). *Vance Packard and American Social Criticism.* Chapel Hill: University of North Carolina Press.

Howard, P. N. (2015). *Pax Technica: How the Internet of Things May Set Us Free or Lock Us Up.* New Haven: Yale University Press.

Hristova, D., Noulas, A., Brown, C., Musolesi, M., and Mascolo, C. (2016). A Multilayer Approach to Multiplexity and Link Prediction in Online Geo-Social Networks. *EPJ Data Science*, *5*(24). doi:10.1140/epjds/s13688-016-0087-z.

Huberman, B. A. (2001). *The Laws of the Web: Patterns in the Ecology of Information.* Cambridge, MA: MIT Press.

Huberman, B. A., and Adamic, L. (1999). Growth Dynamics of the World-Wide Web. *Nature*, *401*, 131.

IBM. (2015). The Internet of Things. Retrieved from http://www.ibm.com/smarterplanet/us/en/overview/article/iot_video.html.

Isaacson, W. (2014). *The Innovators: How a Group of Hackers, Geniuses, and Geeks Created the Digital Revolution.* New York: Simon and Schuster.

Jackman, M., and Kanerva, L. (2016). Evolving the IRB: Building Robust Review for Industry Research. *Washington and Lee Law Review Online* , *72*(3).

Jackson, S. J., and Foucault Welles, B. (2015). Hijacking #myNYPD: Social Media Dissent and Networked Counterpublics. *Journal of Communication*, *65*(6), 932–952. doi:10.1111/jcom.12185.

Jacobs, J. (1961). *The Death and Life of Great American Cities.* London: Pimlico.

Jiang, S., Yang, Y., Gupta, S., Veneziano, D., Athavale, S., and González, M. C. (2016). The TimeGeo Modeling Framework for Urban Mobility without Travel Surveys. *Proceedings of the National Academy of Sciences of the United States of America*, *113*(37), E5370–E5378. doi:10.1073/pnas.1524261113.

Johansen, A. (2004). Probing Human Response Times. *Physica A*, *338*(1–2), 286–291. doi:10.1016/j.physa.2004.02.054.

Johnson, S. (2012). *Future Perfect: The Case for Progress in a Networked Age.* New York: Riverhead Books.

Kahneman, D. (2011). *Thinking, Fast and Slow*. New York: Farrar, Straus and Giroux.

Kahneman, D., Slovic, P., and Tversky, A. (1982). *Judgment under Uncertainty: Heuristics and Biases*. Cambridge: Cambridge University Press.

Kant, I. (2013 [1784]). *An Answer to the Question: "What Is Enlightenment?"* London: Penguin.

Katz, E. (1957). The Two-Step Flow of Communication: An Up-to-Date Report on a Hypothesis. *Public Opinion Quarterly*, *21*(1), 61–78.

Katz, E. (2006). Lazarsfeld's Legacy: The Power of Limited Effects. In E. Katz and P. Lazarsfeld, *Personal Influence: The Part Played by People in the Flow of Mass Communications*. New Brunswick, NJ: Transaction Publishers.

Katz, E., and Lazarsfeld, P. (1955). *Personal Influence: The Part Played by People in the Flow of Mass Communications*. New York: Free Press.

Katz, E., Ali, C., and Kim, J. (2014). *Echoes of Gabriel Tarde: What We Know Better or Different 100 Years Later*. INscribe Digital.

Kearns, M., Roth, A., Wu, Z. S., and Yaroslavtsev, G. (2016). Private Algorithms for the Protected in Social Network Search. *Proceedings of the National Academy of Sciences of the United States of America*, *113*(4), 913–918. doi:10.1073/pnas.1510612113.

Kivelä, M., Arenas, A., Barthelemy, M., Gleeson, J. P., Moreno, Y., and Porter, M. A. (2014). Multilayer Networks. *Journal of Complex Networks*, *2*(3), 203–271. doi:10.1093/comnet/cnu016.

Kleinberg, J. M. (2000). Navigation in a Small World. *Nature*, *406*, 845.

Knibbs, K. (2014). Protesters Are Using FireChat's Mesh Networks to Organize in Hong Kong. *Gizmodo* (September 29). Retrieved from http://gizmodo.com/protesters-are-using-firechat-to-organize-in-hong-kong-1640271776.

Korte, C., and Milgram, S. (1970). Acquaintance Networks between Racial Groups: Application of the Small World Method. *Journal of Personality and Social Psychology*, *15*(2), 101–108.

Kramer, A. D. I., Guillory, J. E., and Hancock, J. T. (2014). Experimental Evidence of Massive-Scale Emotional Contagion through Social Networks. *Proceedings of the National Academy of Sciences of the United States of America*, *111*(24), 8788–8790. doi:10.1073/pnas.1320040111.

Kuhn, T. S. (1962). *The Structure of Scientific Revolutions*. Chicago: University of Chicago Press.

Kwak, H., Lee, C., Park, H., and Moon, S. (2010). What Is Twitter, a Social Network or a News Media? Paper presented at the Proceedings of the 19th International World Wide Web Conference (WWW 2010).

Lancichinetti, A., and Fortunato, S. (2009). Community Detection Algorithms: A Comparative Analysis. *Physical Review. E, 80*(5), 056117.

Lang, K., and Lang, G. E. (1961). *Collective Dynamics*. New York: Crowell.

Lazarsfeld, P., Berelson, B., and Gaudet, H. (1948). *The People's Choice: How the Voter Makes Up His Mind in a Presidential Campaign*. New York: Columbia University Press.

Lazer, D. (2015). The Rise of the Social Algorithm. *Science, 348*(6239), 1090–1091. doi:10.1126/science.aab1422.

Lazer, D., Baum, M. A., Grinberg, N., Friedland, L., Joseph, K., Hobbs, W., et al. (2017). *Combating Fake News: An Agenda for Research and Action. Shorenstein Center on Media, Politics, and Public Policy, Kennedy School of Government*. Harvard University.

Lazer, D., and Friedman, A. (2007). The Network Structure of Exploration and Exploitation. *Administrative Science Quarterly, 52*, 667–694.

Lazer, D., Kennedy, R., King, G., and Vespignani, A. (2014). The Parable of Google Flu: Traps in Big Data Analysis. *Science, 343*(6176), 1203–1205. doi:10.1126/science.1248506.

Lazer, D., Pentland, A., Adamic, L., Aral, S., Barabási, A.-L., Brewer, D., et al. (2009). Computational Social Science. *Science, 323*, 721–723.

Le Bon, G. (1903 [1895]). *The Crowd: A Study of the Popular Mind*. London: T. F. Unwin.

Lehmann, J., Goncalves, B., Ramasco, J. J., and Cattuto, C. (2012). Dynamical Classes of Collective Attention in Twitter. Paper presented at the Proceedings of the 21st International Conference on World Wide Web, Lyon, France.

Leigh, D., and Harding, L. (2011). *Wikileaks: Inside Julian Assange's War on Secrecy*. New York: Public Affairs.

Lessig, L. (2006). *Code 2.0*. New York: Basic Books.

Liben-Nowell, D., and Kleinberg, J. M. (2008). Tracing Information Flow on a Global Scale Using Internet Chain-Letter Data. *Proceedings of the National Academy of Sciences of the United States of America, 105*(12), 4633–4638.

Liben-Nowell, D., Novak, J., Kumar, R., Raghavan, P., and Tomkins, A. (2005). Geographic Routing in Social Networks. *Proceedings of the National Academy of Sciences of the United States of America, 102*(33), 11623–11628. doi:10.1073/pnas.0503018102.

Lin, Z., Zhao, X., Ismail, K. M., and Carley, K. M. (2006). Organizational Design and Restructuring in Response to Crises: Lessons from Computational Modeling and Real-World Cases. *Organization Science, 17*(5), 598–618. doi:10.1287/orsc.1060.0210.

Lintott, C. J., Schawinski, K., Slosar, A., Land, K., Bamford, S., Thomas, D., et al. (2008). Galaxy Zoo: Morphologies Derived from Visual Inspection of Galaxies from the Sloan Digital Sky Survey. *Monthly Notices of the Royal Astronomical Society, 389*(3), 1179–1189.

Lippmann, W. (1920). *Liberty and the News*. New York: Harcourt, Brace and Howe.

Lippmann, W. (1922). *Public Opinion*. New York: Harcourt, Brace.

Lohmann, S. (1994). Dynamics of Informational Cascades: The Monday Demonstrations in Leipzig, East Germany, 1989–1991. *World Politics, 47*(1), 42–101.

Lohr, S. (2015). *Data-ism: The Revolution Transforming Decision Making, Consumer Behavior, and Almost Everything Else*. New York: HarperCollins.

Lorenz, J., Rauhut, H., Schweitzer, F., and Helbing, D. (2011). How Social Influence Can Undermine the Wisdom of Crowd Effect. *Proceedings of the National Academy of Sciences of the United States of America, 108*(22), 9020–9025. doi:10.1073/pnas.1008636108.

Lynch, K. A. (1960). *The Image of the City*. Cambridge, MA: MIT Press.

Mackay, C. (1841). *Memoirs of Extraordinary Popular Delusions and the Madness of Crowds*. London: Richard Bentley.

Madge, C., & Harrisson, T. (1939). *Britain by Mass-Observation*. Harmondsworth: Penguin.

Malmgren, R. D., Stouffer, D. B., Campanharo, A. S. L. O., and Amaral, L. A. N. (2009). On Universality in Human Correspondence Activity. *Science, 325*, 1696–1700.

Malmgren, R. D., Stouffer, D. B., Motter, A. E., and Amaral, L. A. N. (2008). A Poissonian Explanation for Heavy Tails in E-Mail Communication. *Proceedings of the National Academy of Sciences of the United States of America, 105*(47), 18153–18158.

Mandeville, B. (1988 [1714]). *The Fable of the Bees: Or Private Vices, Publick Benefits* (F. B. Kaye, Ed.). 2 vols. Indianapolis: Liberty Fund.

Margetts, H., John, P., Hale, S., and Yasseri, T. (2015). *Political Turbulence: How Social Media Shape Collective Action*. Princeton, NJ: Princeton University Press.

Marinetti, F. T. (1909). Manifeste de Futurisme. *Le Figaro* (February 20). Retrieved from http://gallica.bnf.fr/ark:/12148/bpt6k2883730.langFR.

Marvin, C. (1988). *When Old Technologies Were New: Thinking about Electric Communication in the Late Nineteenth Century*. New York: Oxford University Press.

Marx, G. T., & Wood, J. L. (1975). Strands of Theory and Research in Collective Behavior. *Annual Review of Sociology, 1*, 363–428.

Marx, K. (1992 [1867]). *Capital*. Vol. 1. London: Penguin Classics.

Mason, W., and Watts, D. J. (2012). Collaborative Learning in Networks. *Proceedings of the National Academy of Sciences of the United States of America, 109*(3), 764–769. doi:10.1073/pnas.1110069108.

May, D. (1896). L'enseignement social à Paris. *Revue Internationale de l'Enseignement, 32*, 1–33.

Mayer-Schoenberger, V., and Cukier, K. (2013). *Big Data: A Revolution That Will Transform How We Live, Work and Think.* London: John Murray.

McAdam, D. (1982). *Political Process and the Development of Black Insurgency, 1930–70.* Chicago: University of Chicago Press.

McAdam, D. (1986). Recruitment to High-Risk Activism: The Case of Freedom Summer. *American Journal of Sociology, 92*(1), 64–90.

McAdam, D., & Paulsen, R. (1993). Specifying the Relationship between Social Ties and Activism. *American Journal of Sociology, 99*(3), 640–667.

McAdam, D., Tarrow, S., and Tilly, C. (2001). *Dynamics of Contention.* Cambridge: Cambridge University Press.

McFadden, R. D. (1974). Streaking: A Mad Dash to Where? *New York Times* (March 8), 35, 41.

McNeil, D. G. (2016). Zika Virus Rumors and Theories That You Should Doubt. *New York Times* (February 19). Retrieved from http://nyti.ms/1Rb26XV.

McPhail, C., and Miller, D. (1973). The Assembling Process: A Theoretical and Empirical Examination. *American Sociological Review, 38*(6), 721–735.

Medina, E. (2011). *Cybernetic Revolutionaries: Technology and Politics in Allende's Chile.* Cambridge, MA: MIT Press.

Meier, P. (2015). *Digital Humanitarians: How Big Data Is Changing the Face of Humanitarian Response.* Boca Raton, FL: CRC Press.

Mejova, Y., Weber, I., and Macy, M. W. (2015). *Twitter: A Digital Socioscope.* Cambridge: Cambridge University Press.

Merton, R. K. (1936). The Unanticipated Consequences of Purposive Social Action. *American Sociological Review, 1*(6), 894–904.

Merton, R. K. (1948). The Self-Fulfilling Prophecy. *Antioch Review, 8*(2), 193–210. doi:10.2307/4609267.

Merton, R. K. (1957). Patterns of Influence: Local and Cosmopolitan Influentials. In *Social Theory and Social Structure*, 387–420. New York: Free Press.

Merton, R. K. (1968). The Matthew Effect in Science. *Science, 159*, 56–63.

Michelucci, P., and Dickinson, J. L. (2016). The Power of Crowds. *Science*, *351*(6268), 32–33. doi:10.1126/science.aad6499.

Milgram, S. (1967). The Small World Problem. *Psychology Today*, *2*, 60–67.

Milgram, S. (1970). The Experience of Living in Cities. *Science*, *167*(3924), 1461–1468. doi:10.1126/science.167.3924.1461.

Milgram, S. (1977). *The Individual in a Social World: Essays and Experiments*. London: Pinter and Martin.

Milgram, S., and Toch, H. (1969). Collective Behavior: Crowds and Social Movements. In G. Lindzey and E. Aronson (Eds.), *Handbook of Social Psychology*. 2nd ed. Reading, MA: Addison-Wesley.

Moody, J. (2002). The Importance of Relationship Timing for Diffusion. *Social Forces*, *81*(1), 25–56. doi:10.1353/sof.2002.0056.

Morozov, E. (2011). *The Net Delusion: How Not to Liberate the World*. London: Allen Lane.

Morozov, E. (2013). *To Save Everything, Click Here: The Folly of Technological Solutionism*. New York: Public Affairs.

Muchnik, L., Aral, S., and Taylor, S. J. (2013). Social Influence Bias: A Randomized Experiment. *Science*, *341*(6146), 647–651. doi:10.1126/science.1240466.

Murphy, L. W. (2016). Airbnb's Work to Fight Discrimination and Build Inclusion. Retrieved from http://blog.airbnb.com/wp-content/uploads/2016/09/REPORT _Airbnbs-Work-to-Fight-Discrimination-and-Build-Inclusion.pdf.

Mutz, D. C. (1998). *Impersonal Influence: How Perceptions of Mass Collectives Affect Political Attitudes*. Cambridge: Cambridge University Press.

Negroponte, N. (1995). *Being Digital*. London: Hodder and Stoughton.

Nissenbaum, H. (2009). *Privacy in Context: Technology, Policy, and the Integrity of Social Life*. Stanford, CA: Stanford University Press.

Norris, P. (2001). *Digital Divide: Civic Engagement, Information Poverty, and the Internet Worldwide*. Cambridge: Cambridge University Press.

Noveck, B. S. (2009). *Wiki-Government: How Technology Can Make Government Better, Democracy Stronger, and Citizens More Powerful*. Washington, DC: Brookings Institution.

Noveck, B. S. (2015). *Smart Citizens, Smarter State: The Technologies of Expertise and the Future of Governing*. Cambridge, MA: Harvard University Press.

Oliveira, J. G., and Barabási, A. L. (2005). Darwin and Einstein Correspondence Patterns. *Nature*, *437*, 1251.

O'Neil, C. (2016). *Weapons of Math Destruction: How Big Data Increases Inequality and Threatens Democracy*. New York: Penguin Random House.

Onnela, J.-P., and Reed-Tsochas, F. (2010). Spontaneous Emergence of Social Influence in Online Systems. *Proceedings of the National Academy of Sciences of the United States of America, 107*(43), 18375–18380.

Onnela, J.-P., Saramaki, J., Hyvonen, J., Szabo, G., Lazer, D., Kaski, K., et al. (2007). Structure and Tie Strengths in Mobile Communication Networks. *Proceedings of the National Academy of Sciences of the United States of America, 104*(18), 7332–7336.

O'Reilly, T. (2013). Open Data and Algorithmic Regulation. In B. Goldstein and L. Dyson (Eds.), *Beyond Transparency: Open Data and the Future of Civic Innovation*. San Francisco: Code for America Press.

Packard, V. (1957). *The Hidden Persuaders*. Philadelphia: David McKay.

Packard, V. (1964). *The Naked Society*. Philadelphia: David McKay.

Paldino, S., Bojic, I., Sobolevsky, S., Ratti, C., and Gonzalez, M. C. (2015). Urban Magnetism through the Lens of Geo-tagged Photography. *EPJ Data Science, 4*(1), 17. doi:10.1140/epjds/s13688-015-0043-3.

Papadopoulos, F., Kitsak, M., Serrano, M. A., Boguna, M., and Krioukov, D. (2012). Popularity versus Similarity in Growing Networks. *Nature, 489*(7417), 537–540.

Pariser, E. (2011). *The Filter Bubble: How the New Personalized Web Is Changing What We Read and How We Think*. New York: Penguin Press.

Park, R. E., and Burgess, E. W. (1921). *Introduction to the Science of Sociology*. Chicago: University of Chicago Press.

Park, R. E., and Burgess, E. W. (1984 [1925]). *The City: Suggestions for Investigation of Human Behavior in the Urban Environment*. Chicago: University of Chicago Press.

Pentland, A. (2014). *Social Physics: How Good Ideas Spread—the Lessons from a New Science*. New York: Penguin Press.

Petersen, A. M., Jung, W.-S., Yang, J.-S., and Stanley, H. E. (2011). Quantitative and Empirical Demonstration of the Matthew Effect in a Study of Career Longevity. *Proceedings of the National Academy of Sciences of the United States of America, 108*(1), 18–23. doi:10.1073/pnas.1016733108.

Pickard, G., Pan, W., Rahwan, I., Cebrian, M., Crane, R., Madan, A., et al. (2011). Time-Critical Social Mobilization. *Science, 334*(6055), 509–512. doi:10.1126/science.1205869.

Piedrahita, P., Borge-Holthoefer, J., Moreno, Y., and González-Bailón, S. (2017). The Contagion Effects of Repeated Activation in Social Networks. *Social Networks* (forthcoming).

Piedrahita, P., Borge-Holthoefer, J., Moreno, Y., and Arenas, A. (2013). Modeling Self-Sustained Activity Cascades in Socio-Technical Networks. *EPL* [Europhysics Letters], *104*(4), 48004.

Poitras, L. (Ed.). (2016). *Astro Noise: A Survival Guide for Living under Total Surveillance*. New Haven: Yale University Press.

Popper, K. R. (2002 [1957]). *The Poverty of Historicism*. London: Routledge.

Quercia, D., Pesce, J. P., Almeida, V., and Crowcroft, J. (2013). Psychological Maps 2.0: A Web Engagement Enterprise Starting in London. Paper presented at the World Wide Web Conference, Rio de Janeiro, May 13–17.

Quercia, D., Schifanella, R., and Aiello, L. M. (2014). The Shortest Path to Happiness: Recommending Beautiful, Quiet, and Happy Routes in the City. Paper presented at the Proceedings of the 25th ACM conference on Hypertext and Social Media, Santiago, Chile.

Quételet, A. (1835). *Sur l'homme et le developpement de ses facultés ou Essai de physique sociale*. Paris: Bachelier.

Rainie, L., and Wellman, B. (2012). *Networked: The New Social Operating System*. Cambridge, MA: MIT Press.

Ratti, C., and Claudel, M. (2016). *The City of Tomorrow: Sensors, Networks, Hackers, and the Future of Urban Life*. New Haven: Yale University Press.

Ratti, C., Sobolevsky, S., Calabrese, F., Andris, C., Reades, J., Martino, M., et al. (2010). Redrawing the Map of Great Britain from a Network of Human Interactions. *PLoS One*, *5*(12), e14248. doi:10.1371/journal.pone.0014248.

Rawlinson, K. (2014). Turkey Blocks Use of Twitter after Prime Minister Attacks Social Media Site. *The Guardian* (March 20). Retrieved from http://www.theguardian.com/world/2014/mar/21/turkey-blocks-twitter-prime-minister.

Read, P. P. (2012). *The Dreyfus Affair: The Scandal That Tore France in Two*. London: Bloomsbury Publishing.

Rheingold, H. (1994). *The Virtual Community*. London: Minerva.

Richtel, M. (2011). Egypt Cuts Off Most Internet and Cell Service. *New York Times* (January 28). Retrieved from http://www.nytimes.com/2011/01/29/technology/internet/29cutoff.html.

Roethlisberger, F. J., Dickson, W. J., Wright, H. A., Pforzheimer, C. H., and Western Electric, C. (1939). *Management and the Worker: An Account of a Research Program Conducted by the Western Electric Company, Hawthorne Works, Chicago*. Cambridge, MA: Harvard University Press.

Rogers, E. M. (2003). *Diffusion of Innovations*. 5th ed. New York: Free Press.

Romero, D. M., Meeder, B., and Kleinberg, J. (2011). Differences in the Mechanics of Information Diffusion across Topics: Idioms, Political Hashtags, and Complex Contagion on Twitter. Paper presented at the International World Wide Web Conference, Hyderabad, India.

Ross, J.-M. (2009, March 9). The Rise of the Social Nervous System. *Forbes.* Retrieved from http://www.forbes.com/2009/03/09/internet-innovations-hive-technology -breakthroughs-innovations.html.

Rutherford, A., Cebrian, M., Dsouza, S., Moro, E., Pentland, A., and Rahwan, I. (2013a). Limits of Social Mobilization. *Proceedings of the National Academy of Sciences of the United States of America, 110*(16), 6281–6286. doi:10.1073/pnas.1216338110.

Rutherford, A., Cebrian, M., Rahwan, I., Dsouza, S., McInerney, J., Naroditskiy, V., et al. (2013b). Targeted Social Mobilization in a Global Manhunt. *PLoS One, 8*(9), e74628. doi:10.1371/journal.pone.0074628.

Rutkin, A., and Aron, J. (2014). Hong Kong Protesters Use a Mesh Network to Organize. *New Scientist* (September 30). Retrieved from http://www.newscientist.com/ article/dn26285-hong-kong-protesters-use-a-mesh-network-to-organise.html.

Sainsbury, R. M. (2008). *Paradoxes.* Cambridge: Cambridge University Press.

Sakaki, T., Okazaki, M., and Matsuo, Y. (2010). Earthquake Shakes Twitter Users: Real-Time Event Detection by Social Sensors. Paper presented at the Proceedings of the 19th International Conference on World Wide Web, Raleigh, North Carolina.

Salganik, M. J., Dodds, P. S., and Watts, D. J. (2006). Experimental Study of Inequality and Unpredictability in an Artificial Cultural Market. *Science, 311,* 855–856.

Salganik, M. J., and Levy, K. E. C. (2015). Wiki Surveys: Open and Quantifiable Social Data Collection. *PLoS One, 10*(5), e0123483. doi:10.1371/journal.pone.0123483.

Sauter, M. (2014). *The Coming Swarm: DDOS Actions, Hacktivism, and Civil Disobedience on the Internet.* New York: Bloomsbury Publishing.

Scellato, S., Noulas, A., Lambiotte, R., and Mascolo, C. (2011). Socio-Spatial Properties of Online Location-Based Social Networks. *ICWSM, 11,* 329–336.

Schechner, S. (2014). Google Starts Removing Search Results under Europe's "Right to Be Forgotten." *Wall Street Journal* (June 26). Retrieved from http://www.wsj.com/ articles/google-starts-removing-search-results-under-europes-right-to-be-forgotten -1403774023.

Schelling, T. C. (1969). Models of Segregation. *American Economic Review, 59*(2), 488–493.

Schelling, T. C. (1978). *Micromotives and Macrobehavior.* New York: W. W. Norton.

Schneier, B. (2015). *Data and Goliath: The Hidden Battles to Collect Your Data and Control Your World*. New York: W. W. Norton.

Scott, J. C. (1999). *Seeing Like a State: How Certain Schemes to Improve the Human Condition Have Failed*. New Haven: Yale University Press.

Searle, J. R. (1995). *The Construction of Social Reality*. New York: Free Press.

Seidman, S. B. (1983). Network Structure and Minimum Degree. *Social Networks*, 5, 269–287.

Sengupta, S. (2012). The Soul of the New Hacktivist. *New York Times* (March 17). Retrieved from http://nyti.ms/1D1y6tJ.

Shibutani, T. (1966). *Improvised News: A Sociological Study of Rumor*. Indianapolis: Bobbs-Merrill.

Shirky, C. (2008). *Here Comes Everybody: The Power of Organizing without Organizations*. New York: Allen Lane.

Silver, N. (2012). *The Signal and the Noise: Why So Many Predictions Fail—but Some Don't*. New York: Penguin Press.

Simanowski, R. (2016). *Data Love: The Seduction and Betrayal of Digital Technologies*. New York: Columbia University Press.

Simmel, G. (1971 [1903]). The Metropolis and Mental Life. In Simmel, *On Individuality and Social Forms: Selected Writings* (D. N. Levine, Ed.). Chicago: University of Chicago Press.

Smith, A. (1759). *The Theory of Moral Sentiments*. London: A. Millar.

Smolan, R., and Erwitt, J. (2012). *The Human Face of Big Data*. New York: Against All Odds Productions.

Snijders, T. A. B., van de Bunt, G. G., and Steglich, C. E. G. (2010). Introduction to Stochastic Actor-Based Models for Network Dynamics. *Social Networks*, 32(1), 44–60. doi:10.1016/j.socnet.2009.02.004.

Song, C., Qu, Z., Blumm, N., and Barabási, A.-L. (2010). Limits of Predictability in Human Mobility. *Science*, 327(5968), 1018–1021. doi:10.1126/science.1177170.

Sontag, S. (1991). *Illness as Metaphor, and AIDS and Its Metaphors*. London: Penguin.

Spencer, H. (1873). *The Study of Sociology*. London: D. Appleton.

Spiro, E. S., Acton, R. M., & Butts, C. T. (2013). Extended Structures of Mediation: Re-Examining Brokerage In Dynamic Networks. *Social Networks*, 35(1), 130–143. doi:10.1016/j.socnet.2013.02.001.

Stamp, J. (2013, May 3). Fact of Fiction? The Legend of the QWERTY Keyword. Smithsonian.com. Retrieved from http://www.smithsonianmag.com/arts-culture/fact-of-fiction-the-legend-of-the-qwerty-keyboard-49863249.

Standage, T. (2009 [1998]). *The Victorian Internet: The Remarkable Story of the Telegraph and the Nineteenth Century's On-line Pioneers*. London: Bloomsbury Publishing.

Steel, E. (2014). "Ice Bucket Challenge" Has Raised Millions for ALS Association. *New York Times* (August 17). Retrieved from http://nyti.ms/1oTbWwg.

Steiner, C. (2012). *Automate This: How Algorithms Took Over Our Markets, Our Jobs, and the World*. London: Penguin.

Steinert-Threlkeld, Z. C., Mocanu, D., Vespignani, A., and Fowler, J. (2015). Online Social Networks and Offline Protest. *EPJ Data Science*, *4*(1), 19.

Sun, E., Rosenn, I., Marlow, C. A., and Lento, T. M. (2009). Gesundheit! Modeling Contagion through Facebook News Feed. Proceedings of the Third International Conference on Weblogs and Social Media, ICWSM'09.

Sunstein, C. R. (2016). *The Ethics of Influence: Government in the Age of Behavioral Science*. Cambridge: Cambridge University Press.

Sunstein, C. R. (2017). *#Republic: Divided Democracy in the Age of Social Media*. Princeton, NJ: Princeton University Press.

Surowiecki, J. (2004). *The Wisdom of Crowds*. New York: Anchor Books.

Surowiecki, J. (2016). What Happened to the Ice Bucket Challenge? *New Yorker* (July 25).

Tarde, G. (1969). *On Communication and Social Influence* (T. N. Clark, Ed.). Chicago: University of Chicago Press.

Thaler, R. H., and Sunstein, C. R. (2009). *Nudge: Improving Decisions about Health, Wealth, and Happiness*. New York: Penguin.

Thiemann, C., Theis, F., Grady, D., Brune, R., and Brockmann, D. (2010). The Structure of Borders in a Small World. *PLoS One*, *5*(11), e15422. doi:10.1371/journal.pone.0015422.

Travers, J., and Milgram, S. (1969). An Experimental Study of the Small World Problem. *Sociometry*, *32*(4), 425–443.

Tufekci, Z. (2016, July 25). WikiLeaks Put Women in Turkey in Danger, for No Reason. *Huffington Post*. Retrieved from http://www.huffingtonpost.com/zeyneptufekci/wikileaks-erdogan-emails_b_11158792.html.

Tufekci, Z. (2017). *Twitter and Tear Gas: The Power and Fragility of Networked Protest*. New Haven: Yale University Press.

Turkle, S. (2011). *Alone Together: Why We Expect More from Technology and Less from Each Other*. New York: Basic Books.

Turner, R., and Killian, L. (1957). *Collective Behavior*. Englewood Cliffs, NJ: Prentice-Hall.

Turow, J. (2012). *The Daily You: How the New Advertising Industry Is Defining Your Identity and Your Worth*. New Haven: Yale University Press.

Tversky, A., and Kahneman, D. (1974). Judgment under Uncertainty: Heuristics and Biases. *Science*, *185*(4157), 1124–1131. doi:10.1126/science.185.4157.1124.

Ugander, J., Backstrom, L., Marlow, C., and Kleinberg, J. (2012). Structural Diversity in Social Contagion. *Proceedings of the National Academy of Sciences of the United States of America*, *109*(16), 5962–5966. doi:10.1073/pnas.1116502109.

Ungerleider, N. (2011). The Newest WikiLeaks Problem: Unredacted Cables. *Fast Company* (January 14). Retrieved from https://www.fastcompany.com/1717414/newest-wikileaks-problem-unredacted-cables.

Valente, T. W. (1996). Social Network Thresholds in the Diffusion of Innovations. *Social Networks*, *18*, 69–89.

Valente, T. W. (2012). Network Interventions. *Science*, *337*(6090), 49–53. doi:10.1126/science.1217330.

van de Rijt, A., Kang, S. M., Restivo, M., and Patil, A. (2014). Field Experiments of Success-Breeds-Success Dynamics. *Proceedings of the National Academy of Sciences of the United States of America*, *111*(19), 6934–6939. doi:10.1073/pnas.1316836111.

van den Bulte, C., and Lilien, G. L. (2001). Medical Innovation Revisited: Social Contagion versus Marketing Effort. *American Journal of Sociology*, *106*(5), 1409–1435.

van Ginneken, J. (1992). *Crowds, Psychology, and Politics, 1871–1899*. Cambridge: Cambridge University Press.

Van Laun, H. (1877). *History of French Literature: From the End of the Reign of Louis XIV till the End of the Reign of Louis Philippe*. New York: G. P. Putnam's Sons.

Vazquez, A., Oliveira, J. G., Dezso, Z., Goh, K.-I., Kondor, I., and Barabási, A. L. (2006). Modeling Bursts and Heavy Tails in Human Dynamics. *Physical Review. E*, *73*(036127), 1–19.

Victor, D. (2015). No, You Don't Need to Post a Facebook Copyright Status. *New York Times* (September 28). Retrieved from http://www.nytimes.com/2015/09/29/technology/facebook-copyright-hoax.html.

Wagner, C., Garcia, D., Jadidi, M., and Strohmaier, M. (2015). It's a Man's Wikipedia? Assessing Gender Inequality in an Online Encyclopedia. Paper presented at the Proceedings of the Ninth International AAAI Conference on Web and Social Media, Oxford, UK (May 26–29).

Wagner, C., Graells-Garrido, E., Garcia, D., and Menczer, F. (2016). Women through the Glass Ceiling: Gender Asymmetries in Wikipedia. *EPJ Data Science, 5*(5). doi:10.1140/epjds/s13688-016-0066-4.

Waldrop, M. M. (1992). *Complexity: The Emerging Science at the Edge of Order and Chaos.* New York: Simon and Schuster.

Waller, J. (2009). *The Dancing Plague: The Strange, True Story of an Extraordinary Illness.* Naperville, IL: Sourcebooks, Incorporated.

Wang, W., Kennedy, R., Lazer, D., and Ramakrishnan, N. (2016). Growing Pains for Global Monitoring of Societal Events. *Science, 353*(6307), 1502–1503. doi:10.1126/science.aaf6758.

Watts, D. J. (1999). *Small Worlds: The Dynamics of Networks between Order and Randomness.* Princeton, NJ: Princeton University Press.

Watts, D. J. (2002). A Simple Model of Global Cascades on Random Networks. *Proceedings of the National Academy of Sciences of the United States of America, 99,* 5766–5771.

Watts, D. J. (2011). *Everything Is Obvious.* Once You Know the Answer.* New York: Crown Business.

Watts, D. J. (2014). Common Sense and Sociological Explanations. *American Journal of Sociology, 120*(2), 313–351. doi:10.1086/678271.

Watts, D. J., and Dodds, P. S. (2010). Threshold Models of Social Influence. In P. Bearman and P. Hedström (Eds.), *Handbook of Analytical Sociology.* Oxford: Oxford University Press.

Watts, D. J., and Strogatz, S. H. (1998). Collective Dynamics of "Small World" Networks. *Nature, 393*(4), 440–442.

Watts, D. J., Dodds, P. S., and Newman, M. E. J. (2002). Identity and Search in Social Networks. *Science, 296,* 1302–1305.

Weidmann, N. B., Benitez-Baleato, S., Hunziker, P., Glatz, E., and Dimitropoulos, X. (2016). Digital Discrimination: Political Bias in Internet Service Provision across Ethnic Groups. *Science, 353*(6304), 1151–1155. doi:10.1126/science.aaf5062.

Whyte, W. H. (1980). *The Social Life of Small Urban Spaces.* New York: Project for Public Spaces.

Wiener, N. (1948). *Cybernetics: Control and Communication in the Animal and the Machine.* New York: J. Wiley.

Wiener, N. (1950). *The Human Use of Human Beings: Cybernetics and Society.* New York: Da Capo Press.

Wlezien, C. (1995). The Public as Thermostat: Dynamics of Preferences for Spending. *American Journal of Political Science*, *39*(4), 981–1000. doi:10.2307/2111666.

Woolf, N. (2016). How to Solve Facebook's Fake News Problem: Experts Pitch Their Ideas. *The Guardian* (November 29). https://www.theguardian.com/technology/2016/nov/29/facebook-fake-news-problem-experts-pitch-ideas-algorithms.

Woolley, A. W., Chabris, C. F., Pentland, A., Hashmi, N., and Malone, T. W. (2010). Evidence for a Collective Intelligence Factor in the Performance of Human Groups. *Science*, *330*(6004), 686–688. doi:10.1126/science.1193147.

Wu, S., Hofman, J. M., Mason, W. A., and Watts, D. J. (2011). Who Says What to Whom on Twitter. Paper presented at the World Wide Web Conference, Hyderabad, India (March 28–April 1).

Yasseri, T., Sumi, R., Rung, A., Kornai, A., and Kertész, J. (2012). Dynamics of Conflicts in Wikipedia. *PLoS One*, *7*(6), e38869. doi:10.1371/journal.pone.0038869.

Zelizer, B. (2015). Terms of Choice: Uncertainty, Journalism, and Crisis. *Journal of Communication*, *65*(5), 888–908. doi:10.1111/jcom.12157.

Zittrain, J. (2008). *The Future of the Internet and How to Stop It*. London: Allen Lane.

Zola, E. (1998). *The Dreyfus Affair: "J'accuse" and Other Writings* (A. Pagès, Ed.; E. Levieux, Trans.). New Haven: Yale University Press.

Index

Accountability, 17, 64, 151–152, 162, 177

Activism
  Anonymous and, 150, 166–167, 169, 175
  Big Brother and, 166
  Big Bucks and, 166
  civil disobedience and, 168
  collective behavior and, 67–68
  curation and, 168–169
  DDoS attacks and, 168
  Dreyfus affair and, 63–64
  hashtag, 56, 65, 68, 92, 94
  Indignados and, 133–134
  networks and, 73
  new forms of, 166–169
  obfuscation and, 168–169
  Occupy Wall Street and, 133–134, 136
  policy design and, 152, 166–169
  privacy and, 166
  Snowden and, 167–169
  social influence and, 73, 90, 92
  WikiLeaks and, 150, 166–169, 175
Activity logs, 53–55, 68
Adorno, Theodor W., 172–173
African Americans, 157
Agamemnon (ship), 99
Airbnb, 157–158
AKP, 167

Algorithms, 22
  accountability and, 17
  bias and, 17
  decision making and, 157–162
  discrimination and, 17, 175
  failure of, 7
  future issues and, 173–177, 180
  governance and, 17, 21, 148–150, 154, 160, 169–170
  improving human intelligence by, 156
  increasing sophistication of, 28
  language and, 16–17
  microtasking and, 161
  Morse code and, 4
  obscurantism and, 16
  policy design and, 150, 156–163, 168–169
  privacy and, 162
  Project Cybersyn and, 148–150, 154, 170
  quantification of life and, 15
  questioning, 173–174
  rule of technocrats and, 15
  self-fulfilling prophecies and, 32–33
  sit-ins and, 169
  social distance and, 119
  social influence and, 97
  societal effects of, 15–16
  space and, 142
  unintended consequences and, 28
Allende, Salvador, 147, 150

Amazon, 15
Anglo-Saxons, 48
Anonymous, 150, 166–167, 169, 175
Antisemitism, 45–46
Arab Spring, 113
Archives, 144, 151, 166, 168, 176–177
Arendt, Hannah, 6–7, 12, 45–46, 64
Aristotle, 4
Associated Press, 13
Aurore, L', newspaper, 45–46
Automation, 18, 83, 87, 131, 140, 168
Autonomy, 18, 95, 150–151, 162, 165, 169, 178

Bagehot, Walter, 11–12, 49
Bandwagon effect, 24, 33
Bandwidth, 54, 91–92, 110, 118
Banknote study, 132, 135, 137
Beer, Stafford, 147–150, 156–157
Bell, William, 72
Bell Labs, 5
Berners-Lee, Tim, 26, 175
Bias
  Adorno and, 173
  algorithms and, 17
  antisemitism and, 45–46
  attrition, 105
  cumulative effects and, 37
  digital gaps and, 138–141
  digital technologies and, 30
  ideological polarization and, 29–30
  media, 41, 179
  policy design and, 149–150, 152, 154, 157–158, 160, 169
  power of communication and, 41–43
  preferential attachment and, 36–39
  prejudice and, 31, 33, 43, 45, 150, 157–158, 175
  selection, 138–141, 152, 154
  social distance and, 105
  social influence and, 83–85, 160
  space and, 128, 138–142, 144
Big Brother, 10, 151, 163, 166

Big Bucks, 166
Big data, xvii
  data capitalism and, 179
  decision-making effects of, 169
  Obama administration report and, 164
  as planetary nervous system, 4–5
  as public good, 11
Black Death, 71
Bluetooth, 121
Borges, Jorge Luis, 144
Brain trusts, 153–154, 161
Bronowski, Jacob, 18
Buchanan, James, 99
Burgess, Ernest W., 66–67, 74–75, 141
Butterfly Effect, 28–29
Buzz, 4, 19, 56, 58, 63, 144

Calvino, Italo, 144–145
Cameras, 10
Capta, 177
Carroll, Lewis, 144
Cartographers, 126–127, 131, 139, 144, 177
Cascades
  collective behavior and, 50, 55
  contagion and, 73, 81, 84–85, 90
  herding and, 42–43, 81, 84–85
  information, 1, 18, 20, 50, 55, 73, 81, 84–85, 90, 102, 108, 113, 116, 120, 175
  social distance and, 102, 108, 113, 116, 120
  social influence and, 73, 81, 84–85, 90
  wildfires and, 20, 81, 85, 90, 175
Catholicism, 48
Censorship, 45, 80, 83, 113, 121, 152
Chain letters, 57
Chain reactions
  collective behavior and, 57–58, 64
  contagion and, 73 (*see also* Contagion)
  cumulative effects and, 18, 20, 29, 34, 43, 57–58, 64, 85, 90, 116, 119–120, 175, 178–179

Dreyfus affair and, 63–64
prophecies and, 34
social distance and, 116, 119–120
social influence and, 85, 90
unintended consequences and, 18, 20,
  29, 43, 175, 178–179
Chicago school, 9, 52, 65, 141
Chile, 147–150, 156, 170
Chimes, The (Dickens), 32
China, 120–121, 139
Cholera, 9
Circle, The (Eggers), 15
Citizen science, 161
Civil disobedience, 168
Coates, Robert, 97–98, 169
Collaboration. *See also* Crowdsourcing
  collective behavior and, 60
  cumulative effects and, 39–40
  filtering and, 27, 178
  policy design and, 152–153, 166
  power of communication and, 27
  reference groups and, 90, 92
  space and, 131, 133
  World Wide Web and, 27 (*see also*
    World Wide Web)
Collateral damage, 174–175
Collective action
  networks and, 8, 42, 134, 136
  self-fulfilling prophecies and, 33
  social influence and, 85
  space and, 134, 136
  spatial diffusion of, 85
Collective behavior, xvii
  activism and, 67–68
  buzz and, 4, 19, 56, 58, 63, 144
  cascades and, 50, 55
  chain reactions and, 57–58, 64
  cities as laboratories and, 141–143
  collaboration and, 60
  complexity and, 56, 61–62,
    65–66
  contagion and, 49–50, 58, 65–68,
    73–74

Dreyfus affair and, 45–47, 50, 53, 55–
  57, 63–64, 66, 69, 179
Durkheim and, 47–52, 60, 63, 65
dynamics of collective attention and,
  56–59
effective shelf life of articles and,
  58–59
emotion and, 96–97
feedback effects and, 55–56, 64
herding and, 42–43, 81, 84–85
hoaxes and, 82–83
inequality and, 65
Internet and, 50, 57
logic and, 66, 69
mapping of, 51, 57, 62, 66
mathematics and, 81
measurement of, 50, 52, 57, 60, 62–65,
  68
milling and, 81–82
networks and, 47, 50, 56, 58–59, 62–
  63, 66–68
panic and, 74, 82
paradoxes and, 47, 142
peer effects and, 79–80, 85–87, 95, 119
power of communication and, 59
privacy and, 59
problem of scale and, 50, 52, 57, 60,
  62–63
protest and, 52, 64
rehashing, 65–69
rhythms of communication and,
  53–56
rumors and, 73–74
social facts and, 47–53, 65
social life and, 25, 47, 60, 66
social media and, 57–60, 62, 64, 67–69
social science and, 46–47, 50, 52, 65
sociology and, 47, 60, 65–66
spontaneity and, 20, 28, 49, 52, 58,
  64, 73, 75, 78, 127
statistics and, 48, 50, 53–55, 59, 68
Tarde and, 47–57, 59–60, 62–63, 65–
  66, 68–69

Collective behavior (cont.)
  technology and, 49, 52, 54, 57, 64–67,
    69
  telegraph and, 49, 66
  wildfires and, 20, 81, 85, 90, 175
Collective effervescence
  buzz and, 4, 19, 56, 58, 63, 144
  communication and, 4, 19, 51–52, 56,
    58, 59–64, 68–69, 144
  communication dynamics and, 69
  Durkheim and, 51–52
  tipping point for, 68
  unpacking, 59–64
Collective intelligence, 24, 42, 49, 151–
  155, 159, 170
Collège Libre des Sciences Sociales,
  46–47
Commercialism, 3, 14, 99
Common good, 150–151, 162–163, 169
Communication
  activity logs and, 53–55, 68
  bandwidth and, 54, 91–92, 110, 118
  Bluetooth and, 121
  cascades and, 1, 18, 20, 50, 55, 73, 81,
    84–85, 90, 102, 108, 113, 116, 120,
    175
  censorship and, 45, 80, 83, 113, 121,
    152
  collective effervescence and, 4, 19,
    51–52, 56, 58–64, 68–69, 144
  collective intelligence and, 24, 42,
    49, 151–155, 159, 170 (see also
    Crowdsourcing)
  contagion and, 74–81 (see also
    Contagion)
  conveying meaning and, 5–6
  cracked code and, 179–181
  cryptography and, 5–8, 11, 22, 40,
    122, 174, 180
  decentralized, 26, 44, 63, 66–68, 94,
    131, 147, 150–156, 169–172, 178
  Dreyfus affair and, 45–47, 50, 53, 55–
    57, 63–64, 66, 69, 179

  effective shelf life of articles and,
    58–59
  firewalls and, 72, 80, 101, 111, 178
  hashtags and, 56, 65, 68, 92, 94
  International Telecommunication
    Union and, 139
  as measurement instrument, 1
  multiplied interactions and, 49–50
  nervous system as metaphor of, 1–4,
    7, 148, 154
  networks and, 99–123 (see also
    Networks)
  newspapers and, 10–11, 13–14, 45–46,
    56, 59, 63, 67, 100, 140, 179
  paradoxes and, 1, 23
  photo sharing and, 127–128
  positive impact of, xv–xviii
  printing press and, 14, 66, 171, 179
  radio and, 103
  rhythms of, 53–56, 63
  rumors and, 19, 31, 34, 42, 72–73,
    77–78, 82–83, 94, 118, 120, 175
  Shannon and, 5–6
  smaller world from, 1
  social cryptogram and, 5–8
  social media and, 41 (see also Social
    media)
  statistics of conversation, 53, 55, 68
  technology and, 3, 6, 11 (see also
    Technology)
  telegraph and, 1–3, 7–8, 13–14, 19–20,
    43, 49, 66, 74, 99–102, 115, 118,
    171, 176, 179
  telephone and, 1–3, 10, 20, 103, 134,
    139
  television and, 72, 80
  telex and, 148, 150, 171
  Turing and, 5–6
  WiFi and, 121
  word of mouth, 30, 120
  World Wide Web and, 18, 26–28,
    35–43, 46, 82, 107, 129, 131–132,
    167–168, 175

Complexity
  analytical models for, 174
  Butterfly Effect and, 28–29
  collective behavior and, 56, 61–62,
    65–66
  cumulative effects and, 38
  data science and, 171
  digital technologies and, 171, 180
  distribution of online visibility and,
    38–39
  initial conditions and, 28–29
  mapping and, 177
  policy design and, 149–151
  power of communication and, 41
  as science of systems, 28–29
  social distance and, 114
  space and, 127
  unintended consequences and, 28–29,
    43
Computational social science, 11, 52
Comte, Auguste, 3, 12
Conservatism, 47
Constructivism, 34, 178
Consumer Data Bill of Rights, 164
Contagion
  analyzing viral effects of, 74–81
  behavioral change debate and, 95–97
  cascades and, 73, 81, 84–85, 90
  chain reactions and, 20
  collective behavior and, 49–50, 58,
    65–68, 73–74
  dancing manias and, 71, 73–76, 79,
    86, 141–142
  digital technologies and, 19–20
  double edge of, 95–97
  dynamics of, 74–81
  earthquake fears and, 72
  East Germany and, 72–73, 80
  emotion and, 96–97
  epidemics and, 71–78, 81, 85–86, 95,
    120, 132–133
  exposure and, 86–95
  fads and, 73, 81

  fake news and, 83
  herding and, 42–43, 81, 84–85
  hoaxes and, 82–83
  hysteria and, 74–75
  Ice Bucket Challenge and, 73
  Lippman on, 74–75
  mathematics and, 78
  metaphor for, 74–81
  Middle Ages and, 71, 74, 79
  milling and, 81–82
  networks and, 101, 111, 116–117
  panic and, 74, 82
  peer effects and, 79–80, 85–87, 95, 119
  reducing effects of, 83–84
  reference groups and, 86–95
  reinforcement and, 32–33, 37–38, 43,
    80–81, 83, 88, 90–91, 134, 178, 180
  rumors and, 72–73, 77–78, 83
  social distance and, 101, 111, 116–117
  social influence and, 19–20, 72–97
  social media and, 73, 79–80, 82
  streaking, 71–73, 79–80, 86
  susceptibility and, 51, 76–81, 84, 110
  Tarde and, 74
  Welles hoax and, 82
  wildfires and, 20, 81, 85, 90, 175
Crowdsourcing
  activism and, 166
  brain trusts and, 153–154, 161
  collective intelligence and, 24, 42, 49,
    151–155, 159, 170
  crisis events and, 152
  data visualization and, 152
  governance and, 150–156, 161, 170
  maps and, 151
  Mass Observation and, 141–142
  Peer to Patent initiative and,
    152–153
  policy design and, 150–156
  problem solving and, 151–156, 159,
    161
  selection bias and, 152, 154
  space and, 137–138, 142–143

Crowdsourcing (cont.)
  unintended consequences and, 42
  urban services and, 151
  Wikipedia and, 40, 153–154
Cryptography, 5–8, 11, 22, 40, 122, 174,
    180
Cumberbatch, Benedict, 5
Cumulative effects
  bias and, 37
  chain reactions and, 18, 20, 29, 34,
    43, 57–58, 64, 85, 90, 116, 119–120,
    175, 178–179
  collective action and, 35–37, 39
  complexity and, 38
  digital technologies and, 18–19, 38–40
  distribution of online visibility and,
    38–39
  feedback effects and, 36–40
  Google and, 35
  inequality and, 37–40
  language and, 37
  logic and, 39–40
  markets and, 39
  networks and, 35–37, 39
  paradoxes and, 38, 40
  positive outcomes and, 38
  preferential attachment and, 36–39
  prophecies and, 39–41
  social facts and, 178
  social life and, 37, 40
  social media and, 38
  technology and, 38–40
  unintended consequences and, 37
  World Wide Web and, 18, 26–28,
    35–43, 46, 82, 107, 129, 131–132,
    167–168, 175
Curation, 168–169
Cybernetics, 5, 12, 68, 147–150, 154,
    170

Daily Telegraph, 100
Dancing mania, 71, 73–76, 79, 86,
    141–142

Darwinism, 11
Data capitalism, 179
Data science
  activity logs and, 53–55, 68
  chain reactions and, 18, 20, 29, 34,
    43, 57–58, 64, 85, 90, 116, 119–120,
    175, 178–179
  cities as laboratories and, 141–143
  cybernetics and, 5, 12, 68, 147–150,
    154, 170
  decision making and, 7
  Hammerbacher and, 16
  impact of, 7, 21–22, 170–171, 174,
    177, 180
  Mass Observation and, 141–142
  redefining boundaries and, 131–138
  social influence and, 97
  unintended consequences and, 43
Decision making
  algorithms and, 157–162 (see also
    Algorithms)
  data science and, 7
  fears of automation and, 18
  future issues and, 175
  governance and, 4, 11, 17, 21, 137,
    150, 169
  policy design and, 148, 150, 152–153,
    156–162, 169–170
  privacy and, 162–166
  real-time performance monitoring
    and, 11
  social distance and, 122
  social influence and, 83–85, 88
  space and, 137
Decryption, 7
Defense Advanced Research Projects
    Agency (DARPA), 155
De Sola Pool, Ithiel, 103–106
Dickens, Charles, 32
Diffusion dynamics
  collective behavior and, 67
  epidemics and, 81
  layered connectivity and, 115–118

social distance and, 110–111, 115–120
social influence and, 78, 81, 83–85
space and, 134
Digital gaps, 138–141
Digital technologies
  activity logs and, 54–55
  bias and, 30
  collective behavior and, 52, 54, 57,
    64–69
  complexity and, 171, 180
  contagion metaphor and, 19–20
  cryptography and, 7
  cumulative effects and, 18–19, 38–40
  discrimination and, 150
  distribution of online visibility and,
    38–39
  firewalls and, 72, 80, 101, 111, 178
  future issues and, 171, 179–180
  policy design and, 21, 149–151, 155–
    156, 158, 160, 166, 169
  power of, 11
  predictions on, 3–4
  Project Cybersyn and, 148–150, 154,
    170
  reflexivity problem and, 24
  as revolution, 1–2, 101–102
  self-fulfilling prophecies and, 32, 34
  social distance and, 101, 105, 107,
    110, 117, 122–123
  social influence and, 73, 78, 80–84,
    87, 94–95, 97
  space and, 127–130, 137–143
  surveillance and, 9
  unintended consequences and, 26,
    29–30, 43–44
Discrimination
  algorithms and, 17, 175
  antisemitism and, 45–46
  digital technologies and, 150
  Dreyfus affair and, 45–47, 50, 53, 55–
    57, 63–64, 66, 69, 179
  future issues and, 175
  gender and, 154

Google and, 32, 157
ideological polarization and, 29–30
marginalization and, 139
markets and, 32–33, 157
online, 126, 157
policy design and, 33, 150, 154, 157–
  158, 162
politics and, 139–140
preferential attachment and, 36–39
prejudice and, 31, 33, 43, 45, 150,
  157–158, 175
profiling and, 32–33
racial, 43, 45, 52, 139, 157
regulation and, 157–158
search engines and, 157
segregation and, 29–30, 35, 82, 88
self-defeating prophecies and,
  32–33
self-fulfilling prophecies and, 32
social science and, 32
by statistical inference, 32
transparency and, 162
Disease
  cholera, 9
  epidemics and, 71–78, 81, 85–86, 95,
    120, 132–133
  Flu Trends and, 24, 28
  global monitoring and, 141
  social influence and, 71, 73, 75, 77
Distributed denial of service (DDoS)
    attacks, 168
Division of labor, 72, 113, 138
Dreyfus affair
  activism and, 63–64
  antisemitism and, 45–46
  L'Aurore and, 45–46
  chain reactions and, 63–64
  collective behavior and, 45–47, 50, 53,
    55–57, 63–64, 66, 69, 179
  Durkheim and, 47, 50, 63
  La Libre Parole and, 46
  nature of social facts and, 47, 52
  newspapers and, 45–46, 56, 63–64

Dreyfus affair (cont.)
  presidential pardon and, 53
  Tarde and, 47, 50, 63
  Zola and, 45–47, 53
Durkheim, Émile
  collective behavior and, 47–52, 60,
    63, 65
  Dreyfus affair and, 47, 50, 63
  Elementary Forms of Religious Life and,
    51
  law of unintended consequences and,
    26
  nature of social facts and, 48–52
  school of, 51
  on society, 26
  Tarde and, 47–52, 60, 63, 65

Earthquakes, 72, 81, 152
East Germany, 72–73, 80
Economist, The (journal), 11
Eggers, Dave, 15
Electric Telegraph Company, 2
Elementary Forms of Religious Life
  (Durkheim), 51
Emotion, 96–97
Encryption, 5–7, 22, 40, 180
Encyclopaedia Britannica, 153
Engels, Friedrich, 9
Enigma, 6
Enlightenment, 2, 100
Epidemics
  contagion and, 71–78, 81, 85–86, 95,
    120, 132–133
  diffusion dynamics and, 81
  explaining, 85
Erdogan, Recep Tayyip, 167
Eternal return, 2, 11
Ethnicity
  Dreyfus affair and, 45–47, 50, 53, 55–
    57, 63–64, 66, 69, 179
  marginalization and, 139
  Merton on, 43
  Tarde and, 52

Etzioni, Amitai, 163, 165–166
EU Data Protection Directive, 164–165
Evolution, 11, 27
Exposure
  common, 86–87
  contagion and, 86–95
  defining, 89
  reference groups and, 86–95
  reinforcement and, 88, 90–91
  signal strength and, 91
  social media and, 89–90, 92

Fabian Society, 9
Facebook
  hoaxes and, 82
  quantification of social life and, 15
  reference groups and, 86–87, 89
  social distance and, 108, 111, 116
  social influence and, 78–80, 82, 86–87,
    89, 96–97
Fads, 73, 81
Fairness, 17, 29, 33, 157, 162
Fake news, 83
Fascism, 16
Faust, 15
Feedback
  chain reactions and, 18, 20, 29, 34,
    43, 57–58, 64, 85, 90, 116, 119–120,
    175, 178–179
  collective behavior and, 55–56, 64
  cumulative effects and, 36–40
  cybernetics and, 147–150, 154, 170
  human-machine, 161–162
  industrial regulation and, 148
  model robustness and, 12–13
  newspapers and, 13
  policy design and, 147–148, 159–161
  positive, 13, 34–41, 85
  power of communication and, 41
  reinforcement and, 32–33, 37–38,
    43, 80–81, 83, 88, 90–91, 134, 178,
    180
  reverse engineering and, 19

self-fulfilling prophecies and, 34
social influence and, 81, 85, 90, 179
space and, 134, 143
Wiener and, 147
Ferguson, Adam, 25
15-M. *See* Indignados
Firewalls, 72, 80, 101, 111, 178
Fixmystreet.com, 151
Flickr, 128
Flu Trends, 24, 28
Forbes magazine, 3
France
  Collège Libre des Sciences Sociales,
    46–47
  Dreyfus affair, 45–47, 50, 53, 55–57,
    63–64, 66, 69, 179
  Napoleonic era, 48
French Revolution, 16, 30

Galaxy Zoo, 161
Gender, 12, 48, 79, 154, 167
General Data Protection Regulation,
  165
Gezi Park protests, 113, 121
Global Pulse, 11
Google
  content relevance and, 28
  cumulative effects and, 35
  discrimination and, 32, 157
  European courts and, 35
  Flu Trends and, 24, 28
  link exploitation and, 35
  Page and, 28
  quantification of social life by, 15
  Street View, 130
  voluntary information and, 26
Google Maps, 130, 138–139
Governance
  algorithms and, 17, 21, 148–150, 154,
    160, 169–170
  Big Brother and, 10, 151, 163, 166
  brain trusts and, 153–154, 161
  collective maps and, 128

common good and, 150–151, 162–
  163, 169
crowdsourced, 150–156, 170
decentralized, 26, 44, 63, 66–68, 94,
  131, 147, 150–156, 169–172, 178
decision making and, 4, 11, 17, 21,
  137, 150, 169
government by discussion and, 12
micromanagement and, 169
networks and, 118–119, 151–156,
  169–170
policy design and, 19, 147–156, 161,
  169–170
privacy and, 162–163
problem-solving and, 155, 159, 161
regulation and, 2, 21, 26, 30, 42–44,
  83, 96–97, 119, 145–150, 153, 157–
  160, 163–165, 177, 181
Granovetter, Mark, 88, 91, 104, 106,
  109, 135
Green energy, 128, 161
Greenwald, Glenn, 167

Haiti, 152
Hammerbacher, Jeff, 16–17
Hashtags, 56, 65, 68, 92, 94
Health issues, 9, 21, 161
Herding, 42–43, 81, 84–85
Hirschman, Albert O., 30
Hoaxes, 82–83
Hong Kong, 121
Human Face of Big Data, The (Smolan
  and Erwitt), 3–4
Humanism, 17–18, 174, 176
Hyperlinks, 26
Hysteria, 74–75

IBM, 4, 150
Ice Bucket Challenge, 73
Imitation Game (film), 5
Indignados (15-M), 113, 133–134
Individualism, 48, 125–126, 150,
  162–164

Inequality
  collective behavior and, 65
  cumulative effects and, 37–40
  discrimination and, 33 (*see also*
    Discrimination)
  future issues and, 175, 178–179
  measurement and, 145
  policy design and, 150
  power of communication and, 41–42
  selection bias and, 138–140
  social distance and, 113
  social influence and, 97
Innovation
  digital revolution and, 1–2, 50
  imitation and, 49
  invention and, 1, 4, 12, 17, 26, 39, 43,
    49, 74, 153, 175
  Peer to Patent initiative and, 152–153
  policy design and, 180
  Tarde and, 49–50
  technology and, 1, 13, 18, 43, 49, 95,
    123, 142, 152, 175
  unintended consequences and, 175
International Telecommunication
  Union, 139
Internet. *See also* World Wide Web
  bandwidth and, 54, 91–92, 110, 118
  Bluetooth and, 121
  collective behavior and, 50, 57
  DDoS attacks and, 168
  distribution of online visibility and,
    38–39
  effective shelf life of articles and,
    58–59
  firewalls and, 72, 80, 101, 111, 178
  future issues and, 171
  hyperlinks and, 26
  impact of, 1–2
  networks and, 1, 3–4, 27, 30, 50, 57,
    74, 101, 118–120, 138–140, 150–151,
    169, 171
  online discrimination and, 126, 157
  policy design and, 150–151, 169

  preferential attachment and, 36–39
  search engines and, 35, 38, 41, 157
  social distance and, 101, 118–120
  social influence and, 74
  space and, 138–140
  trust and, 37–38
  unintended consequences and, 26–28,
    30
  WiFi and, 121
Internet of Things, 4
Introduction to the Science of Sociology
    (Park and Burgess), 66
Invention, 1, 4, 12, 17, 26, 39, 43, 49,
    74, 153, 175
Invisible hand, 25, 28, 41

Kant, Immanuel, 33
Kenya, 152
Killian, Lewis M., 75–76
Kochen, Manfred, 103–106
Kuhn, Thomas S., xviii, 38

Lamartine, Alphonse de, 16
Lambeth Walk, 141–142
Lang, Gladys Engel, 75
Lang, Kurt, 75
Language
  algorithms and, 16–17
  bias and, 30
  cumulative effects and, 37
  layers of information and, 174
  networks and, 20, 102
  paradoxes and, 23
  politics and, 7
  printing press and, 14
  probability and, 6
  social influence and, 76
  structure of, 6
  unintended consequences and, 30
"Law, The" (Coates), 98
Laws of Imitation (Tarde), 49
Lazarsfeld, Paul F., 56–57
Le Corbusier, 129

Legal issues
  Dreyfus affair and, 45–47, 50, 53, 55–57, 63–64, 66, 69, 179
  Google and, 35
  policy design and, 154, 165
  privacy and, 162–166
  social distance and, 122
  surveillance and, 9, 11, 121–122, 163, 165–169
  WikiLeaks and, 150, 166–169, 175
Leipzig demonstrations, 73, 80
Liar's Paradox, 23, 34
Liberalism, 11–12, 25, 47, 165
Liberty Machine, 148
Libre Parole, La (newspaper), 46
Lippman, Walter, 74–75
Logic, 7
  algorithms and, 17 (*see also* Algorithms)
  breaking with, 172
  collective behavior and, 66, 69
  deep, 179
  power of communication and, 42
  prophecies and, 34
  research and, 178
  social distance and, 114, 117
  social influence and, 71–98
  space and, 133
  unintended consequences and, 29, 44
London School of Economics, 9
Lutherans, 179

Malthus, Thomas R., 8
Maps
  activity density and, 128
  cartographers and, 126–127, 131, 139, 144, 177
  collective, 127–131
  collective behavior and, 51, 57, 62, 66
  crisis events and, 151
  crowdsourcing and, 151
  dynamic flux and, 51
  geographic distance and, 125, 128–129, 131–139
  individualism and, 48, 125–126
  informational layers and, 129
  information flow and, 66, 171
  magnetism and, 128
  navigation and, 27, 102, 106, 126, 129, 137
  nodes and, 26, 36–39, 92–94, 102, 105–106, 109–121, 129, 133, 160
  OpenStreetMap, 128, 131, 138, 143
  pathway structures and, 108
  policy design and, 151, 160
  poverty, 9
  representational accuracy and, 27, 177
  satellites and, 131
  social distance and, 102, 106, 108, 111–112, 116
  social straitjacketing and, 127
  space and, 125–131, 141, 144–145
  trends and, 62
  useful standard grid of, 126–127
  Ushahidi.com and, 151
  World Wide Web and, 27–28, 35
Marginalization, 139
Marinetti, Filippo Tommaso, 16
Markets
  artificial cultural, 39
  buzz and, 4, 19, 56, 58, 63, 144
  controlling networks and, 178
  cumulative effects and, 39
  discrimination and, 32–33, 157
  invisible hand, 25, 28, 41
  policy design and, 157, 163
  power of communication and, 42
  profiling and, 32–33
  prophecies and, 31–32, 34
  resonance and, 34
  social distance and, 122
  social influence and, 78–79, 87
  telegraph and, 99
  viral campaigns and, 31
Marx, Karl, 27, 94, 147

Mass Observation project, 141–142
Mathematics
  algorithms and, 22 (*see also* Algorithms)
  Bronowski and, 18
  Coates on, 98
  collective behavior and, 81
  cryptography and, 7
  French Revolution and, 16
  Liar's Paradox and, 23
  networks and, 106
  possibility space and, 106
  reference groups and, 90
  Shannon and, 5
  social epidemic models and, 76
  statistics, 8 (*see also* Statistics)
  theory of communication and, 5
  theory of contagion and, 78
  Turing and, 5
  Wiener and, 5
Measurement
  advances in, 24, 34, 150–151, 176, 180
  archives and, 144, 151, 166, 168, 176–177
  collective behavior and, 50, 52, 57, 60, 62–65, 68
  communication as, 1
  data vs. capta, 177
  national barometers and, 8–12
  policy design and, 150–151
  problem of scale and, 50, 52, 57, 60, 62–63
  productivity and, 24, 148
  Project Cybersyn and, 148–150, 154, 170
  representation and, 144–145
  social distance and, 101, 103–106, 105, 109
  social influence and, 90–94
  space and, 144–145
  time series and, 60–63, 133, 136
  unpredictability and, 12–15, 18, 29, 40, 75, 97, 149

Meeting Mediator, 160
Memes, 38
Merton, Robert, 28, 31, 34, 37–38, 43
Microchips, 4
Microtasking, 161
Milgram, Stanley, 104–105, 107, 125–126, 130
Milling, 81–82
Misinformation, 175, 178
  fake news and, 83
  hoaxes and, 82–83
  reducing effects of, 83–84
  social influence and, 73, 82–84, 95, 97
  unintended consequences and, 19
  World War II and, 5
Mobility, 21, 29, 104, 106, 125–128, 132, 137, 143, 145
Morse code, 4

National barometers, 8–12, 19
National Security Agency (NSA), 150, 167
Nature journal, 75–76
Navigation
  maps and, 27, 102, 106, 126, 129, 137
  space and, 20–21, 27, 37, 102, 105–109, 111, 126, 129, 137, 156, 168
  structure and, 106–109
Negroponte, Nicholas, 136
Nervous system, as metaphor, 1–4, 7, 148, 154
Networks
  activism and, 73
  censorship and, 45
  chains and, 102–108, 116–121
  collective action and, 8, 42, 134, 136
  collective behavior and, 47, 50, 56, 58–59, 62–63, 66–68
  communication, 1, 6, 11, 20, 89, 93, 103, 105, 110, 113, 115–117, 121, 135, 152, 160, 175
  communities and, 100, 109–110, 113–119, 132, 135

components of, 109–115
contagion and, 101, 111, 116–117
controlling, 177–179
coordination dynamics and, 33
cumulative effects and, 35–37, 39
diffusion dynamics and, 67, 110–111, 115–120, 134
Facebook and, 15, 78–80, 82, 86–87, 89, 96–97, 108, 111, 116
firewalls and, 72, 80, 101, 111, 178
future issues and, 171–179
governance and, 118–119, 151–156, 169–170
hidden architectures and, 123
hyperlinks and, 26
of interaction, 25
Internet and, 1, 3–4, 27, 30, 50, 57, 74, 101, 118–120, 138–140, 150–151, 169, 171
interventions and, 118–122
layered connectivity and, 115–118
maps and, 172 (*see also* Maps)
markets and, 178
navigation of, 106–109
as nervous system, 1
nodes and, 26, 36–37, 92–94, 102, 105–106, 109–121, 129, 133, 160
paradoxes and, 1
peer effects and, 79–80, 85–87, 95, 119
policy design and, 148–161, 166, 169–170
possibility space and, 106
power of communication and, 41–42
Project Cybersyn and, 148–150
protest and, 89–90, 94, 113–115, 121, 133–134, 178–179
regulation and, 177–179
rumors and, 73, 86–95, 118, 120
search engines and, 35, 38, 41, 157
social distance and, 1, 99–123
social influence and, 73, 79, 88–94, 96, 98

social media and, 113, 115, 118, 120–122 (*see also* Social media)
space and, 128–139, 143, 145
structure of, 106–115
theory of, 20
trans-Atlantic telegraph cable and, 99–100, 102
Twitter and, 108, 113, 118, 120–121, 133
unintended consequences and, 44, 177–179
unpredictability of social life and, 12–13
World Wide Web and, 18, 26–28, 35–43, 46, 82, 107, 129, 131–132, 167–168, 175
YouTube and, 120
Newspapers
antisemitism and, 45–46
Associated Press and, 13
communication and, 10–11, 13–14, 45–46, 56, 59, 63, 67, 100, 140, 179
Dreyfus affair and, 45–46, 56, 63–64
feedback effects and, 13
growing literacy and, 45
telegraph and, 13–14, 100, 179
New York Times, 10, 71–72
Niagara (ship), 99
Nicholas I, emperor of Russia, 101

Obama, Barack, 164
Occupy Wall Street, 133–134, 136
OECD Privacy Framework, 164–165
On the Mode of Communication of Cholera (Snow), 9
OpenStreetMap, 128, 131, 138, 143
Overpopulation, 8–9

Packard, Vance, 10–11
Page, Larry, 28
Panic, 8, 74, 82
Panopticons, xv

Paradoxes, 171
  collective behavior and, 47, 142
  communication and, 1, 23
  cumulative effects and, 38, 40
  Liar's, 23, 34
  networks and, 1
  policy design and, 162–164, 166
  power of communication and, 42–44
  social distance and, 115
  unintended consequences and, 25,
    28, 30
Paris in the Twentieth Century (Verne), 18
Park, Robert E., 66–67, 74–75, 141
Patents, 152–153
Path dependence, 6, 34, 37, 40, 117,
    174
Peer effects, 79–80, 85–87, 95, 119
Peer to Patent initiative, 152–153
Personal computers, 4
Photo sharing, 127–128
Physics and Politics (Bagehot), 11–12, 49
Plato, 4
Poitras, Laura, 167
Policy design
  activism and, 152, 166–169
  algorithms and, 150, 156–163,
    168–169
  Beer and, 147–150, 156–157
  bias and, 149–150, 152, 154, 157–158,
    160, 169
  brain trusts and, 153–154, 161
  collaboration and, 131, 133, 152–153,
    166
  common good and, 150–151, 162–
    163, 169
  complexity and, 149–151
  Consumer Data Bill of Rights, 164
  crowdsourcing and, 150–156
  cybernetics and, 147–150, 154, 170
  decision making and, 148, 150, 152–
    153, 156–162, 169–170
  digital technologies and, 149–151,
    155–156, 158, 160, 166, 169

  discrimination and, 33, 150, 154,
    157–158, 162
  EU Data Protection Directive and,
    164–165
  feedback effects and, 147–148,
    159–161
  General Data Protection Regulation
    and, 165
  governance and, 19, 147–156, 161,
    169–170
  individual rights and, 150, 162–164
  inequality and, 150
  innovation and, 180
  Internet and, 150–151, 169
  legal issues and, 154, 165
  maps and, 151, 160
  markets and, 157, 163
  measurement and, 150–151
  microtasking and, 161
  networks and, 128–139, 143, 145,
    148–161, 166, 169–170
  OECD Privacy Framework and,
    164–165
  paradoxes and, 162–164, 166
  privacy and, 150–151, 162–167, 169
  problem solving and, 151–156, 159,
    161
  Project Cybersyn and, 148–150, 154,
    170
  reference groups and, 158–159
  regulation and, 145, 147–148, 150,
    153, 157–158, 160, 163–165
  social life and, 151, 157
  social media and, 155, 165
  sociology and, 149, 160
  statistics and, 148, 157, 160
  technology and, 12, 21, 138–160,
    163–170
  transparency and, 151, 160, 162,
    166–169
  travel and, 137
  unintended consequences and, 157–
    158, 160, 166

Political economy, 26, 41, 175
Popper, Karl, xviii, 27, 31, 172–173
Positivism, 12, 172–173
Poverty of Historicism, The (Popper), 27
Power of communication
  bias and, 41–43
  collaboration and, 27
  collective behavior and, 59
  complexity and, 41
  distribution of online visibility and,
    38–39
  feedback effects and, 41
  inequality and, 41–42
  logic and, 42
  markets and, 42
  networks and, 41–42
  paradoxes and, 42–44
  prophecies and, 41–43
  regulation and, 42–43
  rumors and, 42
  social life and, 41, 43
  social media and, 41
  technology and, 41, 43
  unintended consequences and, 42–43
Prediction
  digital technologies and, 3–4
  end of newspapers and, 13–14
  Flu Trends and, 24
  model accuracy and, 176
  politics and, 176
  prophecies and, 31 (*see also*
    Prophecies)
  reinforcement and, 43
  social influence and, 72
  social scientists and, 74
  unintended consequences and, 13, 18,
    27–29, 43, 175
  unpredictability of social life and,
    12–15, 18, 29, 40, 75, 97, 149
  word processing software and, 6
Preferential attachment, 36–39
Prejudice, 31, 33, 43, 45, 150, 157–158,
  175

Printing press, 14, 66, 171, 179
Privacy
  activism and, 166
  algorithms and, 162
  autonomy and, 18, 95, 150–151, 162,
    165, 169, 178
  Big Brother and, 163, 166
  collective behavior and, 59
  Consumer Data Bill of Rights and, 164
  cryptography and, 5–8, 11, 122, 174,
    180
  curation and, 168–169
  decision making and, 162–166
  EU Data Protection Directive and,
    164–165
  firewalls and, 72, 80, 101, 111, 178
  General Data Protection Regulation
    and, 165
  governance and, 162–163
  hoaxes and, 82–83
  individual rights and, 150, 162–164
  losses of, 9–10
  OECD Privacy Framework and,
    164–165
  personal information and, 162–166
  policy design and, 150–151, 162–167,
    169
  regulation and, 162–165
  right to be forgotten and, 165
  social distance and, 122
  social influence and, 82–84, 86
  space and, 137
  surveillance and, xv, 9–11, 121–122,
    163, 165–169
  telephone and, 10, 167
  transparency and, 21, 137, 162, 166–
    167, 169
  two sides of, 162–166
  WikiLeaks and, 150, 166–169, 175
Problems of scale, 50, 52, 57, 60, 62–63
Problem solving
  brain trusts and, 153–154, 161
  crowdsourcing and, 151–156, 159, 161

Problem solving (cont.)
  decentralized, 155–156
  microtasking and, 161
  motivations for, 155
  policy design and, 151–156, 159, 161
Productivity, 24, 148
Profiling, 32–33
Project Cybersyn, 148–150, 154, 170
Prophecies
  bandwagon effect and, 33
  benign circles and, 33
  chain reactions and, 34
  cumulative effects and, 39–41
  earthquakes and, 72, 81
  feedback and, 34
  ideological polarization and, 31–32
  logic and, 34
  markets and, 31–32, 34
  power of communication and, 41–43
  rumors and, 31, 34
  self-defeating, 31–34, 174
  self-fulfilling, 31–34, 39–43
  situation definition and, 31–32
  unintended consequences and, 31
  vicious circles and, 32
Protest, 19
  Arab Spring and, 113
  civil disobedience and, 168
  collective behavior and, 52, 64
  DDoS attacks and, 168
  digital gaps and, 140
  Gezi Park and, 113, 121
  networks and, 89–90, 94, 113–115,
    121, 133–134, 178–179
  Occupy Wall Street and, 133–134,
    136
  printing press and, 179
  social distance and, 113–115, 121
  social influence and, 71–73, 80–81,
    85–86, 89–90, 94
  umbrella revolution and, 92, 121
Protestants, 14, 48
Proust, Marcel, 56

Public good, 11, 25, 41–42, 44, 69, 119,
  154
Public opinion, 24, 45, 64–65, 68, 69,
  100–101, 167

Quételet, Adolphe, 12
QWERTY keyboard, 34

Racial issues, 43, 52, 139
  African Americans and, 157
  Airbnb and, 157–158
  Anglo-Saxons and, 48
  antisemitism and, 45–46
  Dreyfus affair and, 45–47, 50, 53, 55–
    57, 63–64, 66, 69, 179
  profiling and, 32–33
Radio, 103
Rating systems, 42
Reference groups
  collective behavior and, 86
  common exposure and, 86–95
  Facebook and, 86–87, 89
  policy design and, 158–159
  size of, 89–90
  social influence and, 86–95
  social media and, 89–90, 92
  threshold models and, 88, 88–94
Reflexivity, 23–24, 31, 33
Regulation
  censorship and, 45, 80, 83, 113, 121,
    152
  cybernetics and, 148
  discrimination and, 157–158
  EU Data Protection Directive,
    164–165
  feedback and, 148
  future issues and, 177, 181
  General Data Protection Regulation,
    165
  governance and, 2, 21, 147, 150
  networks and, 177–179
  policy design and, 145, 147–148, 150,
    153, 157–158, 160, 163–165

power of communication and, 42–43
privacy and, 162–165
Project Cybersyn and, 148–150, 154, 170
social distance and, 119
social influence and, 83, 96–97
unintended consequences and, 26, 30, 44
WikiLeaks and, 150, 166–169, 175
Reinforcement, 178, 180
cumulative effects and, 37–38
exposure and, 88, 90–91
prediction and, 43
prophecies and, 32–33
redefining boundaries and, 134
social influence and, 80–81, 83, 88, 90–91
Religion, 14, 25, 48, 51, 179
Rhetoric of Reaction, The (Hirschman), 30
"Rise of the Social Nervous System, The" (Ross), 3
Roosevelt, Franklin D., 153
Rumors
bank runs and, 31, 34
boundaries of, 93
collective behavior and, 73–74
contagion and, 72–73, 77–78, 83
fake news and, 83
hoaxes and, 82–83
misinformation and, 5, 19, 73, 82–84, 95, 97, 175, 178
networks and, 73, 118, 120
politics and, 73
power of communication and, 42
reducing effects of, 83–84
reference groups and, 94
research on propagation of, 83
self-defeating prophecies and, 31
social distance and, 118, 120
social influence and, 72–73, 77–78, 82–83
Zika virus and, 73

Satellites, 131
Schelling, Thomas C., 29–30, 32, 35, 88
Schneier, Bruce, 11
Scientific American magazine, 2–3, 99–100
Screening, 162
Search engines, 35, 38, 41, 157
Security, 141, 150, 162–163, 167
Seeclickfix.com, 151
Segregation, 29–30, 35, 82, 88
Selection bias, 138–141, 152, 154
Self-defeating prophecies, 31–34, 174
Self-fulfilling prophecies
algorithms and, 32–33
bandwagon effect and, 33
cumulative effects and, 39–41
digital technologies and, 32, 34
discrimination and, 32
feedback effects and, 34
power of communication and, 41–43
social life and, 31, 33
sociology and, 32
technology and, 32–34
Shannon, Claude, 5–6
Silicon Valley, 7
Snow, John, 9, 21
Snowden, Edward, 167–169
Social cryptogram, 5–8, 174
Social distance
activity density and, 128
algorithms and, 119
bias and, 105
cascades and, 102, 108, 113, 116, 120
chain reactions and, 116, 119–120
complexity and, 114
contagion and, 101, 111, 116–117
decision making and, 122
de Sola Pool and, 103–106
Facebook and, 108, 111, 116
inequality and, 113
Internet and, 101, 118–120
Kochen and, 103–106
legal issues and, 122

Social distance (cont.)
  logic and, 114, 117
  mapping and, 102, 106, 108, 111–112,
    116
  markets and, 122
  measurement and, 101, 103–106,
    109
  Milgram and, 104–105, 107, 125–126,
    130
  networks and, 1
  paradoxes and, 115
  privacy and, 122
  protest and, 113–115, 121
  regulation and, 119
  rumors and, 118, 120
  social life and, 101, 106, 111, 116,
    122–123
  social media and, 113, 115, 118,
    120–122
  statistics and, 108
  technology and, 101–107, 110, 117–
    119, 122–123
  telegraph and, 99–102, 115, 118
Social facts
  collective behavior and, 47–53, 65
  cumulative effects and, 178
  nature of, 48–53
  prophecies and, 34
Social influence
  activism and, 73, 90, 92
  algorithms and, 97
  behavioral change debate and, 95–97
  bias and, 83–85, 160
  cascades and, 73, 81, 84–85, 90
  chain reactions and, 85, 90
  collective action and, 85
  contagion and, 19–20, 72–97
  dancing manias and, 71, 73–76, 79,
    86, 141–142
  data science and, 97
  decision making and, 83–85, 88
  emotion and, 96–97
  exposure and, 86–95
  Facebook and, 78–80, 82, 86–87, 89,
    96–97
  feedback effects and, 81, 85, 90, 179
  herding and, 42–43, 81, 84–85
  hoaxes and, 82–83
  inequality and, 97
  Internet and, 74
  markets and, 78–79, 87
  measurement and, 90–94
  milling and, 81–82
  networks and, 73, 79, 88–94, 96, 98
  panic and, 74, 82
  peer effects and, 79–80, 85–87, 95, 119
  prediction and, 72
  privacy and, 82–84, 86
  protest and, 71–73, 80–81, 85–86,
    89–90, 94
  regulation and, 83, 96–97
  reinforcement and, 32–33, 37–38, 43,
    80–81, 83, 88, 90–91, 134, 178, 180
  rumors and, 72–73, 77–78, 82–83
  signal strength and, 91
  social media and, 73, 78–80, 82, 86–
    92, 96–97
  sociology and, 74–75, 79
  spontaneity and, 73, 75, 78
  streaking and, 71–72, 79–80, 86
  susceptibility and, 51, 76–81, 84, 110
  technology and, 19–20, 73–74, 78–84,
    87, 89, 94–95, 97
  telegraph and, 74
  transparency and, 97
  unintended consequences and, 85, 88,
    94, 97–98
  unpredictability of, 97–98
  wildfires and, 20, 81, 85, 90, 175
Social life
  collective behavior and, 25, 47, 60,
    66
  communication's impact on, 23
  cumulative effects and, 37, 40
  Dreyfus affair and, 45–47, 50, 53, 55–
    57, 63–64, 66, 69, 179

future issues and, 171–175, 178–181
Google's quantification of, 15
hidden structure of, 6–7
layers of, 1
logic of, xv, 7, 40, 69 (*see also* Social influence)
maps and, 172 (*see also* Maps)
national barometers for, 8–12
overpopulation and, 8–9
path dependence and, 6, 34, 37, 40, 117, 174
policy design and, 151, 157
power of communication and, 41, 43
self-fulfilling prophecies and, 31, 33
social distance and, 101, 106, 111, 116, 122–123
space and, 126
structure of, 6–7
technology and, 2 (*see also* Technology)
unintended consequences and, 19, 27–28
unpredictability of, 12–15, 18, 27, 29, 40, 75, 97, 149
World Wide Web and, 18, 26–28, 35–43, 46, 82, 107, 129, 131–132, 167–168, 175
Social Life (game), 116
Social media. *See also specific platforms by name*
  collective behavior and, 57–60, 62, 64, 67–69, 73–74
  contagion and, 73, 79, 80, 82
  cumulative effects and, 38
  Eggers on, 15
  emotion and, 96–97
  memes and, 38
  news and, 38
  photo sharing and, 127–128
  policy design and, 155, 165
  power of communication and, 41
  reference groups and, 89–90, 92

rumors and, 73–74
  social distance and, 113, 115, 118, 120–122
  social influence and, 73, 78–80, 82, 86–92, 96–97
  space and, 128, 133–136, 142
Social movements, 9, 65, 67, 85, 94, 134, 179
Social physics, 11–12, 49, 53
Social science
  Adorno and, 172
  autonomy and, 18, 95, 150–151, 162, 165, 169, 178
  barometers for, 9, 11
  Chicago school and, 9, 52, 65
  collective behavior and, 46–47, 50, 52, 65
  computational, 11, 52
  data tradition of, 17
  discrimination and, 32
  evolution and, 27
  future issues and, 172
  national barometers and, 8–12
  paradoxes in, 25
  positivism and, 12, 172–173
  reflexivity and, 23–24
  social cryptogram and, 5, 7
  social distance and, 20, 99–123
  society as living organism, 2, 19–20
  statistics and, 8–9, 12
  unintended consequences and, 18 (*see also* Unintended consequences)
Social theory, 21, 172
Sociology
  collective behavior and, 47, 60, 65–66
  Comte and, 3, 12
  policy design and, 149, 160
  reflexivity and, 23–24
  self-fulfilling prophecies and, 32
  social influence and, 74–75, 79
  space and, 141, 143
  Spencer and, 3, 5

Sociology (cont.)
  survival of the fittest and, 12
  Watts and, 15
  Webb and, 9
Sontag, Susan, 4
Space
  activity density and, 128
  administrative partitioning of, 126,
    130–132, 137
  algorithms and, 142
  banknote study and, 132, 135, 137
  bias and, 128, 138–142, 144
  cities as laboratories, 141–143
  collective action and, 134, 136
  complexity and, 127
  decision making and, 137
  digital gaps and, 138–141
  diversity and, 126–127, 135–136
  feedback effects and, 134, 143
  geographic distance and, 125, 128–
    129, 131–139
  human interaction and, 133–137, 143
  informational layers and, 129
  Internet and, 138–140
  logic and, 133
  magnetism and, 128
  maps and, 125–138, 141, 144–145
  Mass Observation and, 141–142
  meaningful places and, 125
  measurement and, 143–145
  mobility and, 21, 29, 104, 106, 125–
    128, 132, 137, 143, 145
  navigation of, 20–21, 27, 37, 102,
    105–109, 111, 126, 129, 137, 156,
    168
  OpenStreetMap and, 128, 131, 138,
    143
  possibility, 106
  prediction and, 140
  privacy and, 137
  recognition and, 129–130
  redefining boundaries, 131–138
  representation and, 143–145

  satellites and, 131
  social life and, 20–21, 126
  social media and, 128, 133–136, 142
  social straitjacketing and, 127
  sociology and, 141, 143
  technology and, 20–21, 127–130,
    136–143
  telegraph and, 19–20
  telephone study and, 134–135
  transparency and, 137
  urban, 9, 21, 125–130, 141–142, 151
Spencer, Herbert, 3, 5
Spontaneity
  collective behavior and, 20, 28, 49, 52,
    58, 64, 73, 75, 78, 127
  social influence and, 73, 75, 78
  unintended consequences and, 28
Statistics
  algorithms and, 176 (see also
    Algorithms)
  cholera and, 9
  collective behavior and, 48, 50, 53–55,
    59, 68
  of conversation, 53, 55, 68
  crowd estimation and, 160
  discrimination and, 32
  Internet penetration and, 139
  policy design and, 148, 157, 160
  politics and, 132, 135
  social distance and, 108
  social science and, 8–9, 12
Streaking, 71–73, 79–80, 86
Street View, 130
Surveillance, xv, 9–11, 121–122, 163,
    165–169
Susceptibility, 51, 76–81, 84, 110
Sweeney, Latanya, 157

Tarde, Gabriel
  collective behavior and, 47–57, 59–60,
    62–63, 65–66, 68–69
  conservatism of, 47
  contagion and, 74

Durkheim and, 47–52, 60, 63, 65
dynamics of collective action and,
  56–57, 59
higher aggregations of, 60, 63
languishing ideas of, 51
Laws of Imitation and, 49
nature of social facts and, 48–52
solidarity of the brains and, 49
statistics of conversation and, 53, 55,
  68
technology and, 49–50
trickle down of imitation and, 62
Technology
algorithms and, 15–17 (*see also*
  Algorithms)
automation and, 18, 83, 87, 131, 140,
  168
bandwidth, 54, 91–92, 110, 118
Bluetooth, 121
breakthroughs in, 2, 66, 123
cameras, 10
collective behavior and, 49, 52, 54, 57,
  64–67, 69
communication, 3, 6, 11, 14, 18–23,
  41, 43, 49, 74, 102–103, 119, 123,
  127–130, 136–143, 153, 179
cumulative effects and, 38–40
cybernetics and, 5, 12, 68, 147–150,
  154, 170
decryption and, 7
digital, 3, 7, 9, 11 (*see also* Digital
  technologies)
encryption and, 5–7, 22, 40, 180
future issues and, 171–181
innovation and, 1–2, 13, 18, 43, 49–
  50, 95, 123, 142, 152, 175, 180
Internet, 1, 3–4, 27, 30, 50, 57, 74,
  101, 118–120, 138–140, 150–151,
  169, 171
invention and, 1, 4, 12, 17, 26, 39, 43,
  49, 74, 153, 175
microchips, 4
multiplied interactions and, 49–50

nervous system metaphor, 1–4, 7, 148,
  154
networks and, 1 (*see also* Networks)
newspapers and, 10–11, 13–14, 45–46,
  56, 59, 63, 67, 100, 140, 179
older, 10, 171
Peer to Patent initiative, 152–153
personal computers, 4
policy design and, 12, 21, 138–160,
  163–170
printing press, 14, 66, 171, 179
radio, 103
reflexivity and, 24
repurposing, 15
satellites, 131
search engines and, 35, 38, 41, 157
self-fulfilling prophecies and, 32–34
social distance and, 101–107, 110,
  117–119, 122–123
social influence and, 19–20, 73–74,
  78–84, 87, 89, 94–95, 97
space and, 20–21, 127–130,
  136–143
surveillance and, xv, 9–11, 121–122,
  163, 165–169
telegraph, 1–3, 7–8, 13–14, 19–20, 43,
  49, 66, 74, 99–102, 115, 118, 171,
  176, 179
telephones, 1–3, 10, 20, 103, 109, 118,
  134–135, 137, 139, 145, 160
television, 72, 80
telex, 148, 150, 171
typewriters, 34
unintended consequences and, 26–30,
  43–44
UPC codes and, 4
WiFi, 121
Telegraph
collective behavior and, 49, 66
commerce and, 3
Electric Telegraph Company, 2
end of newspapers and, 13–14
fears of, 101

Telegraph (cont.)
impact of, 1–3, 7–8, 13, 99–101, 171,
176, 179
Morse code, 4
as national barometer, 8, 19
as nervous system, 2–3
newspapers and, 13–14, 100, 179
public opinion and, 100–101
social distance and, 99–102, 115, 118
social influence and, 74
space and, 19–20
spread of, 99–100
trans-Atlantic cable for, 99–100, 102
unintended consequences and, 43
Western Union, 3
Telephones, 1–3, 20
as disruptive technology, 10
impact of, 134–135, 137, 139, 145
Meeting Mediator and, 160
networks and, 103, 109, 118
privacy and, 10, 167
Television, 72, 80
Telex, 148, 150, 171
Third Republic, xvii, 47
Time series, 60–63, 133, 136
Transparency
discrimination and, 162
future issues and, 173, 177
policy design and, 151, 160, 162,
166–169
privacy and, 21, 137, 162, 166–167,
169
social influence and, 97
space and, 20–21, 137
Transportation, 128, 132, 162
Travel
airport screening and, 162
banknote study and, 132, 135, 137
cities as laboratories and, 141–143
contagion and, 78
of information, 13–14, 20, 22, 58, 68,
73, 101, 112, 115, 118, 145, 177–179
policy design and, 137

"slower is faster" effect, 142
social media and, 128
social signals and, 90
transportation and, 128, 132, 162
Turing, Alan, 5–6
Turkey, 113, 120–121, 166–167
Turner, Ralph H., 75–76
Twitter, 38, 57, 92, 108, 113, 118, 120–
121, 133, 136
Typewriters, 34

Umbrella revolution, 92, 121
"Unanticipated Consequences of
Purposive Social Action, The"
(Merton), 28
Uncertainty principle, 145
Underdog effect, 24, 31
Unintended consequences
algorithms and, 28
cascades and, 1, 18, 20, 50, 55, 73, 81,
84–85, 90, 102, 108, 113, 116, 120,
175
chain reactions and, 18, 20, 29, 43,
175, 178–179
collateral damage and, 174–175
complexity and, 28–29, 43
crowdsourcing and, 42
cumulative effects and, 37
data science and, 43
digital technologies and, 43–44
feedback mechanisms and, 19
focusing on, 43–44
future issues and, 171–175, 178
ideological polarization and, 29–30
innovation and, 175
Internet and, 26–28, 30
language and, 30
law of, 25–30
logic and, 29, 44
misinformation and, 19
networks and, 44, 177–179
paradoxes and, 25, 28, 30
policy design and, 157–158, 160, 166

power of communication and, 42–43
prediction and, 13, 18, 27–29, 43, 175
preferential attachment and, 37–38
prophecies and, 31
reasons for focusing on, 43–44
regulation and, 26, 30
segregation and, 29–30, 35, 82, 88
social change and, 29
social influence and, 85, 88, 94, 97–98
social life and, 19, 27–28
space and, 140
technology and, 26–30, 43–44
telegraph and, 43
United Nations, 11
Universal suffrage, 30
Unpredictability
    Butterfly Effect and, 28–29 (*see also*
        Complexity)
    effects of, 12–15, 18, 29, 40, 75, 97,
        149
    social influence and, 97–98
    uncertainty principle and, 145
UPC chips, 4
Ushahidi.com, 151
US Patent and Trademark Office, 153
US State Department, 166
US Transportation Security
    Administration, 162

Verne, Jules, 18
Victoria (queen), 99

War of the Worlds hoax, 82
Watts, Duncan, 15, 106
Webb, Beatrice, 9
Weill, Jeanne, 46
Welfare state, 30
Welles, Orson, 82
Western Union, 3
Wiener, Norbert, 5, 12, 147–148
WiFi, 121
WikiLeaks, 150, 166–169, 175
Wikipedia, 40, 153–154

Wildfires, 20, 81, 85, 90, 175
Women, 12, 48, 167
Word of mouth communication, 30,
    120
World Economic Forum, 11
"World Memory" (Calvino), 144
World Wide Web
    as collaboration system, 27
    cumulative effects and, 18, 26–28, 35–
        43, 46, 82, 107, 129–132, 167–168,
        175
    effective shelf life of articles, 58–59
    firewalls and, 72, 80, 101, 111, 178
    Ice Bucket Challenge and, 73
    mapping, 27–28, 35
    preferential attachment and, 36–39
    trust and, 37–38

Yahoo, 131
YouTube, 120

Zika virus, 73
Zola, Émile, 45–47, 53